LIONS RAMPANT

LIONS RAMPANT

The Story of No 602 Spitfire Squadron

Douglas McRoberts

Foreword by
Air Vice Marshal Sandy Johnstone
CB, DFC, AE, DL, RAF (Retd)

WILLIAM KIMBER · LONDON

First published in 1985 by
WILLIAM KIMBER & CO. LIMITED
100 Jermyn Street, London, SW1Y 6EE

© Douglas McRoberts, 1985
ISBN 0-7183-0572-8

Typeset by Jubal Typesetting Ltd.
and printed in Great Britain by
Redwood Burn Limited, Trowbridge

Dedicated to
The Officers and Men
of
No 602 (City of Glasgow) Squadron, AAF
and to
Kenneth, Graham, and Alistair,
who only ever knew freedom

Contents

List of Illustrations

Foreword

By

Air Vice Marshal Sandy Johnstone

CB, DFC, AE, DL, RAF (Retd)

It is not often that an individual squadron of the Royal Air Force merits an entire book being written about it, but No 602 (City of Glasgow) Squadron was no run-of-the-mill outfit, as I well know, having first joined it in the ninth year of its existence. By then the squadron had already hit the headlines because of the exploits of two of its members, The Marquess of Douglas and Clydesdale and David McIntyre, who had just made their historic flight over Mount Everest in 1933, when the former was its Commanding Officer and McIntyre the senior Flight Commander. These officers set a standard of exceptional proficiency for the unit which their successors were to maintain throughout its entire history.

It was a stroke of genius which inspired Lord Trenchard to start up the Auxiliary Air Force in 1924, for it was a concept that immediately seized the imagination of enterprising young men from all walks of life who were eagerly prepared to devote most of their spare time to learning and performing tasks normally undertaken by the Royal Air Force itself: And this enthusiasm was not confined to the pilots, for there grew up in those early Auxiliary squadrons an incredible atmosphere of enjoyment which could have been achieved only through the combined efforts of ground and air crews alike. The result was that the AAF put in as much flying as the regular RAF, soon showing such a high degree of operational skill that, when the war came in 1939, the Auxiliary squadrons were able immediately to play their full part as front line operational units in the defence of the country. Indeed the Glasgow and Edinburgh Squadrons were the first to go into action in October 1939.

Time has a nasty habit of slipping by unnoticed and I find it hard to believe it is now twelve years since Douglas McRoberts first approached me with his plan to write the squadron's history, but he has obviously put the intervening years to very good use, for he has come up with a story of such unrivalled interest that, once I began reading the manuscript, I found it almost impossible to lay it down. Of course, being intimately involved in the day by day goings on of the squadron from the mid-thirties until the spring of 1941, I obviously failed to recognise the significance of what we were doing at the time and it has taken the inspired pen of McRoberts to make me, and I suspect most of my colleagues, appreciate how privileged we were to have been in a position to contribute in some small measure to 602 Squadron's remarkable successes during its all-too-short existence. Sufficient to say, there can be few flying units anywhere in the world which have left such a mark in aviation history as the City of Glasgow Squadron, and its glory will surely live for ever.

London   S.J.
15th December 1984

Author's Introduction

This is a story – better than that, it's a true story. I learned the beginnings of it on my father's knee. I inherited his old flying helmet and goggles, and would gaze through the cracked left eyepiece at the field near Renfrew where he'd learned his circuits and bumps, a seven year old's imagination taking me into the skies to tangle with the Huns. Then we'd drive to the wooded field at Floors Farm where he'd seen the smoking wreckage of Hess's aircraft, and my daydreams would take off again.

I loved that helmet, and when, at my grandmother's insistence, it was put into a church jumble sale, I spent my last sixpence buying it back.

The story surfaced again years later, when, as a student, I was given a tattered copy of Nancarrow's *Glasgow's Fighter Squadron*, published in 1941 – and I met once again McKellar, Boyd, Farquhar and the others. I began digging, at first around my native Glasgow, and one by one they turned up, those that were left, intrigued that a young divinity student should be tracking them down.

I found others had tried to tell the story:– Vivian Bell, who'd been stopped by the post-war censors; Max Sutherland, who wrote his own unpublished account of his time with 602, and had to tell it to someone . . .

And I discovered why 602 became legend. It wasn't just the aces – though the statisticians will discover that eight of the RAF's forty top scorers flew with 602 – and it wasn't just the conquering of Everest, or the way in which they pushed their Spitfires, and themselves, to the limit and beyond. It has something to do with the spirit of the Lion, carried so proudly on the Spitfires.

Above all, this is a story of machines and of men – and of their actions and reactions during what was, for many, at once the most exhilarating and yet terrifying time of their lives. The events all took place; so, too, the conversations, which represent an honest attempt not by the author, but by the men who were there, to recall exactly what was said – and to tell the story exactly as it was.

My thanks are due to everyone who helped in the creation of the book, far too numerous to mention here, but who are listed at the end of this book. The pilots, who welcomed me to their homes, and opened their logbooks and memories; aircraftmen like Smithy, who found himself writing a thirty page letter; professional writers who have touched on the story, and who, almost to a man, proved so helpful to me; William Kimber who saw the possibilities; Mary Ann Day who typed it so painstakingly; and my wife Lesley, who knew just when to cajole, when to turn up with coffee, and when to switch off the light.

I am particularly indebted to Air Vice Marshal Sandy Johnstone, CB, DFC for his constant encouragement, and for his foreword, and to Dugald Cameron for painstakingly searching out the photographic gems from over four hundred prints he's collected. He, too, painted the originals for the cover – and his brush seems to me to have recaptured that most intangible, but vital atmosphere that tells you, 'This is how it really was'.

I don't have the helmet any more, but my two-year-old son, Scott, has inherited the feeling. At eighteen months, he raided a forbidden cupboard, and now he's at his happiest racing through the house with a large, combat-scarred model Spitfire. With, of course, a Lion Rampant on its side.

This story is for him, too.

D McR
Inverness, 1985

Prologue

16th October 1939 09.43 Weather inland fine, visibility good, scattered cloud 4/10 to 5/10. To sea, haze. Low sun made visibility to east difficult. Wind 4–5 mph. Reported to Turnhouse U/A flying over 'drome above clouds.

Extract, 602 Sqn Operations Record

Helmut Pohle was not a happy man. The commanding officer of 1/ KG30 'Verband', the only Luftwaffe operational unit flying the Junkers Ju88 'wonder bomber', he was under pressure from all sides. Just three weeks earlier, four of his aircraft, with the assistance of large helpings of propaganda from Dr Goebbels, had 'sunk' the aircraft carrier *Ark Royal* – which in point of fact was now heading for the South Atlantic. And exactly one week ago, the whole unit had returned with their bombs from an abortive attempt to find the Home Fleet. On landing, he was called to the telephone to give Goering a personal report. He answered bitterly, 'We were just sent to an area where there was no enemy'. The next morning, summoned to a conference at the Reich Air Ministry in Berlin, he faced the sweating bulk of the Reichsmarschall, and was told, 'Pohle, we've got to score a success! There are only a few British ships that stand in our way – the *Repulse*, the *Renown*, the *Hood*. And of course the aircraft carriers. You owe me an aircraft carrier.'

The U-boats, of course, had already got one – the *Courageous*, sunk by *U-29* west of Ireland on 17th September – and only two nights ago, hadn't Günther Prien in *U-47* penetrated Scapa Flow and put two salvoes of torpedoes into the *Royal Oak*? If the 'wonder bomber's' reputation was on the line, so was Pohle's. At KG30's base at Westerland, on the island of Sylt, he received his orders of the day on the telephone from the Luftwaffe's Chief of General Staff, Hans Jeschonnek. The battlecruiser *Hood* was reported by Luftwaffe Intelligence as having entered the Firth of Forth. 1/KG30 was to attack it – and Jeschonnek added, 'I also have to convey to you a personal order from the Führer. Should the *Hood* already be in dock when KG30 reaches the Firth of Forth, no attack is to be made. I make you personally responsible for acquainting every

crew with this order. The Führer won't have a single civilian killed.'
More restrictions – more pressure.

Pohle wasn't to know that once again the intelligence service had
let KG30 down. The *Hood* wasn't even in the Forth. But they made
one other, much more serious, mistake – one which Pohle wouldn't
discover until he was over his target. . . .

*

The three Spitfires entered the landing circuit in line astern, coming
in low and fast from the north-east, over the Bass Rock. An eerie,
whistling note accompanied the snarl and crackle of the Merlins as
they throttled back, and eager ground crews heard, and saw, the
evidence of action. The canvas patches over the gun ports in the
leading edges had been shot away, the undersides of the wings were
streaked with black gun oil and blast. The section leader, Flight
Lieutenant George Pinkerton, clambered out and gave his report to
the intelligence officer. Yes, they'd sighted an enemy aircraft. Yes,
they'd chased it through scattered cloud, going east beyond May
Isle. No, he couldn't confirm it as a kill. Just before 10.20 that
morning, No 602 (City of Glasgow) Fighter Squadron, had fired the
opening shots of the air war over Britain. Excitement was now running high at RAF Drem, a peacetime Flying Training Station hastily,
and uncomfortably, converting to a fighter base after the arrival,
just three days earlier, of the Spitfires of the Glasgow Squadron.

Throughout the day, the Radio Direction Finding stations at St
Abbs Head and Drone Hill had suffered intermittent power
failures, and predictions of incoming aircraft were far from reliable.
That something was brewing was clear. Single enemy aircraft, Heinkel
111s from KG26 'Löwengeschwader', had been flying reconnaissance missions through the morning – it was one of these that
George Pinkerton had chased out to sea. Before the day was out,
he'd fire his guns again – and this time, he wouldn't miss.

*

13.00 hours. The nine Ju88s of 1/KG30 take off from Westerland,
1,000 lb bombs slung beneath them, the crews tense after Pohle has
briefed them for the first raid of the war over Britain itself. As they
head west into a slightly misty sky, the unsynchronised beat of the
twin Jumo engines is comforting, familiar. Equally comforting is

the thought that the worst they will have to contend with is naval anti-aircraft fire. Department 5 (of the Luftwaffe General Staff) have informed them that there are no Hurricanes or Spitfires stationed in Scotland. At 14.10, they sight land, and in a straggled formation of ones and twos, slide in past Elie, heading for Rosyth. So far, they're lucky. 603 Squadron's standing patrol has been vectored onto an unidentified aircraft which they never sighted, Red Section of 602 had been scrambled after two Fleet Air Arm Skuas, and are now returning to base, while Green Section of 602 have just been instructed to land at Leuchars to refuel. With the RDF stations 'out', the Ju88s are clear as far as the Forth Bridge.

14.22 hours. Blue Section of 602 Squadron is ordered to patrol Dalkeith at 20,000 feet. Excitement is high –the three Spitfires, already warmed up and with George Pinkerton, Flying Officer Archie McKellar and Flying Officer Paul Webb in the cockpits, are all in the air within 90 seconds. It's their third flight of the day –since the morning flurry of action, they've flown another abortive patrol. This time, there's confusion. Over the R/T, Pinkerton is ordered first to Tranent, after a sighting of two 'bogeys' – unidentified aircraft. Then it comes – 'Enemy aircraft bombing Rosyth. Enemy aircraft bombing Rosyth. Patrol five miles north.'

14.27 hours. At the head of his loose formation, Pohle saw exactly what he didn't want to. Right at the dock gates at Rosyth, a large naval vessel (although not the *Hood*) – too close inshore for a bombing run. He circled over the naval base, taking in the scene, the inner and outer Firth of Forth, separated by the great triple span of the bridge. Just beyond it, to the east, he sighted two cruisers and a destroyer . . . and he tipped the Junkers into a steep dive, coming down over the bridge at a sharp angle. Lined up in his primitive sights was the cruiser *Southampton*. The speed increased rapidly as the Ju88 came down the sky; at about 4,000 feet it was bracketed by surprisingly accurate flak from the other cruiser, the *Edinburgh*, and then, at a speed of about 400mph and an angle of eighty degrees, it happened – a sharp explosion, followed by a crashing, tearing sound and an icy blast of air. The cabin roof had blown clean off. Pohle kept control, though, and at 3,000 feet released his bomb. It wasn't his day – he hit the ship, but his bomb failed to explode.

But the bomber crew had no time to assess the results of their attack. No sooner had they pulled out from their dive, than the radio operator's voice screamed the warning: '*Achtung! Schpitfeuren . . . drei Schpitfeuren!*'

14.32 hours. Pinkerton, leading McKellar and Webb north-west towards Kirkcaldy, sights the leading German aircraft heading east. 'Villa Blue Section, Tally ho . . . Buster . . .' The throttles are shoved against the stops, and the Spitfires lunge forward, exhaust stacks bellowing, with guns armed, and the little orange rings lighting the reflector sights. McKellar, on Pinkerton's right, sights two more air-craft, even nearer – but just in time they're identified as the two Skuas, flying serenely through Britain's first air raid. The Spitfires close in on their original target, tearing through scattered cloud. The Ju88, already low over the water, takes no avoiding action as Pinkerton, for the second time that day, thumbs the firing button, and the eight Browning guns chatter furiously. Rapidly overhauling the 'wonder bomber', the token resistance of its single backwards-firing machine gun already knocked out, Pinkerton sees his bullets strike home – there's a puff of smoke from the port engine. As Pin-kerton breaks away, McKellar attacks from the starboard side – again there are strikes. Once again, Pinkerton closes on the wounded bomber, as it climbs briefly, and dives to port. The Brownings hammer, the Junkers drops right down low over the water. Pinkerton once again thumbs the button, but hears only the hiss of compressed air and the clatter of empty breech blocks. Ammunition expended, he circles as his victim flattens out over a trawler.

On board the Junkers, Pohle is losing consciousness. In the first attack, bullets have raked the cabin, killing the radio operator seconds after his warning shout, and reducing the rear gun position to a shambles. The port engine is hit. As the second Spitfire closes in, the bomber's tail surfaces are lashed, and control becomes dif-ficult. Pohle, already wounded, exerts all his strength to keep the bomber in the air; his last faint hope is to head out to sea, to where the Germans have stationed the fishing cutter *Hornum*. But then, Pinkerton's long second burst badly wounds the Ju's observer, and the starboard motor fails. Pohle was unconscious as the bomber hit the water, level, at 140mph.

15.00 hours. The Spitfires sweep low and fast into the circuit, wind whistling through the gun ports, Archie McKellar whipping into an impromptu low roll. The fitters, riggers and armourers cluster round, eager for the pilot's news. Yes, this time we got one . . . yes, definitely down.

*

Helmut Pohle awakened, some days later, in hospital. And one of his first visitors was George Pinkerton, who remembers, 'He didn't talk much. His face was a bit bashed where he'd hit the dashboard when he landed in the sea. I sent him some sweets, and some cigarettes. He wrote back to me.' The letter, written from one airman to another, reads:

> Dear Flight Lieutenant Pinkerton,
>   You have me make with your surprising present a very much gladness, especially I just learn in this days to comprehend the doleful fate of the prisoner of war. I thank you for the friendly conduct, wish you the best, and greet you. Likewise the other pilot. To old airmen comradeship.
>
> Helmut C.W. Pohle,
Hauptmann der Luftwaffe.

For Pohle, the war was already over. For the men of 602 (City of Glasgow) Squadron, it was just beginning.

CHAPTER ONE

'Per Ardua . . .'

. . . a corps d'élite of mechanical yeomanry, organised on a territorial basis – men who in earlier times would have served on horseback.

Extract, Sir Hugh Trenchard's 1919 Memorandum
for a Reserve Air Force, incorporated in the
1924 Auxiliary Air Force Act

7th October 1925. Squadron Leader Lowe flew DH 9A H.144 to Renfrew from Henlow. This is notable inasmuch that this aeroplane was the first aircraft flown in an Auxiliary Air Force unit.

Extract, 602 Squadron Operations Record Book

Flight Lieutenant Gilbert Martyn, known universally as 'Dan', was making history – though the thought was probably far from his mind as he piloted his little Jowett saloon skilfully between the puddles and derelict buildings on the deserted wartime acceptance airfield on the Moorpark Road at Renfrew. As rain spattered the windscreen, and the car lurched into a deep trough once again, he reflected on his orders. On the face of it, they were simple enough. He, newly appointed as Adjutant of Britain's first Auxiliary Air Force squadron, had the task of bringing Trenchard's dream to reality. The theorists had worked it all out; each of the squadrons would have a Regular nucleus, to supervise administration, stores, and the training of volunteers.

Dan, experienced in the ways of the Postings Department, was not in the least surprised to find himself the sole member of Number 602 (City of Glasgow) Squadron actually at Renfrew that Saturday morning, the 12th September 1925, without so much as a standard-issue blanket for company, wondering how long it would be before somebody else turned up and doubled the squadron's strength. He surveyed his new charge. The field wasn't very promising. It was bumpy, it sprouted puddles at the least hint of rain, and it lay (appropriately enough, as many would later claim) adjacent to Arkleston Cemetery. He stopped the Jowett and stuck an exploratory finger into the damp air; sure enough, if that wind was anything like typical, the landing approach would be right over the gravestones. He'd never doubted it, somehow. He put the Jowett into gear, only to stick fast in the mud. He had, he thought, spent better weekends.

On the Monday, the CO turned up. Squadron Leader C.N. Lowe, MC, DFC, was a Regular, who'd picked up his decorations flying SE5As in the Great War as a Flight Commander on 24 Squadron. He was also an English international wing threequarter, with a disconcerting habit of doing a pre-breakfast run across whichever airfield he happened to be stationed at; the problem was he insisted on taking the Permanent Staff with him in the early days at Renfrew. The first of these had arrived on the Tuesday. So had some transport, and a Hucks starter – but no aircraft for it to start. Lowe was undismayed. One of the few crates so far delivered contained some Air Force stationery, and a Great War vintage typewriter. most of whose keys still functioned. 'Good show,' said the CO to the Adjutant. 'Type them a letter at Air Ministry and let them know there's a squadron here. They might even send us a plane.'

On 7th October, Their Airships obliged – though Lowe had to go down to Henlow to fetch it. Waiting for him there was H.144 – a newly-overhauled De Havilland DH9A two-seat day bomber. He signed the Acceptance Form, climbed in, and flew it back to Renfrew and into the history books, as 602 became the first Auxiliary Squadron actually to fly a plane, a full week before the London or Edinburgh squadrons began to form. The angular, silver 'Nine Ack', with its distinctive square radiator, 400 hp 'Liberty' engine and 450 lb bomb load, was a Great War vintage bi-plane. Armed in standard pattern with a Vickers machine gun forward, and a ring-mounted Lewis gun aft, it was still in first-line RAF service, and was in some ways ideal for the Auxiliaries. Easy to fly, it was described by one pilot as, 'A gentleman's machine – she flew like a demure lady, with no vices, and always responded well to a bit of encouragement'.

For Renfrew, though, with its steep approaches over the graveyard, she wasn't completely perfect – the Nine Ack floated forever on finals. 'She was a bit too demure, actually. You couldn't get her to lay down at all sometimes.'

They had the base, the Regulars, and the aircraft. All that was missing was the volunteers themselves. A recruiting campaign was mounted in the squadron's temporary Town Headquarters – a wooden hut in the back yard of the 52nd (Lowland) Division Drill Hall in Kelvinbridge – and launched by a flypast from some Fleet

Air Arm Fairey Flycatchers. They certainly caught public interest, as did the offer of a £3 annual bounty, no doubt, and within a few days, Clydeside's natural engineers and craftsmen were signing on the dotted line.

The authorities had thoughtfully warned the Regular staff to be on their guard against possible Communist infiltration. The unit on 'Red Clydeside' was to be doubly vigilant. Sergeant E.G. Hill, taking down the names of would-be fitters and riggers remembers one man who listed his occupation as 'Red Leader'. The Adjutant, checking the forms, promptly informed London that the first Marxist plot had been uncovered; he was surprised at the sheer arrogance of the infiltrator, until it was established that the unfortunate 'Marxist' was a painter who daubed the hulls in John Brown's shipyard with red lead!

Within a year, the squadron had trained its first generation of fitters, riggers, MT drivers, and tradesmen, and acquired its first three Auxiliary pilots – Messrs J.P. Drew, H.G. Davidson, and C.A.S. Parker – who had first of all to pass their 'A' licences. Only later were they able to train pilots from scratch. They got their first Auxiliary CO, too – Captain John David Latta, MC, an Ayrshire man who'd flown Scouts in the Great War, and who didn't go for early morning squadron runs, to everyone's relief. They also acquired Dr J.C.H. Allan of Paisley, commissioned as a Flight Lieutenant. Doc Allan, with 602 until the outbreak of war, would become Senior Medical Officer in Fighter Command's 11 Group, which bore the brunt of the fighting during the Battle of Britain. The officers were particularly glad they hadn't needed his services during the first Annual Camp, which saw the squadron going to RAF Leuchars for a fortnight, and getting a taste of real Service life. In accordance with a new regulation, they each had to make a parachute jump, parachutes having been finally adopted as standard RAF equipment only the previous year. A helpful officer explained the procedure: 'Ah, well, yes – we're not really too confident that the damned things will open on demand, as it were, but it's all right, we've worked out a foolproof system. What happens, you see, is that you stand on the wing – uh, we've strengthened them, y'know – and then you release the parachute. If it opens, which usually happens, it pulls you off and you're all set for a nice drop. If it doesn't, well, you should still be on the wing, and you can bring the thing back and we'll swop it. All clear? Jolly good, carry on'. Which is exactly what 602's intrepid birdmen did, thankfully with complete success.

Back at Renfrew, Dan Martyn urged his fledglings to ever greater efforts – 'Come on, man, lower. If you can't read the names on the gravestones, you're too high.' 'Boom' Trenchard came to inspect the squadron, and discussed Renfrew's unique problems. The possibility of another airfield was mooted; meanwhile, promised the Great Man, he'd look into the question of alternative aircraft. 602 thanked him. Next year, when their Fairey Fawns arrived, they wished they hadn't.

The pilots of 602 gazed in some awe at their new mounts. Opinions varied – but not much. 'Without doubt the ugliest aircraft I have ever seen,' said one. 'God, it was awful,' remembered another, 'and mine actually smelled of mothballs. We soon discovered why the Regulars didn't fly them. They had all the aerodynamic qualities of a half brick.'

Along with their little Avro 504k trainers, though, the week-enders kept doggedly flying through even the worst of Glasgow's weather. While sensible birds walked, 602 persisted in hauling the Fawns off Renfrew's waterlogged surfaces into hopefully clearer skies beyond, seeking to notch up further flying-hours records. To see one of these heavy biplanes lumbering through Moorpark's lakes, and then laboriously picking up speed in a cloud of freezing spray, before clambering into leaden skies, shaking itself like a dog, and finally droning on up through the cloud base, was to begin to understand the dedication and enthusiasm of the week-end fliers.

The pilots, typically, made light of their efforts. Denis McNab, who'd just joined, reckoned, 'The Fawn was the ideal aircraft for the job. With others, you might have worried about aquaplaning on landing – but not the Fawn. It swam like it flew – like a brick!' They wondered about fitting floats, but decided it would make no appreciable difference to the plane's landing characteristics – 'Much better', said James Lennox, 'to equip the damn things with lifeboats.'

Lennox and McNab had both been commissioned in 1928; Lennox was an ex-RFC pilot returning to his first love. His experience arrived at just the right moment, as 602 were recovering from the death of Bobby Drew, who'd killed himself looping an Avro dangerously close to the ground. Lennox, demonstrably, was a natural survivor.

Denis McNab was as determined as they come. A bobsleigh enthusiast who'd already cheated death on the Cresta Run, he was told at his first attempt to join 602 that a lazy eye would prevent him from judging speed and distance; 'You'll never be able to fly,' said the medic. Young Denis promptly joined the new Scottish Flying Club at Renfrew, took lessons from the Chief Instructor, and soloed after only 3½ hours of dual training, right under the noses of 602 Squadron – a club record which stood for years (and possibly still does!) 'I went back to 602 – they had to pass me this time, only this time they spotted my red/green colour blindness. I was accepted on condition I did no night flying, when mistaking the colour of a flare could prove embarrassing.' He was still flying when the Spitfires came, despite having been officially put on the Reserve list. Of such men was the Auxiliary Air Force formed.

The previous year, they'd signed up four successive Commanding Officers. John Fullerton took over from Latta in May, but of much more significance was the arrival of David McIntyre, Douglas Farquhar, and the Marquess of Douglas and Clydesdale.

'Douglo', as he was known to colleagues, (or, to the ACs, the 'Marquess of Govan and Clydebank') was a boxing champion who was willing to take on all comers – of any rank – in the Town HQ. It's not recorded that he was ever beaten! He was destined, along with McIntyre, to be the first to fly over Everest, and, right from the start, it was agreed his presence gave the squadron that extra 'something'. A few days after he joined, came the great day when the long-awaited Town Headquarters were opened, at No 49 Coplaw Street, Eglinton Toll, on Glasgow's South Side. It had everything – permanent staff accommodation, messes, hall, lecture rooms – and 602 was now well equipped to handle everything from training to social events with style. The opening, on Tuesday 12th July 1927, was performed by the King and Queen themselves. 602's lower ranks weren't particularly surprised. 'It's because we've got the Marquess,' went the rumour. 'They're obviously old friends.'

David Fowler McIntyre, a name which would become equally famous in aviation history as the founder of Scottish Aviation and Prestwick Airport, began his flying career by taking his 'A' Licence at Beardmore's Flying School, and joined 602 in March 1927. He soon made his mark. On one occasion, he was standing with a few other pilots, watching some crows landing and taking off. He noticed the birds would approach *downwind*, finally executing a tight 180° turn before touching down. 'We should try that', he muttered, half to himself, 'It would solve the problem of approaching over the graves'. A knot of interested spectators were shortly afterwards treated to the sight of Mac's aircraft approaching the field downwind, and travelling pretty fast. A couple of feet off the grass, it lurched round in an almost flat spin, before dropping heavily to earth, shearing its undercarriage off as it slewed to an ignominious halt. Unabashed, Mac later declared it was time the crows learned some basic aerodynamics.

Douglas Farquhar, who would lead 602 to war, arrived almost by chance. The dapper young stockbroker was at the Stock Exchange one day, when business was suspended for five minutes to allow Colonel Connal to 'plug' the City of Glasgow squadron's activities. 'Sounds interesting,' said Farquhar to his companion. 'I think I'll take a spin out there on Saturday.' He did – and found himself taking a spin of a different kind in the cockpit of an Avro, with the ground whirling round over his head. After they landed, his instructor invited him to afternoon tea. The tea stayed down – and Farquhar was in.

In 1929, the search for a new airfield was still going on, with the Fawns and Avros scouring the countryside looking for fields which were big enough, and with clear approaches. On Saturday, 5th January, Flying Officer Finney, the squadron's Regular Assistant Adjutant, thought he'd finally hit the jackpot near Howwood – though he couldn't understand why nobody had noticed the field before. He put the Avro into its landing approach.

Down below, Denis McNab, skating with some friends on the frozen lake, couldn't believe his eyes; 'Even more to my surprise, the Avro actually landed successfully – the lying snow prevented a skid. The problem came when it turned at the end of the run, putting all the weight on one wheel. The ice couldn't take it. There was a crack, and the undercart vanished through the ice. Luckily, the rest didn't follow.' Finney stepped out gingerly, and crept his way to *terra firma*.

There appeared to be no immediate danger, but just in case souvenir hunters appeared, the unfortunate Finney was detailed to stand guard over the Avro, by now locked solid in the ice, overnight, until a rescue squad could dismantle it. 'I suppose it was fair enough,' said McNab. 'I think he got pneumonia.' He also collected a severe reprimand from a Court of Inquiry – but 602 collected a unique piece of aviation legendry ('We landed the first Avro on ice, you know, old boy – nothing to it, really.')

News came of new aircraft, as the ground crews were sent on maintenance courses on the Westland Wapiti, a two-seat general purpose aircraft which had only recently come into RAF service, and which promised to be a vast improvement on the Fawns, with its 500 hp Bristol Jupiter engine, increased bomb load and immeasurably better flying characteristics. 'I was certainly keen as hell to fly it,' remembers John Feather, 'something –anything – other than the Fawn!'

Meanwhile, Annual Camp at Leuchars had still to be flown with the Fawns, much to the pilots' chagrin, for it was at camp that much of the competition took place towards the presentation of the Esher Trophy, presented by Lord Esher for all-round efficiency. With Fawns, lamented the Glasgow boys, they didn't stand a chance. Yet perhaps it was simply that extra challenge which spurred on the determined Scots. It came as a pleasant thrill, and certainly a surprise, when it was announced that 602 had done the impossible, and wrested the trophy from the grasp of the southern squadrons.

Four days after they returned from camp, the first of the Wapitis arrived. Then, in early November, Group Captain Fletcher and the Works and Buildings Department arrived to check out the site of what was to be their new airfield, at a place called Abbots' Inch.

As the year came to a close, many of the original volunteer groundstaff came to the end of their 'tour'; almost to a man, they signed on for another, proudly sewing the small cloth star to their right sleeve; the overall mood was one of satisfaction, confidence, and eagerness.

It was only fitting that one of the last official acts of 'Boom' Trenchard as Chief of Air Staff should be the presentation of the Esher Trophy to the City of Glasgow Squadron, in so many ways the premier Auxiliary unit, at a ceremony in the City Chambers on Friday, 22nd November. It marked a satisfactory end to the decade, but the real story was just beginning . . . and the legend had been born.

CHAPTER TWO

'. . . Ad Astra'

No 602 Squadron is as good as the best squadron in the Air Force so far as its handling of its machines is concerned. Judging by a close inspection of those machines on the ground, it is equally good in its care and maintenance. However the London squadrons pride themselves on their smart appearance they certainly will not beat Glasgow.

Extract, article by C. G. Grey, 'The Aeroplane', June 1931

The Guards Officers cruising through the leafy lanes of Windsor Great Park in their Rolls Royce were a little surprised when the silver biplane appeared just over the trees, low enough for them to read the squadron number – 602 – painted in red on the fuselage. The Park, after all, was a prohibited flying area – at any height.

On board the Hawker Hart, Pilot Officer Edward Howell got a nasty shock too, when the usually reliable Rolls-Royce Kestrel engine spluttered, coughed a couple of times, and then died. At fifty feet above the trees, he was in real trouble, but as luck would have it, a tree-lined lane suddenly appeared ahead, and he somehow managed to get the Hart down in one piece, running her round a slight bend and fetching up close to Queen Anne's Gate. He sat in the cockpit, wondering what on earth to do next.

The Rolls-Royce purred up, causing the young pilot more than a little nervous anticipation – but it was the Guards Officers who stepped out. 'You know you shouldn't be here, don't you?'

'No choice, old boy.' He nodded, and waved to the Rolls. 'You'd better hop in. . . .' He shouted a couple of crisp orders, and troops appeared as if by magic from the trees, mounting a guard on the Hart. Howell was whisked off to HQ, still wondering how he'd explain to Clydesdale the unfortunate consequences of a little low-level flying on a cross-country exercise.

'When we got there, I was more than a little disconcerted to be met by the local CO – a full colonel. He couldn't have been more accommodating though. 'Have a drink, old boy, I expect you could do with one.' After my narrow escape, the realisation where I'd landed, then confrontation with an Army Colonel, I heartily agreed. Actually, I had several – I was plied from all sides. All thoughts of telephoning base, a standing rule for pilots down, soon vanished, and a great friendship began to blossom rapidly. I accepted an invitation to lunch, and it was only after I'd been there a couple of hours that I dragged my thoughts back to my predicament. I was puzzling over why it should have happened, particularly as the Rolls-Royce engine was so reliable, when suddenly it hit me like a thunderbolt – I had committed the classic boob. The Hart takes off on a gravity tank, and the pilot then switches to his main tank. I had completely forgotten. I sheepishly confided to the colonel, and, in great humour, he just laughed, and said, 'Splendid, we'll get you back there and you can go off the way you came in.'

Back purred the Rolls, to find the Hart still under its imposing guard. A brief check confirmed Howell's suspicions, and after refilling the gravity tank, he bade his rescuers a hasty and somewhat red-faced farewell, started up, and despite the narrowness of the 'runway', and the effects of the slightly alcoholic lunch (or just possibly, as he admitted later, because of it) succeeded in lifting off, swerving round the trees, and waggling his wings in a farewell salute.

Back at Lympne, a grim-faced reception committee was waiting, headed by the CO.

'Where the hell have you been?'

'Windsor Great Park – had a great time!'

'I suppose you realise they're taking overdue action – they're searching the Channel for a corpse'.

'Don't be silly, I'm not dead, I'm here!'

'Yes, well, that's not good enough, you know.'

Shortly afterwards, a telegram arrived, in true Auxiliary style, from friends in Glasgow. Substituting 'Pop' for 'Stop', every word began with a P. PAISLEY PILOT PLUNGES PARKWARD POP POURQUOIS? POP PETROL? POP PERHAPS PALS PIMMS PARTY PRODUCED PARTIAL PARALYSIS POP.'

The story made the national newspapers – not the first, or the last, of 602's escapades to do so – and the Air Officer Commanding, Air Commodore Baldwin, came to deliver a rocket from the Air Council. 'I showed him the telegram, and his eyes twinkled. He issued a reprimand – I suppose he had to, I'd broken about six cardinal rules all at once – but we parted on good terms after some drinks in the Mess. Pimms. . . .'

Edward Howell was one of the new generation of 602 pilots – men who, almost without exception, would distinguish themselves in the war which was now less than a decade away. And who even broke the rules with style that was uniquely Auxiliary.

*

As the twenties gave way to the thirties, morale in 602 was high – in marked contrast to the depression which pervaded most of the country. With the Esher Trophy displayed at Town HQ, and with recruiting reaching an all-time high, the squadron was re-organised into three Flights, each with its own aircraft (three to a Flight), its own pilots, and its own fitters and riggers. Inter-Flight rivalry led to increased efficiency, and each Flight took on something of the character of its leadership.

The senior Flight Commander, Lennox, gave 'A' Flight a disciplined approach, while McIntyre gave 'B' Flight a slightly freer rein, emphasising flying skills. The squadron's finest aerobatics came from his Flight, which included McNab and Mitchell. Clydesdale's leadership of 'C' Flight was much more unobtrusive – as was his style when he took over the squadron in 1931. In the air, he had his foibles – he wasn't averse to leading the whole squadron down to zero feet on cross-country flights in order to read station name boards to see where he was, or even, on one occasion, actually landing to relieve the needs of nature in a little copse. Such incidents, of course, raised him ever higher in the squadron's estimation – as did one episode at the summer camp of 1932 when the squadron was at Hawkinge on the south coast.

One day when they were all up, the entire airfield and surrounding countryside were suddenly enveloped in a thick white mist, for which the English Channel is notorious. On the ground, the fitters and riggers waited, listening anxiously to the sound of aircraft circling above the mist, and then landing 'blind'. John F. Davies remembers, 'Eventually all except one came down safely, and the pilot of this machine made several attempts to land, but always at the last moment, apparently unable to judge accurately his height, he roared off again into the white void.

'Our CO stood for some time at the edge of the tarmac apron in front of the hangar, and then grimly strode to his aircraft, started up, and took off into the mist. Some minutes later we faintly discerned the CO's machine leading in the other pilot, with the aircraft almost nose to tail, and there was a general feeling of relief when they both touched down safely. I suppose that to the Marquess it was all in a CO's day's work, but the incident did earn him that little extra respect.'

'C' Flight was in turn taken over by Douglas Farquhar, while John Feather took over 'A' Flight from Lennox, who was transferred onto the Reserve List. The unit's capability in the air was further enhanced by the new adjutant, Flight Lieutenant George Stacey Hodson, AFC, who, like Clydesdale, was a Central Flying School instructor.

But perhaps the most notable addition to the ranks was their new chaplain. The Rev Lewis Albert Sutherland, commissioned in the rank of Squadron Leader in May 1931, was to prove a great asset – and was indeed to become 602's longest serving officer, finally taking his leave in 1954. He had – of course – an immaculate pedigree. Born in 1889, he was a son of the manse, and a direct descendant of the reformer John Knox. He was an accomplished piper, and could entertain 'his lads' at squadron functions in a way that might not have succeeded at any of his church meetings. A non-smoker, he nevertheless carried a perennial pack of twenty 'to give you lads some spiritual uplift!' During the Second World War, he would win the Air Efficiency Award, and be mentioned in despatches – and was awarded the OBE in the New Year Honours List of 1945. And when 602 reformed – he was one of the first to volunteer.

Throughout the early thirties, 602's reputation spread – largely through increased contact with the Regulars. In 1930, Denis McNab and David Lloyd, a new pilot from the famous steel family, became the first Auxiliaries to attend a Regular Armaments and Gunnery Course, at Eastchurch – and in the autumn, Farquhar, with his air gunner/bomb aimer R.B. 'Nobby' Clark took on the Regulars at their own game, and beat them. The occasion was the annual RAF bombing competition, for the Laurence Minot Trophy, at North Coates Fittes, near Grimsby.

September 30th was the first day of competition. In bumpy conditions, Farquhar and Clark made two runs, dropping their white smoke practice bombs plumb on target; at the end of the day, they found they were in the lead. The Regulars couldn't believe it – aerial bombing was understood to be more of an art than a science, and well beyond the capabilities of the weekenders. 602 confounded the critics, though, and after four days of competition, the Glasgow Wapiti – J9598 – emerged as runner-up in the overall rankings.

'How on earth did you get in so much practice?' demanded the defeated Regulars. 'Easy,' replied Farquhar. 'We've got our own private range. Over at the Duke of Hamilton's castle!'

David McIntyre obtained a year's attachment to one of the RAF's premier units, No 12 (Bomber) Squadron, at Andover. The 'Shiny Twelfth' was the only squadron flying the Fairey Fox, replaced during Mac's time with the advanced Hawker Hart, and was experimenting with blind formation flying, using new gyroscopic instruments. The disciplined and adaptable Mac learned fast –or, as he put it on his return, 'I soon showed 'em how to do it.'

In other fields too, 602 were showing 'How to do it.' After a cross-country exercise to Hendon, the two London squadrons, now joined by 604 (County of Middlesex) Squadron, brought up the old argument as to which unit was first to form, 600 claiming an early birth at Finsbury Barracks in August 1925, and 601 ('The Millionaires' Mob') claiming an ever earlier beginning, over cigars and port at White's Club, St James's. Andrew Rintoul recalled, 'It was decided to settle the matter with a game of rugby . . . on their pitch. I think they reckoned it to be 'their' game, and in any case doubted our ability to find our way all the way to London again in our planes. Not only did we get there, we thrashed them. In fact, we beat them three times in a row, until they gave up the practice of asking for a return game in order to satisfy honour.' Here endeth the argument.

*

Back up in the north, work continued apace on the new airfield site, while at Renfrew, a new batch of Wapiti IIas were received, and eagerly stripped, checked, reassembled, put on the 'top line' by skilled hands. . .and then shot down in flames, metaphorically speaking, by the Bulldogs of 19 Squadron, up on an Affiliation Exercise. For the first time in years, 602 found themselves technically outclassed. Edward Howell, commissioned in 1932, said of the Wapiti, hailed a few years before as a welcome advance, 'It was an awful old cow.' *Sic transit gloria.*

Howell himself, the son of the minister of Paisley Abbey, was typical of the new generation of pilots. Professional in his approach to flying, and convinced the next war would be won and lost in the air, nevertheless the appeal of the Auxiliary squadrons 'like a rather exciting club' was greater than that of the Regular RAF. He'd end up commanding the last Hurricanes in Crete.

Others agreed: George Pinkerton, one of the first speedway riders, who'd open the shooting war over our shores; Donald Law, who took over 20 Squadron in India in 1939; James Hosier Hodge, who'd become a Senior Fighter Controller, along with David Lloyd, in the Battle of Britain; the erudite Vivian Bell; tall, good-looking Marcus Robinson, who'd been impressed with the reaction of girls to an Air Force blue uniform; seventeen-year-old Sandy Johnstone, banned by his doctor from playing any more rugby for Kelvinside Academy, and looking for something interesting to do on Saturday afternoons.

As 1933 began with unusually mild weather, the new Adjutant, Stacey Hodson, celebrated by making the first official landing at Abbotsinch, now ready for occupation. He had, of course, been pre-empted by one of the Auxiliaries – Andrew Rintoul. 'It was completely unceremonious. I had engine failure, and I couldn't go anywhere else.' It was another first, though.

The move was complete by the end of January, and 602 could boast their own purpose-built airfield, complete with Abbotsburn House, formerly John Fullerton's home, and now one of the finest officers' messes anywhere.

*

Style was, of course, the keynote – and 602 together with 603, proud of their Scottish roots, hit upon the ideal scheme; form pipe bands!

Eagerly, volunteers were sought for instruments, permission from their Airships, and then they hit their first problem. They could hardly have pipe bands without Highland dress, and such a break from RAF dress regulations would clearly require permission from the very top. Clydesdale obtained permission from his father, the Duke of Hamilton, whose other sons served with 603, for both units to wear the Grey Douglas tartan. Sketches were prepared and sent off, and the Marquess began pulling some high-level strings. The final result was a letter, dated 17th June 1933 at St James' Palace, to the Chief of Air Staff: '. . . I have submitted to the King your letter . . . together with the sketch . . . of which His Majesty approves.'

Nothing like going to the top! The bandsmen, by now practising hard on chanter and drums, weren't in the least surprised. They

'...an awful old cow...'
Westland Wapiti IIs at Abbotsinch, 1933.

'As near as you get to the perfect aeroplane.'
Hawker Harts at Abbotsinch, 1934.

'With agonising slowness, they climbed straight up the wind...'
Clydesdale's Westland, photographed from McIntyre's, approaching the summit of
Everest on the first flight. 0945 hours, April 3rd, 1933.

knew their CO and the King were old friends. . .

The two pipe bands were the first in the Air Force, and continued right through until disbandment in 1957 – with a slight interruption occasioned by Hitler – and remain, to this day, the only pipe bands attached to operational squadrons, a unique distinction for the Scots Auxiliaries.

In the air, the training on the old Wapitis continued – and on one occasion came something new, when 602 were asked to provide an aircraft to take part in Royal Navy Fleet manoeuvres far out to sea. Consternation! Who could navigate accurately enough even to find the ships? Enter the squadron's resident mathematical wizard and navigational genius, newly-arrived Pilot Officer T.A.B. Smith, who coped magnificently, earning a pat on the back, and a few pink gins, from the Senior Service. Brian Smith was an intriguing character; one of those quiet, unassuming people about whom stories abound, and round whom legend persistently grows. It was said that he found it difficult to acquire a permanent air gunner, or, for that matter, even a permanent ground crew. The reason? He was always airsick – but persistently refused to let such a trifling drawback hinder his career as an aviator.

Employed by precision instrument makers Barr and Stroud of Anniesland, Smith was brilliant, and creative with it. Serving with 602 through the thirties, he was employed during the war as a Scientific Advisor by the Air Ministry developing gunsights and bombsights. His Auxiliary training made him that rarest of species – an inventor who had practical insight into the problems of using gadgets under operational conditions.

In February of 1934, 602 at last took delivery of their first Hawker Harts, two-seat day bombers of such performance that they'd easily outflown some single-seat fighters sent up against them in Air Defence exercises over London. A metal-framed fabric-covered biplane with a top speed of 184 mph, a ceiling of over 21,000 feet, and a bomb load of 500 lbs, it had a wing span of just over 37 feet, and was armed, in the accepted pattern, with a fixed forward-firing Vickers machine gun, and a ring-mounted Lewis gun aft. These are the bare statistics, but what no figures can convey is the impact this elegant, silver aircraft had upon her pilots.

Denis McNab reckoned the Hart to be '. . . as near as you get to the perfect aeroplane. No matter how adventurous you were, it could accommodate you with ease – and we were certainly adventurous. We used to fly 'em nose inside tail in formation. And – we got 'em before 603!'

Edward Howell, forty years later, was still almost lyrical in his praise of the Hart – and particularly its Rolls-Royce Kestrel engine: 'Ah, now there was a beautiful engine. Our fitters liked them too. They ran so well they practically maintained themselves. I was never once let down. Of course, there was that one little occasion when I let the Kestrel down.'

Which is where we came in. But if Edward Howell's low-level exploits made the inner pages of the national newspapers, two of 602's senior pilots had made front page headlines with one of the most daring high altitude flights of the decade. The RAF has as its motto '*Per Ardua Ad Astra*' – through effort to the stars. The City of Glasgow Squadron had just come as close as any man could.

CHAPTER THREE

Everest

> To the pilots, the recollection is at once romantic and a little unreal. Something of the mystery has been overcome and something of the unknown revealed; yet the Mistress of the World remains remote, immense and magnificent.
>
> *Extract, The Pilots' Book of Everest,*
> *(Clydesdale & McIntyre)*

At precisely 10.05 am local time, on 3rd April 1933, man first looked down on the summit of the highest point on earth – and Everest had been conquered. It was, though, the briefest of glimpses. As the large Westland biplane was lifted bodily over the Mistress of the World in an airstream rushing up the western slopes and tearing powdered snow into a plume stretching four miles downwind, the pilot, the Marquess of Douglas and Clydesdale, with Lt Colonel L.V. Stewart Blacker in the observer's cockpit, was frantically correcting for drift, checking survey cameras, and searching for the second aircraft, last seen fighting 100 mph winds as it struggled towards the summit. At its controls, his senior Flight Commander on 602 Squadron, David McIntyre.

The involvement of 602 in the Houston–Mount Everest Expedition began in early 1932, when Clydesdale was approached by Blacker and Colonel P.T. Etherton, who were planning a survey flight over Everest. The object was threefold: to show what British aircraft and pilots could do; to make the first survey of the region, which would lead to more accurate maps; and to investigate some of the practicalities – and mysteries – of high altitude flying.

Clydesdale, accepted as first pilot with his Central Flying School experience, suggested McIntyre as second pilot, and 602's John Feather as reserve. All were accepted, though Feather had to pull out through illness. He also involved Lady Houston, who'd already provided £100,000 to back the development of the Supermarine S6B seaplane which, without official government backing, had won the Schneider Trophy for Britain the year before.

Over the next year, the planning was completed.

In equipment terms, the most important item was the engine. The choice was obvious, since the Bristol Pegasus had recently set a new world's height record when Cyril Uwins climbed to 44,000 feet. The aircraft to carry it was a natural consequence – one of the large general purpose RAF biplane types, similar to the Westland Wapiti flown by 602. And Westlands it was who provided the goods. One was the PV3, a private development of the firm's, soon renamed the Houston-Westland. The second machine, the PV6, was an adapted prototype of the Westland Wallace, fitted with the supercharged Pegasus engine and a closed rear cockpit with angled side windows for oblique photography. This would be McIntyre's machine.

Bit by bit, thousands of items of gear were tested and assembled, from electrically heated flying suits to big game rifles, and in February of 1933 the adventurers finally set off on an epic flight across Europe and the Middle East.

After some incredible escapades, including the loss of a Fox Moth in a storm, blind flying over an African desert, and a short stay in an Italian gaol, they all made it, and the assault on Everest was planned from their base – the tiny landing strip of Lalbalu, nine miles east of Purnea in Bihar State.

April 3rd, 08.25 hours. With a shattering roar, the two Westlands threw up an enormous dust cloud as they lumbered into the air, fully laden, and set course at last for Everest; for weeks, they'd waited for the weather to improve. Conditions today were marginal, but time was running out. At a relatively low throttle setting, the big machines climbed steadily and powerfully through the thick morning air, vanishing into the red dust haze which hung over the plains, and covered the skirts of the Mistress of the World.

At 19,000 feet, they finally broke through, and the pilots found their breath taken away by the magnificent sight which appeared before them. They were at the centre of a vast amphitheatre of the most gigantic mountains in the world. In unlimited visibility, they gazed 100 miles east to the massif of Kangchenjunga; 100 miles west, the remarkable pointed peak of Gauri Sankar. And just to starboard of their track, Everest, 50 miles distant.

That final fifty miles saw them fighting a continuing battle with the westerly winds, rising in strength as the Westlands clawed for height. As they passed the 24,012 foot peak of Chamlang, it loomed over their port wings; it should have been slipping underneath, well to starboard. They turned further west, forcing the big machines higher.

Disaster struck on the final run-in. Just where they would have expected an upcurrent of air off the slopes of Lhotse, they hit an enormous, violent downdraught – wind deflected at some 70 mph off Everest itself. Within seconds, they lost 2,000 feet, and were blown directly towards the knife-edge ridges of Makalu.

Clydesdale, a few hundred feet higher to start with, recovered first, and with infinite patience and skill, fought his way right up through the plume of ice particles and vapour whipping from the summit of Everest itself. With agonising slowness, they climbed straight up the wind, and as they felt themselves lifted over the top by a final, jolting updraught, Clydesdale dropped the right wing slightly, and they caught a brief glimpse of a rocky, windswept platform big enough for perhaps four people to stand on, but never before seen by man. Automatically, Clydesdale checked his watch: 10.05 am.

As the Houston-Westland swept away downwind, McIntyre in the Wallace was having serious problems. He'd lost even more height, and had to crab right up to the knife-edge ridge stretching between Everest and Makalu four times, gaining a little precious height each time, before finally crossing it to the north and approaching their target. In the rear cockpit, British Gaumont film photographer Sidney Bonnett worked nervelessly away with the cine and stills cameras, shooting memorable close-ups of the enormous rock formations and ice sheets as his pilot continued to take enormous, but calculated, risks.

As they cleared the north-west ridge, Bonnett dived down, rapidly reloaded his camera, and accidentally trod on his oxygen line as he stood up again. In the intense, brittle cold, the feed pipe fractured close to his face mask. With the Wallace banking for the final run-in to the summit, he collapsed, and with the last of his failing strength, wrapped a handkerchief around the split. As McIntyre lifted over the summit, he turned again to check on Bonnett's predicament, and felt his own face mask come away. As the big biplane swept back downwind, Mac had to hold his mask with one hand, and fly with the other.

For sixty miles of the return journey, he was convinced Bonnett was dead; at 8,000 feet over Forbesganj, however, something flickered in his rear-view mirror, and he turned round to see Bonnett shakily standing up, his face a 'nasty dark green shade', gulping the warmer, thicker air for all he was worth.

They touched down at 11.25, handed over Bonnett to the team's medic, and set about exposing the survey films. Consternation – both the main survey cameras had jammed. They decided to do the whole thing again!

In the interim, Fellowes and the replacement pilot, Dick Ellison, did a survey flight over Kangchenjunga, at 28,146 feet the third highest in the Himalayas, and hit similar troubles. Fellowes, in fact, ran out of fuel, and had to be rescued the following day from his emergency landing ground. In Britain, the company insuring the expedition telegraphed that they'd taken enough risks already, and wouldn't be insured for any more. Lady Houston cabled: 'Be content. Do not tempt the evil spirits of the mountain to bring disaster.' After a fortnight's wrangling, during which the weather only added to the gloom, a final telegram was much blunter; 'Pack up and return to England.'

Now, even Fellowes admitted defeat, but not so the pilots. McIntyre, disgusted by the failure of the survey cameras, had personally stripped, cleaned, and reassembled his. He wouldn't let anybody near it. Then Fortune played her hand. Fellowes fell ill, and while he was thus otherwise occupied, the two 602 men seized their chance on a day with even more marginal weather than on the first flight. At 07.52 on 19th April, they were off, having secured permission for a 'test flight'. This time, they flew at low level far to the south-west of their target, before climbing hard to windward of Everest. The oxygen systems and cameras functioned perfectly. Climbing to 31,000 feet in hurricane force winds, they swept over towards their target. Clydesdale, marginally miscalculating the drift, missed it by just over three miles, and turned back into wind to try again; he failed. At an indicated airspeed of 122 mph, the Houston-Westland was actually being slowly blown *backwards* over the ground. But McIntyre got it exactly right. Bearing further and further to the left after crossing the Dingboche Monastery, he crabbed almost sideways at 34,000 feet towards the summit, before turning squarely into wind and fighting for fully fifteen minutes at full throttle before crossing it with 'a terrific bump – just one terrific impact such as one might receive flying low over an explosives factory as it blew up.'

When the Wallace finally touched down, fifteen minutes after Clydesdale, it had been in the air a few minutes short of four hours, and its fuel exhaustion time had, on paper, been reached. It had been a close thing. Fortune favours the bold, however, and the pilots were delighted to discover that not only had both survey cameras functioned, but they'd both, by an incredible coincidence, exposed their last frames over exactly the same spot – a perfect datum point for the map-makers. And, as Mac pointed out to an irate Fellowes, the question of insurance hardly mattered –now.

They'd accomplished all their objectives, scientific, geographical, and aeronautical. On the way, they'd also become household names, their pictures flashed round the world. Their exploits would be celebrated in books, and in the film *Wings Over Everest*.

The mountain known to local sherpas as Chomolungma – 'The Mountain So High No Bird Can Fly Over It' – had finally surrendered to man's skill, resourcefulness, and courage – and the employment of a rather Nelsonian blind eye towards authority. But then isn't that just how 602 would do it?

CHAPTER FOUR

'Beware the Crossed Lion!'

The conclusion which might have to be drawn from the above figures,
if they are correct, is that this country is seriously open to the threat of
sudden attack by a continental power in a degree to which it has not
been exposed for hundreds of years.

*Extract, letter dated 10th April 1935, from Sir John Simon, the Foreign
Secretary, to the Prime Minister, following a visit to Berlin, during which
Hitler had told him that the German Air Force was already as strong as the
RAF, and was expanding.*

Young Sandy Johnstone was disobeying doctor's orders, as he
climbed into the observer's seat of Douglas Farquhar's Hart for his
first trip in the type. Not that he was forbidden to fly – but the 602
men were bound for a rugby match against an English Auxiliary
XV. The date was Sunday, 25th February 1935; the weather was
cold, crisp and clear as the five 602 Harts left Abbotsinch for
Turnhouse, where they were joined by five more from 603. All ten
aircraft wheeled, and set course for RAF Usworth, on the outskirts
of Newcastle. At first, all went well, but shortly after crossing the
border into 'enemy territory', the formation ran into snow.

Minutes passed: the swirling white flakes grew denser, and soon
the Scots felt their aircraft being increasingly buffeted about in the
face of a gale, which was by now whipping the snow into a
blizzard.

All five 602 aircraft instinctively turned for the coast, intending to
fly back to Turnhouse, where the weather would hopefully be
clearer. Three Harts flew in tight 'nose inside tail' formation –
Farquhar's, Jimmie Hodge's and Andrew Rintoul's. These three
pilots all had considerable experience. Less experienced, but
nevertheless grimly hanging on, were Marcus Robinson and John
Shewell, whose Harts could be seen intermittently through freak
clear patches. Hitting the coast just south of Alnwick, the 602 men
blindly groped their way northwards; navigation was by dead
reckoning, since the ground was almost totally lost to view, and in
addition they had no idea of wind strength.

By the time they reached the Firth of Forth, all the 602 aircraft were very low on fuel, and with visibility worse, even the largest landmarks were invisible through the blizzard. Suddenly the 602 men found themselves right over the Forth Bridge; they were extremely lucky – flying below the level of the bridge top, they burst through into a clearer patch, to discover the huge structure slap in front of their eyes, unavoidably close, but as luck would have it they were approaching the bridge midway between two of the three enormous cantilevers. Safely past this obstacle, Farquhar signalled the other pilots to break off; it was every man for himself, as the Harts desperately sought landing ground.

Farquhar swung round to eastwards, and began to creep back along the coast. Suddenly, with the Hart at only fifty feet and one hundred yards offshore, the Kestrel's even note died abruptly. The fuel tank was empty. Farquhar swung towards the shore, and the Hart silently glided through the eddying storm, buffeted this way and that; an eerie experience for young Johnstone.

Suddenly Farquhar glimpsed some sand, just when the Hart was running out of usable height. Swiftly and skilfully he set her down on the only flat stretch of shore for miles around – Portobello beach. The sturdy biplane bounced and slewed over the semi-frozen, skidding surface, lurched over a couple of sewage pipes, and finally ground to a halt near the water's edge.

An old man with a dog nodded amiably to them, as though the sight of a bomber arriving in a storm on the beach was an everyday occurrence. Soon a crowd had gathered, and Farquhar enlisted their aid. By this time water was lapping at the Hart's wheels, as the tide rose, and so the aircraft was dragged by willing helpers along the beach and up a slipway to the road. Farquhar and Johnstone tethered it – one wing to a lamp-post and the other to a drinking fountain – and then left a bemused local policeman standing guard over it, while they set off for the local police station.

One by one, all the other pilots turned up safe and more or less in one piece – though Jimmie Hodge had his temper (and more) inflamed as he slid down the cowling of his upended Hart which had buried its nose in a field. The aluminium was rather hot.

Young Johnstone never did get his game of rugby, though he'd certainly had a weekend to remember.

Later in the year, George Pinkerton's air gunner, Johnny Strain, added another chapter. During an exercise at 15,000 feet over the Trossachs, while leaping about in the rear cockpit trying to get his sights on one of the attacking Hawker Furies of No 1 Squadron, he trod on the control wires. Pinkerton, feeling the elevators and rudder stiffening up, and guessing what had happened, turned round and pointed down, mouthing silent but obviously urgent words. Strain, completely misunderstanding, leapt smartly over the side and pulled his ripcord. Pinkerton could only return to Abbotsinch, and it was a highly disgruntled pilot who motored to Kippen to pick up his gunner. The squadron, of course, were delighted, particularly when it was established that Strain's impromptu performance had set some kind of height record.

Later, Strain would train in the RAFVR as a pilot, and serve two tours as a Hampden pilot on 489 (Torpedo) Squadron, picking up the DFC. This was a statistical miracle; he should have been shot down at least four times – but he never once had to use his parachute in earnest.

One way and another, 1935 was proving a memorable year. Training continued apace under their new Adjutant, Flight Lieutenant A.D. 'Mark' Selway, whose methods were inspired: 'I'd post up a complete programme for the weekend, and leave them to it. Sunday evening was devoted to finding out what they'd *actually* been up to. As often as not, instead of doing simulated bombing on the range, they'd be bucking the winds over Corryvreckan or somewhere equally risky. But I believe in a loose rein, for pilots need initiative and imagination, and ought to be left to themselves to cogitate on the mysteries of the air.'

A wise man, whose methods were fully vindicated when, in the summer, 602 became the first Auxiliary Squadron to attend an Armaments Training Camp, at North Coates. At the end of a fortnight's intensive air firing and bombing, they turned in better results than any of the Regulars had been getting.

That summer also saw the great Royal Review at RAF Mildenhall, on the occasion of King George V's Jubilee. All the Auxiliary units were detailed to send three aircraft and pilots, 602 being represented by Farquhar, Rintoul and Selway. They arrived, set the aircraft in the static display line, and set off for the officers' mess, where they received the unwelcome news that, with so many visiting aircrew, there was no room to put them up overnight, and, along with other Auxiliaries, they were to sleep in tents. Fair enough, they thought, and duly went under canvas. But then, they discovered that they weren't allowed into the hallowed precincts of the officers' mess at all – not even for a drink. Rintoul: 'We adjourned to the local, and, suitably fortified, hatched our plot. If we couldn't get in, then they weren't going to get out, either. Round about two in the morning, with the airfield settled for the night and nothing but snores wafting from the mess windows, we crept over to where some construction work had been going on. All the ingredients were there, and we quietly bricked up all the entrances. The weather was on our side; the cement set fast, and they couldn't sort it out the next morning before the King arrived. It was beautiful, and not a word was said.'

As they celebrated their tenth anniversary, with Mess Secretary Jimmie Hodge organising special cards through the family publishing firm ('They sold well – so we did Christmas cards and postcards too. Good, sound, profitable enterprise . . .') new faces appeared: Dunlop Urie and Hector MacLean, both destined to have a nasty run-in with the Luftwaffe over the English Channel; Findlay Boyd, the fair-haired coalmaster's son with the piercing blue eyes, who'd become the most successful of all the Scots Auxiliaries; lean, lanky Donald Jack; the handsome P.J. 'Ian' Ferguson; and the little man who'd fly and fight like no other in his Hurricane over London, Archie McKellar.

The Regulars came in 1936, when Wing Comander Brian Baker arrived to command Abbotsinch, and No 34 Squadron flew in from Bircham Newton in their Hinds. They parked them in five new canvas Bessoneaux hangars – and were promptly blown almost literally away by a 90 mph gale which uprooted the hangars. 602's spanking new Hinds were safely under cover in the airfield's only permanent hangar. Even then, they'd learned the art of keeping their heads down when it mattered.

In 1937, they went to summer camp at RAF Rochford, near (to the delight of many) Southend, and, at a special guest night at the Palace Hotel, attended by the local council, 602 notched up another 'first'.

Just before they left Abbotsinch, the word had finally come through that permission had at last been granted for the officers of the Glasgow and Edinburgh Squadrons to wear Grey Douglas kilts with their Mess Dress. Both units had sought permission the year before, since, apart from sartorial considerations (important in the Auxiliary lifestyle) it would be another Air Force 'first' (even more important).

Thanks to some high-level contacts, 602 were well prepared with the result that the officers appeared in full Grey Douglas splendour at the Palace Hotel; the first to go 'operational' with their new equipment. A great time was had by all – in fact, rumour has it that the inevitable Sassenach question about the kilt was answered. But alas, modesty forbids. . .

Camp was also notable for one other reason – the official presentation, by Air Commodore Goble, of the squadron crest, and thereby (of course) hangs a tale. Some while previously, the Auxiliary squadrons had all been requested to design appropriate badges, within the standard Air Force crest pattern. The Glasgow unit, with due regard to the squadron's origins, submitted a design featuring a winged bowler hat over crossed umbrellas, with the legend 'No 602 (City of Glasgow) Gentlemen's Bomber Squadron'. They were told in no uncertain terms to stop messing about.

Their final design at first glance, was appropriate enough; even inspired. It bore the two Scottish symbols – the Lion Rampant superimposed on a St Andrew's Cross, with the impressive Latin legend '*Cave Leonem Cruciatum*'. This, they said, translates as 'Beware the Crucified Lion', or, more idiomatically, 'Beware the Lion When Crossed'. 'Fine', said the authorities, relieved that the Glasgow unit were at last approaching the thing in the right spirit. The design was submitted to the King, and approved by the Chester Herald. Only when it was a fait accompli did 602 quietly spread the true idiomatic translation – 'Beware the Castrated Lion!' 'Still the squadron badge to this day,' points out one of the perpetrators, Dunlop Urie, 'and still pretty sound advice too.'

In October, 602 said farewell to McIntyre, who had succeeded Clydesdale as CO, but who was now destined to write his name into aviation history as the man who, by his drive, enthusiasm, and vision, built up Prestwick Airport, Scottish Aviation Ltd, and who ran the RAFVR training schemes which provided much-needed pilots and aircrew; the eastern end of the Atlantic Bridge ferrying aircraft and men in their thousands during the war years; and then, in peacetime, developed internal and European air routes, and the manufacturing centre which started with the Prestwick Pioneer, expanded with the distinctive triple-tailed Twin Pioneer, and which still produces Bulldog trainers and Jetstream feederliners.

His successor was Douglas Farquhar, who'd just come fourth in the RAF's dive-bombing competition at Upper Heyford, and who was destined to lead 602 to war just two short years hence.

Nineteen thirty-eight was Glasgow's big year. In defiance of growing international tension, the city staged the great Empire

Exhibition, from April to October. 602, of course, were at the centre of things, with a flypast at the close of the King's speech at the opening, and mounting exhibitions, and pipe band displays, throughout the summer in Bellahouston Park.

At the close of the whole thing, they staged something special. Three Hinds, piloted by Pinkerton, McKellar and Paul Webb, a new pilot, co-operated with searchlights in the night sky over Ibrox Stadium. As thousands of heads craned upwards, the three aircraft shimmered, held in the crossed beams, and then dived, with flares streaming from their wingtips, tracing fiery patterns in the night sky over the city; it was beautiful, but ominous. Would these same searchlights soon be seeking other targets – Heinkels and Dorniers?

Working hard under their new CO, 602 set new flying hours records. But if the squadron worked hard it also, of course, played hard. At the summer camp of 1938, when they went again to Hawkinge, Farquhar decided the men had earned a break.

Each year, the CO was given a certain amount of money by the local Territorial Association, for 'the recreation of airmen during annual training'. The CO decided on a bold venture: a day in France for the whole squadron; the officers ard 150 men set sail on the *Maid of Kent*, and the aircraftmen were each given a few shillings' pocket money. Volunteer guides in Boulogne were arranged through the British Legion, and the officers watched as the men, under strict orders to return to the dock by 7.00 pm, hit the town in a wave.

The officers chartered a few taxis, and headed along the coast to Le Touquet, to try their luck at the tables. No one came away any richer, though, and at the end of the day they returned to the ship, where a Warrant Officer stood by the gangway checking off names from his roster as the men came aboard; some carried parcels for home, others had bottles of wine, some came arm-in-arm with ladies who'd shown them the sights the British Legion wouldn't – and all were clean and sober. The local Gendarmerie hadn't a single complaint all day.

There was a problem, though, as Vivian Bell remembered: 'Five minutes before we sailed, five men were still missing, when round the warehouse building skidded a fast-moving Citroën, and out leapt the missing men, hotly pursued by an equal number of girls, who threw their arms around them, shouting various things in French as they came aboard. The squadron, it seemed, had indeed acquitted itself with distinction on its first overseas operation. On the passage back, I asked one of the late arrivals where he had learned French, only to be told that he knew not a word of it; neither did any of his pals, but they had "got along just fine". He added, "You don't half get a lot for a few bob, though, sir." He appeared empty-handed, so I asked, "A lot of what?" He just grinned. "Anything at all . . . sir!" '

Ironically enough, the only man to encounter slight problems was one of the officers, Findlay Boyd, who was asked to leave a certain hotel. Vengeance comes to him who waits, however, 'In 1942, when I was commanding a Spitfire Wing at Kenley, we were ordered to send a couple of aircraft to shoot up a Gestapo HQ in a certain hotel – guess which one! I took the job on myself; I only had to do it once.'

CHAPTER FIVE
'Spitfire!'

Item no.	Time Over aerodrome	Pilots	Aircraft	
14	17.30	F/Lt Pinkerton	Avro 504N	(1925)
	17.32	F/O Urie	Avro Tutor	(1931)
	17.34	F/Lt Robinson	Hind 7229	(1936)
	17.36	F/O Johnstone	Gauntlet 'L'	(1938)
	17.38	S/L Farquhar	Spitfire	(1939)

Extract, Flying Programme, Empire Air Day,
RAF Abbotsinch, 20th May 1939.

The peace of the airfield was shattered. 'B-brroom – bang!' From behind a hangar came the full-throated, crackling roar which was to become the audible symbol of Britain's fight for survival. For the first time, the crowd heard a Rolls-Royce Merlin in full song – and, with the power of over a thousand horses beating the eardrums of the spectators, a lean camouflaged fighter swung into wind, accelerated across the grass and leapt into the sky. The awkward, splayed legs which had held it to earth vanished into its slim, bird-like wings, and the snarling Merlin carried it swiftly, cleanly, into its element. As the echoes rolled around the hills of Renfrewshire, excited chatter broke out. What was it? Almost out of earshot, the tiny shape banked gracefully, silhouetted briefly against the late afternoon sky, beautiful to watch. But as it swooped like a hawk and shot past the crowd once more, the bellow of the Merlin, the sharpness of the form, the momentary blurring of the outline, left one overriding impression. This was a killer. A Spitfire.

More significantly, it was a 602 Squadron Spitfire, flown by Douglas Farquhar. They were, at that point, the only Auxiliaries flying them, at a time when many Regular units were just forsaking biplanes for the slower Hurricane. It had been a far-sighted, and indeed inspired, decision to make 602 only the eighth squadron overall to receive the aircraft which would make the first kills over Britain, and which they would fly in its many forms throughout the war.

As the last few months of 'peace for our time' ran out like the grains in an hour glass, 602 found themselves switched first to Army Co-operation duties ('They gave us bloody Hawker Hectors,' lamented Boyd, 'and we fooled around for a couple of months in unreliable planes getting thoroughly brassed off') – and then to fighters. The nimble Gloster Gauntlets were a delight to fly, and in common with 603, the Glasgow squadron adjusted to their new role, practising fighter tactics and filling the Renfrewshire skies with the snarl of Bristol Mercury radials.

They prepared for war. The clean, silver lines of the biplanes were covered with drab olive green and earth-coloured camouflage paint and – horror of horrors – the proud squadron letters substituted by the anonymous grey code letters LO. The last of the Auxiliary pilots appeared – solicitor Norman Stone from Whitecraigs, and N.S. Graeme, who would transfer to 607, the Durham squadron, and go off to fight in France. The first of McIntyre's VR Sergeant Pilots came from Prestwick; Andy McDowall, who'd knock down a dozen enemy aircraft over the green fields of England, and Bryden, who'd be the first to die. LAC Randall Phillips gained another 'first' for 602 by wangling a long leave from the Clydesdale Bank, becoming, in April 1939, the first Auxiliary 'tradesman' to volunteer for the newly-instituted NCO pilot category in the Auxiliary Air Force itself; he would return to 602 just in time for the Battle of Britain.

Others, unable to train within the Air Force, found other ways; the Civil Air Guard was a scheme by which flying clubs around the country were assisted officially in the training of pilots who would retain civilian status, but who would be available should the need arise. At Renfrew, the Scottish Flying Club operated the scheme with over sixty pupils, including the author's father, who'd tried to join a war once before. In 1918, as a lad of fifteen, he'd lied about his age – but they'd caught him out. In 1937, he'd tried the RAF, but they'd told him that due to his hands being deformed, he'd never be able to fly a plane, and anyway he was too old. An excellent driver and golfer, he wasn't too worried. He lied about his age again – the other way round – and enrolled in the Air Guard. Soon he, too, was flying Tiger Moths and Gypsy Moths around Renfrew. Nobody could deny that Glasgow was preparing for war in the air.

No 602 received a couple of docile Fairey Battles – their first experience of low-wing monoplanes with retractable undercarriages and flaps. Definitely, they agreed, the shape of things to

'All clear – Chocks away!'
Hawker Hind K5507, Abbotsinch, 1937.
Note underwing bomb shackles.

George Pinkerton with his newly-camouflaged Gloster Gauntlet, at Abbotsinch in May 1939. Note the gunsight, prominent atop the cowling.

At this point, the Spitfires had just begun to arrive. It's interesting to speculate what might have happened if 602 had gone to war in the Gauntlets – Pinkerton might never have caught Pohle's Ju88 at all . . .

The code letters are interesting, too. LO was originally allocated to the squadron, and carried at the Empire Air Day display in May 1939. Then they were switched to ZT – carried by the early Spitfires – no doubt to confuse enemy observers. At the outbreak of war, they reverted to LO.

'You take the high road...'
602 over Loch Lomond.

'Aces High?'
As Findlay Boyd throws down the gauntlet to Archie McKellar, Sandy Johnstone gets on the blower to Dunlop Urie. Marcus Robinson is already developing a Flight Commander's frown... Summer Camp, Rochford, 1937.

come. And clearly something was coming. But what? Everyone knew the Auxiliaries only ever got second-hand planes; hadn't the Edinburgh boys just taken delivery of a batch of hand-me-down Gloster Gladiators from 54 Squadron when they received their precious Spitties?

Then, in the spring, she came, in all her wicked beauty.

*

She made her entrance early in May, as the Glasgow pilots were flying their Gauntlets in preparation for the Air Day. As she banked across the western sky, her stark silhouette, her thin, eerie whistle, and her sheer speed somehow stilled the thousand activities of a busy airfield. A captive audience watched as she straightened, sideslipped a little height off, and throttled back on her approach, exhausts popping and crackling. The slender undercarriage appeared, and, with a final burst of power, she settled neatly on the grass, sitting back arrogantly on her tailwheel, before taxiing over to the dispersal area, swinging her tail tantalisingly.

And the men gathered round her; pilots and groundcrews alike, with pulses beating just a little faster, began to let her presence fill their senses – and she gave pleasure. The slenderness of the fuselage, the graceful ellipse of those elegant, slim wings, the threat of the eight .303 Browning guns, their flash eliminators protruding through the leading edges . . . the power of the Merlin, betrayed by the depth of the nose cowling, the soft tinkling of cooling metal, and the size of the huge propeller that had to absorb all the torque . . . and her lingering aroma – a subtle mix of hot aluminium, high-octane fuel, glycol, burnt oil and camouflage paint – hers and hers alone, it excited; the warm, familiar scent of a lover.

Reginald Mitchell, despite the cancer which was slowly but surely taking his life, had laboured on his final creation, and lived long enough to see just one – the prototype K5054 – take to the air. And he knew it was right. His masterpiece would continue in production throughout the war. It would fly to the edge of the stratosphere; it would dive to near the speed of sound; it would endure terrible battle damage and carry its pilots back to fight another day; it would stalk the enemy over the sands of the desert, the depths of the ocean, and the scarred earth of Europe; and it would kill. When told that they were going to give it a name from an abandoned project – 'Spitfire', Mitchell grunted, 'Just the sort of bloody silly name they would choose!' But did ever a name turn out to be more apt?

No 602's early Spitfires were from the first production batch, and they weren't exactly perfect. They had three-bladed two-pitch props, with one setting for take-off, and another for flight; woe betide any pilot who attempted to take off in coarse pitch –result, one hole in the airfield boundary hedge, one bent Spitfire, and a pilot who wouldn't do it again, either because he'd learned his lesson, or else because he'd never fly again.

Another problem was oil slinging – the early Merlins leaked oil in copious quantities, most of which whipped down the fuselage and blew off around the tail. Things got worse when the propeller problem was solved by the introduction of constant-speed propellers. These threw off their own oil too. It wasn't just messy – it deposited an oily film over the cockpit, which impaired long-range vision, and which turned soapy in the rain. But this problem was solved on Clydeside. At the Rolls-Royce Aero Engine plant at Hillington, new oil seals for the Merlins were developed; while Douglas Farquhar, along with some of 602's engineering types, designed an oil collector ring which drew off the slipstreaming propeller oil. This device was subsequently approved by Fighter Command, and fitted to all the Spitfires. A minor, but significant, 602 'first'.

As each new Spitfire arrived at Abbotsinch, fresh in her warpaint, the fitters, riggers and armourers would transform her; the airframe checked, the engine, hydraulics, electrics, and control runs stripped and carefully reassembled, the radios tuned, and the eight Brownings mounted in the wings. Then the fighter would spit lead for the first time at the butts, as the guns were harmonised to the reflector sights. Finally, she would receive her grey code letters – ZT – her own individual letter, and, most important of all, the Lion Rampant crest on her cowling, marking her out as a City of Glasgow Spitfire.

Forty years on, Dunlop Urie still had a gleam in his eye: 'My first flight in a Spitfire was the greatest thrill of my life – bar *none*. I sat in her, went through the drill – BTFCPUR, which stood for Brakes, Trim, Flaps, Contacts, Petrol, Undercarriage, and Radiator – but there was a much easier, and completely unprintable, way of memorising it of course. Then, tighten the harness, press the button, and after a few flicks of that enormous prop, the Merlin roared into life. I could see the chocks being pulled away through the blue smoke that whipped back; I checked the dials, eased the throttle forward, let the brakes off, and she moved. A final check, and then I ran up the engine, with the noise mounting and short blue flames stabbing back from the exhausts. She was away, and I was aware of a swing to the right as the tail came up at sixty. I checked it with the rudder, she lifted and accelerated, and as I raised the wheels, she leapt forward. Before I knew where I was, Dunoon was in sight below the wing root. She was in her element: so, at last, was I.'

*

The letters came on a Wednesday in August. On the blue envelope, 'ON HIS MAJESTY'S SERVICE. URGENT. EMBODIMENT'. Inside, the message 'NOTICE OF CALLING OUT.'

And so the weekenders went to a war that they knew had come, ten days before Chamberlain's announcement. The fitters and riggers reported for duty, and, across the country, the pilots hastily packed their bags and took their leave of wives, sweethearts, loved ones. Pinkerton hadn't far to travel, he was one of the first to arrive. Bell was harvesting at his farm in Wiltshire when he got the telephone call from Farquhar – 'Be up here by first light tomorrow.' John Feather, holidaying in the South of France, was last in – just a day late. Sandy Johnstone, after a day's sailing on the Clyde, finally got to Abbotsinch at two in the morning, to find the whole airfield ablaze with lights, and 269 Squadron's Ansons already leaving for their forward base at Montrose. 602 had investigated the possibilities of a detachment going to Grangemouth, recently opened as a civil airport by David McIntyre. A few days later, Farquhar and Johnstone set off, on a Sunday morning, to check it out. They landed to find the place deserted; taxying up to the buildings, Farquhar had just finished muttering 'Where the hell is everyone?', when two figures emerged from an air raid shelter, looking very relieved. One of them recognised Sandy. 'Och, it's you, Mr Johnstone! We were told you were Germans. Haven't you heard? The sirens went off ten minutes ago. We're at war.'

CHAPTER SIX

'Suicide Corner'

October 17th 1939. Normal routine.
Telegrams received:
1. From A,C,M. Sir Hugh Dowding, GCVO, KCB, CMG, ADC,
   AOC-IN-C Fighter Command: "Well done. First blood to the
   Auxiliaries".

Extract, 602 Squadron Operations Record

Christ, I joined for the dancing, not for the fighting . . .
Flying Officer Archie McKellar, on hearing
Chamberlain's Sunday morning broadcast

Flight Lieutenant John Dunlop Urie was beginning to suspect
someone was leading him a merry dance, too. Orbiting May Island,
he peered through the curved perspex of his Spitfire's cockpit
canopy, only too award that the fighter had its blind spots – behind,
under the wing roots, and ahead of the long nose cowling with its
flared exhaust stacks. He was searching for the enemy – the enemy
he'd opened his own shooting war against the previous day, when
he'd shared in the destruction of one of the reconnaissance Heinkels
brought down during the Forth raid. Now, with the telegrams of
congratulations arriving, the BBC broadcasting 602's success to the
nation, and Drem at a high state of readiness, he'd been scrambled
to intercept an incoming aircraft, plotted on the primitive radar
screens at Drone Hill and St Abb's head.

The fighter controller's voice crackled through the static – 'Bogey
now at 5,000 feet. Steer 180 degrees. He's close. . . .'

Urie hauled the Spitfire round to the south, craning his neck
round, quartering the sky. Nothing. A 'bogey' meant an unidentified aircraft. Friend or foe – a definite enemy sighting was a 'bandit'.
But they all knew the form now – a succession of single recce aircraft
had come over before yesterday's raid. Urie was searching for the
Heinkel that would be carrying back today's information on ship
dispositions, fighter reaction, and damage inflicted by Pohle's
efforts. Still nothing. He banked round towards the island as the
controller's voice crackled again – 'Villa One Five, Bogey now at
Angels 10' (10,000 feet).

'Roger. Angels 10. Climbing.' He eased the Spitfire's nose up, and climbed over May Island, circling, searching . . . and with a nasty suspicion beginning to dawn . . .

'Hullo, Villa One Five. Bogey appears to be circling. Now at Angels 13. Climb on 270 degrees.'

Urie glanced down at his compass, below the flight panel. He was already on 270, as near as dammit. His altimeter flicked round to 13,000 feet – and he knew. He was chasing himself! The other aircraft, whatever it was, had long since disappeared. He'd been flying in ever-decreasing circles, in perfect imitation of the legendary Greater Ogo Pogo Bird, which performs a similar stunt, before vanishing up its own backside, from which it continues to throw abuse at its hunters.

Disgusted, he levelled off, straightened out, and headed for Drem, determined to collect at least a drink from a certain fighter controller.

They were all still learning. Vivian Bell, inheriting the keys to the safe, the squadron's war book, and a pile of mysterious documents marked 'MOST SECRET. ONLY TO BE OPENED IN TIME OF WAR', from the Regular Adjutant. Hodder – who returned, on the day war was declared, to marry Hermione Jones, the station CO's daughter; the couple would have no trouble in future remembering their anniversary – 'Yes, that's when all the trouble started officially, old boy.' 602 were thoughtful. They'd read up on the aces of the Great War, and couldn't help noticing most of them were dead. Within a week of war breaking out, Donald Jack, Findlay Boyd and Dunlop Urie had all got married – and they were all wondering how long that lifelong vow might last.

Farquhar, the leader, the master of air fighting technique, was busy. Not just training his tender young VR sergeant pilots, but working on ways to improve the Spitfire as a fighting machine. The oil thrown off by the VP airscrews was causing problems, but this was solved by a collector ring designed by 602's engineering types – it was photographed in action, details forwarded to Fighter Command, and became a standard fitting. The armourers, led by R.T. Richards, Bert Simpson and Corporal Emerson, designed new quick-loading curved metal feeds for the gunbelts, and cut the re-arming time for the fighter in half.

Day and night, the Spitfires incessantly flew their patrols and circuits. Two days into the war, George Pinkerton broke the first one, landing at night through haze, in minimal lighting; Ian Ferguson only got down safely courtesy of a hastily-gathered collection of vehicles, lined up with their headlights on.

And then Bryden crashed – and burned.

When Spitfire K 9965 lined up for take-off at 22.10, it was the young sergeant's first night flight. No one would ever know what went wrong – it could have been complete disorientation as he struggled, in the darkness, with a new set of problems in his high-powered machine, its exhaust flames destroying his night vision; it could have been control failure. The watchers saw him roar into the darkness, banking at about 500 feet, and then the Spitfire came down the sky at full throttle, impacting with a heart-wrenching WHOOMPH! And instantly, the flames. Sergeant Pilot J.M.C. Bryden never got to face his chosen enemy, but was the first Fighter Command pilot 'killed on active service' – one of the many who would die simply because the war demanded, daily, near-impossible little feats of heroism from a generation of young men who hadn't asked to be heroes.

Sandy Johnstone nearly became victim number two.

1st October 1939, 02.28 hours: George Pinkerton ducked involuntarily as the shadow of Johnstone's Spitfire swept overhead, quickly swallowed in the mist; Sandy had only been able to take off in the clag after Pinkerton had driven to the end of the strip and unmasked his headlights. George went back to his tent to find some warmer clothing, before returning to the watch hut.

02.48 hours: Johnstone, shivering in his pyjamas under the damp greatcoat, was completely lost. His radio crackled uselessly, the fog was dazzling in the diffused glare of the Merlin's exhausts, and he'd been unable to find somewhere to get down at all, let alone locate the radar plot which had caused Control to send him off on Fighter Command's first Spitfire night operational sortie. As his fuel gauge wound inexorably down, he gingerly descended over the rolling hills of Renfewshire, and pulled off his solitary parachute flare. From 3,000 feet, in the bright orange glow, he saw it – the perfect flat field.

Muscles tensed, he dived, levelled out, dropped the wheels, and throttled back – and then, in the dying flickers of the flare, glimpsed the tell-tale ripples on the surface of the reservoir! He banged the throttle wide open, hauled up the undercarriage, and prayed. Suddenly, just as he was thinking he'd got away with it, there was a momentary blur ahead, a terrific clatter as the airscrew shattered, and with a rending, tearing noise, the fighter thumped onto rising ground, bucking and slewing, with mud and debris flying up inside the cockpit. A final, gut-wrenching impact as the starboard wing slammed into a cairn, and the young pilot's head crashed into the side of the armoured glass windscreen. Consciousness disappeared.

Further down the hill, shotgun in one hand and torch in the other, reservoir warden John McColl picked his way up towards the crash, expecting to find a German wreck, and puzzled by the sound which echoed through the mist. It was a motor horn – but how on earth had somebody driven up there?

What he found, of course, was a dazed young Spitfire pilot, in mud-spattered pyjamas, sitting in his shattered aircraft, with the undercarriage warning horn sounding, set off when Johnstone chopped the throttle with his wheels up. With the luck that was never to desert him, he'd survived, flying not so much into the hill as onto it. Three feet lower, and he'd have died.

One by one, the Spitfires were getting bent, but hadn't as yet fired their guns in anger. Farquhar, eager for action, finally gained approval for their move to Grangemouth, and on 7th October, he led the Spitfires over, while Vivian Bell took the rest by road. The convoy was halted just outside the town, the men fell in at the roadside, and the City of Glasgow Squadron, led by the pipe band, marched in and through the town, with the Lord Provost taking the salute. It was a nice touch. There aren't many Air Force squadrons who can actually march to war in such style.

Their stay at Grangemouth was short – Farquhar, anxious to cut interception times to the minimum, had his sights set on RAF Drem, near North Berwick, which had been opened as a Flying Training Station. Farquhar and Bell flew over to check it out, and went to see the CO, Group Captain Charles Keary. It wasn't a pleasant meeting. Keary just didn't want to know. Furious, Farquhar flew back to Grangemouth, and phoned the Air Officer Commanding No 13 Group, Air Vice Marshal R.E. 'Birdie' Saul. A week later, 602 got their move, and so, eventually, did the Flying Training Unit. There was only one slight problem – Keary didn't. By the time he finally did give up the unequal struggle against the fighter boys on the ground, eight months later, he was a sadder, if not wiser, man, with a fine collection of grey hairs and lines on his forehead, and (of course) a still-immaculate uniform, which couldn't quite disguise the droop of those once-proud shoulders.

No 602's move wasn't for the superstitious. On Friday, 13th October, thirteen pilots flew the thirteen serviceable Spitfires, on orders from No 13 Group, to the erstwhile base of No 13 Flying Training School. Unlucky, as it turned out, for Johnstone, making his first flight after recovering from concussion he'd suffered on the hilltop. Touching down at Drem, he found his machine running down a slope at rather too high a speed, before hitting a muddy patch at the bottom, and digging its nose in. Then there were twelve – for the rest of the day, at any rate.

At 09.30 the following morning, came the first 'scramble', when four of the Spitfires went up after a suspicious plot, but nothing was seen. Two days later, George Pinkerton opened the shooting war over Britain.

*

16th October, 14.15 hours: Helmut Pohle leads the nine Ju88s of KG30 in from the east, through scattered cloud along the north of the Firth of Forth. They're lucky – up to a point. Green Section of 602, Farquhar, Ferguson and Johnstone, are on the ground at Leuchars, munching sandwiches, as the Spitfires, low on fuel after a fruitless high-speed chase over Fife, are checked and refuelled. The Coastal Command Station, unfamiliar with the fighters, hasn't the gear to do the job swiftly. Red Section are just about to land at Drem, having been scrambled after two Fleet Air Arm Skuas; they, too, are short on fuel. The RDF stations on the coast are temporarily 'out' – and 603's standing patrol out of Turnhouse has been vectored onto an aircraft they never sighted, but which was real enough – a reconnaissance Heinkel of KG26, flying over the Lothians.

14.22 hours: Pinkerton takes Blue Section into the air for their third patrol of the day, his own Spitfire sporting fresh canvas patches doped over the gun ports after his long-range target practice in the morning. Ten minutes later, Yellow Section are ordered off, to patrol Turnhouse at 10,000 feet, in response to unconfirmed sighting reports of a formation of machines heading towards the Forth Bridge.

On the ground at Turnhouse itself, Flight Lieutenant George Denholm of 603 Squadron is ordered off, with Pilot Officer George 'Sheep' Gilroy and Pilot Officer James 'Black' Morton. Yellow Section, 603 Squadron, take to the air and swing towards Dalkeith – their target, the Heinkel which is still dodging clouds over the Lothians.

In the air, Pohle leads his 'wonder bombers' in to attack the cruisers *Southampton* and *Edinburgh*, just off the Forth Bridge, and passengers on a train crossing the bridge are amazed to see the ships opening up with their high angle guns. As ripples of fire burst from the superstructure, the first waterspouts blossom and crash back, as the crack Luftwaffe pilots score near misses on both ships.

And that's when Pohle's luck runs out. Diving at close on 400 mph, bracketed by a flak burst from the *Edinburgh*, his cabin roof blows off, and as the bomber pulls out and streaks towards May Island, above the fearful racket comes the scream from the radio operator: '*Achtung! Schpitfeuren . . . drei Schpitfeuren!*'

Sighted by Pinkerton and Webb, Pohle's aircraft is doomed. The Spitfires, trailing black smoke from the exhaust ports as the throttles are banged forward, sweep in; Webb, taken by surprise at the speed of events, a little behind Pinkerton and McKellar, who open fire in turn at the twisting, weaving German machine.

Right along the seafront at Kirkcaldy, watchers are treated to a grandstand view of the RAF's first kill, as Pinkerton's Spitfire, on its first and third passes, knocks out both the Junkers' engines.

The end comes swiftly. Off Crail, the Junkers, like a great wounded bird, makes a last, despairing lunge for the sky, then hits the water, level, with a fearful impact. Pohle, unconscious, will survive to meet his conqueror in hospital. The rest of the crew are already dead or dying.

*

Pohle's aircraft was the first to fall – although official records, put together long after the excitement had died down, would say otherwise. Even today, it's impossible to establish the precise order of events, but by collating eye-witness reports, combat records (German as well as British) and contemporary news sources, the overall pattern is clear. Pinkerton fired the opening shots of the battle, and destroyed Pohle's aircraft – interestingly, he correctly identified the bomber as a Ju88, but official reports persisted in calling them Heinkels; KG30 was at this time the only Luftwaffe unit operating the new bomber over the North Sea.

The German pilots were, for the most part, already experienced. They included Walter Storp, who'd been blooded in the Spanish Civil War, and who succeeded in putting one of his bombs into the cruiser *Southampton*. It struck a glancing blow on the ship's bow, and failed to explode; the cruiser, already hit by Pohle's dud, was leading a charmed life. Storp, at full throttle, made his escape low over the water. Others, though, weren't so lucky.

Pinkerton's 'Tally Ho' over the radio had triggered frantic activity on the ground. At Turnhouse, they could hardly keep up with the action. Minutes later, Red Section of 603 Squadron also found the enemy. Squadron Leader E.H. 'Count' Stevens radioed his 'Tally Ho!' Just north of Dalkeith, he closed in on what he reported as a Heinkel. And this one really was – time had run out for the recce machine which had earlier proved such a convenient diversion as Pohle slipped in with his Junkers. The three Spitfires closed, in line astern formation, as the Heinkel dived and turned for the coast. Golfers on a course below looked up in astonishment as the great, black machine blasted over them, followed by the snarling fighters. Then, as they dived for cover as a cascade of cartridge cases and belt links rained down from the Spitfires' wings – and, suddenly, they'd gone, the sound of straining aero engines and chattering machine guns echoing across the course.

At Drem, just after Red Section had landed, they'd got the news of Pinkerton's sighting – and they could hear the naval guns and coastal batteries opening up. Frantically, the armourers rechecked the Brownings, fuel was poured into thirsty tanks, and Dunlop Urie and the others dashed to the watch hut for the latest 'gen', before racing back to their machines. The Merlins, still hot, caused a moment's anxiety, before they fired – and three more Spitfires rose to the fray.

At Turnhouse, 603's Flight Lieutenant Pat Gifford, respected solicitor, councillor and fiscal, was seething. If the Controller wouldn't order him up, he'd go anyway. He telephoned the Ops Room and simply told them he was taking off. Two minutes later, he was in the air, with Flying Officer Ken MacDonald and Flying Officer Colin Robertson, heading north-east, climbing flat out, determined to catch the fast-departing Junkers.

Over the Forth Bridge, the rest of the Junkers pilots circled, chose their targets, and dived. A couple never even got that far – two stragglers, coming in from the east, saw Dunlop Urie's Spitfires racing across the Firth, and, pursued by some .303 ammunition fired at

extreme range, turned tail and headed out to sea past May Island.
By this time, all was confusion, as Spitfires converged on Rosyth
from Turnhouse and Drem, the Junkers dived from 12,000 feet on
the naval vessels offshore, and the guns below sent their flak bursting in black puffs across the sky.

Gifford held the Heinkel squarely in his sights. As they rocketed
out over the shoreline, coming right down 'on the deck', the
Luftwaffe pilot saw the ripple of tiny splashes ahead of his aircraft;
momentarily puzzled, he gazed at them, then realised they were
British bullets. They slammed into his engines and control surfaces. Spitfires, it seemed, were coming at him from all angles. In
fact, they were – a couple of 602's Yellow Section were helping 603
to their first kill. The Heinkel came down in the sea just off Port
Seton, with one dead crew member – the gunner, knocked out in
Gifford's first attack. The other three, soaked and shocked, were
picked up by the crew of a fishing boat. Their war, too, was over –
like Pohle, they would spend most of the next six years in Canada,
as prisoners of war. They hit the water at 14.50 – the second aircraft
to fall.

Meanwhile, at Leuchars, Douglas Farquhar, Ian Ferguson and
Sandy Johnstone had just had their second rude awakening. They'd
been contentedly munching their sandwiches, watching some
Blenheims coming over in the distance, when the air raid alarms
went. They were bundled apologetically into a shelter by one of the
Regulars. 'Sorry – this is the third practice alert today, but the Old
Man's a stickler for going by the book.' After a while, Farquhar
strolled over to the ops building to find out how long they were liable
to be stuck on the ground. He shot out of the building seconds later
– 'Sandy, come on, for Pete's sake. These weren't Blenheims,
they're 88s!' They flung themselves into a little van, and shot across
to where the Spitfires, now thankfully refuelled, were sitting,
Merlins already grumbling, against the chocks. With some pointed
comments from Group Captain Brian Baker ringing in their ears,
they belted across the airfield and curved round to the south, throttles through the gate.

Farquhar, in K9962, was first to sight the enemy – a Ju88 going
east at about 2,000 feet off Aberdour. He closed rapidly, and felt the
Spitfire shudder as the Brownings hammered. 'Blast – too low,' he
thought, and hauled the Spitfire round to come in slightly below
the German machine, which was taking no avoiding action. This
time, he saw strikes, and a cloud of white smoke belched from one

of the engines, whipping away in the bomber's slipstream as it went into a shallow dive. Two other Spitfires (Ian Ferguson, and Flying Officer Boulter of 603) helped it on its way – and Farquhar then followed it down, watching with some satisfaction as it broke up on impact. No one got out.

The last Junkers to dive on the warships was piloted by Leutnant Horst von Riesen. Dodging the heavier anti-aircraft fire of the two cruisers, he attacked the destroyer *Mohawk*, just returning from convoy escort duty. The bomb came away cleanly at 3,000 feet, and it was a near miss. The bridge of the destroyer was raked with splinters; her captain, Commander Jolly, was mortally wounded. As von Riesen climbed away, his radio operator called the words that would become only too familiar to Luftwaffe crews just under a year later over England. '*Schpitfeuren! Schpitfeuren!*' and the Junkers dived for the water, weaving and jinking. The Spitfires, piloted by Robertson and Morton of 603, easily caught up with the bomber, and attacked alternately. The chase went right out to sea; one burst of fire knocked out the starboard motor, but still the bomber wouldn't go down. The Spitfires, low on fuel, had to break off, and von Riesen was left with a dilemma. They'd been told the Ju88 wouldn't maintain its height on one engine – and they were only just doing so. What's more, they had no height left to play with. With their speed reduced to about 110 mph, they faced a flight of nearly four hours in a damaged machine. Von Riesen spelt out the alternatives to the crew. They couldn't ditch – it was already getting dark, and there was little chance of rescue. Should they cut their losses and turn back to crash-land in Scotland? One of the crew said it for all of them: 'No, no, never! If we go back there those Spitfires will certainly get us.' Four hours later, exhausted, and with the remaining motor almost red-hot, they made it, to find their leader and one other crew gone, and three other Junkers battle-damaged. It was the first, and the last, raid the Luftwaffe mounted in any strength against the Firth of Forth that winter.

At Drem and Turnhouse, there was jubilation – as each Spitfire landed, gun patches shot away, black oil and blast streaking the wings, and one or two pilots whipping into impromptu rolls over the ground crews. The fighters were fuelled, rearmed, and, section by section, went up once again on patrol. The wires were humming with news of Britain's first air raid of the war; the British machines had returned virtually without a scratch, and the Junkers had inflicted no serious damage on the ships either.

About an hour later, the sirens sounded again. This time, 603 were quicker – they slightly damaged a reconnaissance Heinkel over Rosyth, and then put a second down in the North Sea. Three survivors were later picked up by HMS *Gurkha*. The first Heinkel made it back to base; one of its pictures was subsequently published in a Berlin newspaper. It shows the Forth Bridge, with the train clearly visible blowing off steam, and the two cruisers with the destroyer lying off to seaward, along with a tanker (which was near-missed, although the Germans didn't even claim it). Banner headlines proclaimed that it showed a direct hit on the bridge – interesting in view of their stated policy of hitting only military targets clear of the shore – but closer examination reveals that the white blur at the base of the pier is in fact Inch Garvie Island, on which the bridge was built. The first shots in the propaganda war were being fired.

Radio listeners that night in Britain heard of four German machines being shot down, and of the safe return of all our fighters. German listeners heard of two of their bombers failing to return, and of two RAF fighters shot down.

In fact, the British reports were fairly accurate – surprisingly so, in the light of later exaggerations at the height of the Battle of Britain. During the raid itself, the Germans lost two Ju88s from the bomber *Gruppe*, and also the Heinkel off Port Seton, which was from a different unit; the fourth victim, the other Heinkel, was, in a sense, a separate action.

The two dead Germans who had been picked up, the Heinkel's gunner and Pohle's radio operator, who was actually alive when they first got to him, were buried in Portobello Cemetery with military honours; the squadrons' pipe bandsmen playing in salute.

While newspapers still talked of the 'phoney war', around the Firth of Forth, the reality had arrived.

*

28th November 1939: Red Section scrambled just after coming 'on state' in the morning, rapidly followed by Yellow and Blue. A pair of Heinkels were over Scotland, one circling near Dalkeith, the other over Rosyth.

Archie McKellar was the first to sight the enemy – the Heinkel over Dalkeith. With the advantage of that first sighting, he drew ahead of the other fighters, already accelerating to combat speed, his guns and sight switched on. Last time, he'd been too eager, firing before he was properly in range. This time, he made sure. Closing in for a quarter attack, he opened fire from around 200 yards. Two bursts did all the damage – the first knocked out the bomber's dorsal gunner and struck the starboard wing root, the second lashed the sensitive tail control surfaces. Overshooting the shuddering Heinkel, Archie watched as three more Spitfires – Red Section of 603 – swept in and fired, this time hitting the starboard wing, and the perspex nose cabin. The Heinkel came down in a sloping field at Kidlaw, near Haddington, with the pilot wounded, the observer unhurt, but both gunners dead. It was the first enemy aircraft to fall on the British mainland – and 602 had another notable 'first' to their credit. The Heinkel was subsequently dismantled, and taken bit by bit to Farnborough, where it was minutely examined – the fifty-nine page report covered everything from the airframe to a detailed examination of a stopwatch. It didn't appear until August 1941 – by which time dozens of other Heinkels littered the countryside.

The photographers, newshounds, and propagandists had a field day, of course, and the public, courtesy of 602, could at last gaze on a defeated enemy. Archie was quite pleased with himself, and the squadron reckoned he'd at least made up for his antics on the Forth raid, when he'd rolled his Spitfire so low over the airfield, he'd actually bent the wings. The rivets had all sprung, and the Vickers representative who'd come to examine them was amazed the plane had kept flying at all.

At Drem, Keary was having something of a personal nightmare. His once well-ordered establishment was now a sea of mud, the Spitfires, on 24-hours-a-day readiness, continually shattered the silence by night and by day; the fighter pilots, top tunic buttons undone, sauntered about the field, even getting covered in engine oil and grease as they fiddled with the Spits, seeking the last ounce of performance.

Almost daily, the Luftwaffe put in their fleeting appearances, and 602 shot off to intercept. Time, on these operations, was very much of the essence. Climbing wasn't one of the Spitfire's strongest points, and any interception was frequently out to sea, at extreme range. Pilots went in ready to fire at any opportunity, however remote.

One cloudy day, a section just off Fife caught a fleeting glance of a 'twin' diving into the mist. They belted after it, and sent a tentative ranging burst as it disappeared. Nothing more was seen, though, and they landed to report their contact. The news had travelled ahead of them, though – right down the telephone line from Dyce, where one of the Aberdeen Squadron's Ansons had landed, its fuselage full of holes. After some angry exchanges, everything, including the holes, was more or less patched up. Still, as Findlay Boyd observed, it was 'damn good long-range shooting'. Four days after Christmas, they did it again, this time with more serious results.

Just after 15.00, Dunlop Urie, Norman Stone, and Archie McKellar were scrambled to intercept an incoming formation of bombers over North Berwick, at just over 1,000 feet. Dusk was closing in, there was a sea mist, and to make things worse, Control told them to search for 'bandits'. That meant the aircraft were definitely hostile, as opposed to unidentified ('bogey'). The three fighters, guns switched on, sighted the bombers, and, before they could take cover in cloud, delivered their attack on the slim, twin-tailed machines which looked like Dorniers – the first 602 had encountered. They weren't. They were RAF Hampdens, returning from an operation over the North Sea. The tired bomber crews watched in mounting horror as the Spitfires curved in, the flashes on their leading edges bright in the gloom.

After their firing pass, Urie and the others realised their mistake, but for two of the Hampdens, it was already too late. Both went down. With a terrible irony, the rest, low on fuel, landed at Drem. After a strained evening in the Mess, the Glasgow pilots awoke the following morning to find there were no toilet rolls left. The surviving Hampdens, taking off at first light, duly returned them – in a bombing raid over the buildings. The pilots, wisely, avoided Keary completely for the next couple of days.

By that time, Urie had made amends. Along with Hector MacLean and 'Fumff' Strong, he'd intercepted a pair of Heinkel 115 floatplanes, on a minelaying mission fifteen miles east of May Island. Attacking in line astern, they each took potshots at the nearer machine, which promptly hit the water and sank, while the other made off home at a rather higher speed than Ernst Heinkel himself could have believed.

As the winter wore on, some of the old faces departed. John Feather had long since left for Training Command. Jimmie Hodge, once he was operational on the Spitfire, headed south to turn his expertise to good effect as a Fighter Controller. In December, 602's Adjutant, Vivian Bell, left on promotion to become a Senior Fighter Controller at 11 Group. He was replaced by Flight Lieutenant Wheeldon, who already had a DSO from an earlier war, and who was in distinguished company. Bill Scarnell boasted a VC, and the Military Medal, from the First World War as well. But, by now, the City of Glasgow Squadron had its first decoration too – George Pinkerton had been awarded the DFC, following the Forth raid. In November, he too had left, promoted to command a Regular Spitfire squadron, No 65 at Northolt. There, along with Bob Tuck, soon to become famous in the Battle of Britain, he flew in exercises with Bomber Command Blenheims which had survived the early raids over German naval bases. This sharing of experience was invaluable in working out fighter tactics.

Up at Drem, 602 were working on their tactics, too. The book said that fighters must fly in tight 'vics' of three, with the leader in the centre, and his wing men tucked in astern, to port and starboard. The Glasgow pilots were already doubting the wisdom of this; it meant that numbers two and three were too busy concentrating on formation flying – they couldn't keep such an effective lookout, and when they went into action, somebody was always on the wrong side.

Despite frequent orders to 'Strictly adhere to Fighter Command Regulations governing Fighter Attacks', dutifully noted in the Operations Record Book, they went their own way. The weather, and the hit-and-miss scrambles against single unidentified aircraft, all aided the change to the tactics which would put 602 at a distinct advantage in the Battle of Britain, where they'd come across Messerschmitt 109s flying exactly the same way. Each time 602 were sent up against a plot, three aircraft had to go. It wore down the pilots' patience, and it wore out the Spitfires, too; regular maintenance checks came round so frequently that the servicing facilities couldn't cope. And there were an alarming number of bent Spitfires, too, as the field at Drem alternated between a bog and an ice rink. Late in November, two of Yellow Section's three fighters collided on landing; next month, Urie broke a prop overshooting on a night landing. Undercarriage legs were frequently written off as Spitfires bounced; the ground crews got used to this. Their record time in rendering a machine serviceable again (replace airscrew, jack the wings, change the oleo leg, fit the wheel, check the hydraulics, clean the wing, dope the scratches and *Look sharp you lazy*

Ogo Pogo Bird
Dunlop Urie prepares for a convoy patrol in the Spitfire that kept chasing itself. Drem, 17th
January, 1940.

Suicide Corner
Heinkel IIIk of KG 26, shot down by Douglas Farquhar on 9th February 1940. He fired 625
rounds of .303, most of which ended up in the engines and centre section.

'A' Flight at readiness, Drem 1940.

Braving the wind. The first winter at Drem

buggers!) was a whisker under four hours. 602 began flying in pairs.

Alastair Grant reckoned he came close to collecting an Iron Cross, Second Class. 'I bent three. Nothing spectacular really, but Goering was pinning medals on Messerschmitt pilots for similar feats.'

But the unlucky one was John McAdam. During one memorable week in January, he put one Spitfire on its back at Acklington, after a gunnery exercise; back at Drem, he tipped a second onto its nose, and the following day nearly landed a third with its wheels up. Only a quick-witted Bill Scarnell, firing off a Very Light across his landing path, averted the hat trick. John was not to be denied, however. A couple of months later, as the fighters were being dispersed for the night, he gently taxied his Flight Commander's into another one.

Pilot error and raw recruits apart, it was happening because of Drem's inherent problems. It was far from being the ideal fighter base; too small for high performance machines to operate with a generous safety margin, it had a slight hill right in the middle. And, of course, the weather produced such extraordinary ground conditions that on one occasion a Spitfire skidded sideways landing on ice, and then promptly dug its nose into an unfrozen patch of mud at the bottom of the more sheltered slope. Some of the pilots didn't even get to their machines that winter. A number went down with flu, while Harry Moody slipped climbing onto the wing of his Spitfire. Somersaulting spectacularly on the ice, he broke his collar bone.

In one of the harshest winters on record, flight mechanics, their breath freezing in tiny particles, worked 24 hours a day with numbed hands on the Spitfires. The Merlins had to be fired and run every few minutes to stop the oil freezing in feed pipes. To these men must go the highest credit – throughout the winter, the pilots were never let down once by engines seizing, and whenever they were called to go, the Spitfires were ready to take off.

On 13th January, 602 struck lucky again – Marcus Robinson led Red Section off against a 'hostile' north of St Andrews. They found it flying north, and attacked the single Heinkel 111 at close range, knocking an engine out and watching as it descended. 111 Squadron's Hurricanes then got in on the act, and the bomber came down fifteen miles east of Carnoustie. The pilot, fished from his waterlogged dinghy, later ended up under lock and key at

Leuchars, from where he rather cheekily sent his compliments and congratulations on 602's good shooting. Hector MacLean wasn't inclined to return the compliment – the Heinkel's gunner had put a bullet through his windscreen, nearly ending his war prematurely.

The young Luftwaffe pilot did come out with another gem, though. During interrogation, he revealed that the aircrews of his unit, KG26, had nicknamed the Firth of Forth 'Suicide Corner' – they were far happier facing even the anti-aircraft fire of the Home Fleet than Drem's Spitfires and Hurricanes. He also claimed that all the fighters that attacked him were Spitfires – which didn't particularly please Treble One's Hurricane Aces. This was one of the first cases of what became known as 'Spitfire snobbery' – the Luftwaffe crews reckoned it rather infra dig to be knocked down by the slower Hurricanes, but to be shot down by a Spitfire? Well, that was something you could live with in prison camp.

In February, Douglas Farquhar wrote himself into aviation history. 602's CO took off on the duty patrol just after 09.00, in K9962, in company with Alastair Grant – the pairs were now standard 602 routine. Half an hour into the patrol, an enemy aircraft was reported; the two Glasgow Spitfires swung east and accelerated. Then they saw it – a Heinkel 111K, about twenty miles out to sea, heading slightly south of east. Racing through the clouds, Farquhar and Grant overhauled the bomber, and Farquhar, closing from almost dead astern, briefly thumbed the gun button, the Heinkel filling his sight. He broke away, as the bomber dived for cloud.

His combat report stated: 'Enemy aircraft entered cloud and I followed.' While Grant circled, covering the exits, Farquhar, travelling something approaching six miles a minute, plunged into dense, grey mist, straining his eyes for an elusive shadow. He deserved to be lucky. He was.

As the Spitfire raced into a clear patch, there was the Heinkel, sitting just ahead and below. Almost instantly, he observed red flashes from its rear gun, but he pressed home his attack. Closing to less than a hundred yards, he triggered the Brownings. Six of them fired, the outer two already frozen. In less than a second, the bomber again disappeared in the clag. Douglas lost it, climbed, and rejoined Grant. As they flew back towards Scotland, Sandy Johnstone, by now up with Yellow Section, caught sight of the Heinkel, obviously badly damaged with thick smoke belching from one engine. As they watched, it slid in past North Berwick, and landed, wheels up, on a hill just beyond. Three men got out – the gunner, seriously wounded, was taken to the station hospital at Drem, where he later died.

Meanwhile, Farquhar's armourers, alerted by the whistling of air through the gun ports, eagerly whipped the panels off as the Spitfire rolled to a standstill, and made a startling discovery that their CO's kill had used only 625 rounds of ammunition altogether – just a shade under four seconds' total firing time, with two of the Brownings out of action. It was a remarkable piece of marksmanship.

Some of the pilots later went to see the crashed bomber. Fighting their way through newshounds, photographers, spectators and police, they were amused to note that the Heinkel, from KG26 'Löwengeschwader', had the unit badge painted on its fuselage – a lion, 'not quite so rampant as ours.' Sandy Johnstone was intrigued by the tyres. They had 'Made in Germany' printed on them – in English!

On the 21st, Birdie Saul telephone Farquhar with the news that he had been awarded the DFC. That night, there was a celebration at the Marine Hotel, so it was with rather a thick head that Douglas took Red Section into the air the following morning, on the second scramble of the day. This time, there were three; Farquhar and Sergeant Andy McDowall were accompanied by George Proudman, flying L1007 – the only Spitfire in the squadron, or indeed the entire RAF, to be equipped with 20mm Hispano cannon. This machine, which had arrived at Drem on 14th January complete with Flying Officer Proudman, had a chequered career to say the least. The cannons, which would eventually become the standard armament of later marks of Spitfire, were capable of throwing out a tremendous weight of explosive ammunition, much more effective in destroying aircraft in a concentrated burst of fire, but there were a lot of problems in fitting the unit into the Spitfire's slim wings. L1007 was the prototype, and on trial in the south it had suffered frequent stoppages. Some of the bugs had been ironed out, however, and the aircraft was allocated to 65 Squadron, where, of course, it never came into contact with the enemy.

George Pinkerton, though, after he took over the squadron, arranged for plane and pilot to be attached to his old unit, 602, who were actually shooting down enemy aircraft. At Drem, neither L1007 nor her pilot worked particularly effectively. They fired the cannons into the sea just to prove they worked – sometimes – and together they also flew into the windsock at Drem, neatly severing the pole.

And so, on the 22nd, they still had something to prove. They got their chance. Just before midday, Farquhar sighted their quarry – a Heinkel 111P over St Abb's Head. Closing for the kill, Douglas decided that they'd better make sure of the bomber before Proudman let fly with the cannons – just in case nothing happened – so he made the first firing pass. K9962, equipped with a gun camera, now produced Fighter Command's first pictures of combat. The film ran for just over six seconds, the camera triggered by Farquhar's shooting. It shows the flickering image of the bomber square in the sight. Four seconds in, there's a puff of white smoke from the port engine. Less than a second later, and it explodes – and the bomber staggers, dips a wing, and slides out of sight.

On board the Heinkel, the gunner cries out his warning: '*Achtung, Jäger! Jäger!*' He fires, briefly, then feels the Spitfire's bullets smashing into his legs. There's noise and confusion, as splinters fly forward, and bullets ricochet around the cabin. Then the engine goes, and the pilot, uninjured, knows he has no choice but to crash land. He pulls the stricken bomber round in a wide, flat turn – and his wireless operator, face against the perspex, calls out that another fighter is curving in.

They needn't have worried. L1007, true to form, looses off a few rounds, and before Proudman can correct his aim, the cannons wheeze to a halt.

The Luftwaffe pilot managed to pull off a reasonably good landing at Coldingham. As the Spitfires circled overhead, they saw the Germans clamber out, seemingly unharmed, and it occurred to Farquhar that they might just try to set fire to their machine. Anxious that evidence of what the cannons might have achieved shouldn't be destroyed, and unable to attract any worthwhile attention on the ground, he did the only thing possible. The other pilots were surprised to see his Spitfire descend and land further down the field from the German machine, whose crew, incredulous, could only watch in amazement as the Spitfire hit a patch of mud, dug its nose in, and flipped neatly over onto its back.

They ran down to assist, and found Farquhar hanging upside down in his straps, inches above the morass. Gingerly, they eased him out. Now, the potential tragedy, already magically transformed to comedy, became pure farce. A bunch of Dad's Army types were scrambling over the countryside, intent on capturing the Nazi aircrew. The Germans, pleasant enough fellows but aware of their duty, had run back up the hill and were trying to set the bomber alight. Douglas Farquhar followed. 'Look here, you chaps. You'd be better surrendering to me. There's no telling what these soldiers will do. You'd better hand over your guns.'

By the time the Local Defence Volunteers arrived, he'd collected three Lugers, and was promptly arrested by the Great War veteran who led the LDV. Only the production of an Income Tax form which he'd received in that morning's post saved the day. By the time they'd sorted themselves out, the nose section of the Heinkel was burnt out, and Farquhar was disgusted when he found that the cannons had missed the Heinkel completely. His Spitfire, its back broken, would never fly again. Still, things began to improve when Dad's Army led them all back to Mrs Millican's farm, where she dressed the gunner's wounds and brewed a pot of tea. By the time he got back to Drem, he'd collected a stiff neck, three Lugers, and an immortal piece of the 602 legend.

Four days later, he received his DFC from the hands of the King, at Drem, with the whole squadron for once doing Keary proud, and feeling pretty proud themselves.

And the next week, Proudman, short of fuel, put L1007 into a field, rather untidily. Patched up, she finally slunk off back to her makers. The cannon shells she left behind, they discovered, made rather nice candlesticks.

In March, the 13th once again proved to be a red-letter day for 602, when Farquhar's promotion to Wing Commander was announced. Three weeks later, after thirteen years' service with 602, he left, to take command of Martlesham Heath, a fighter station in Suffolk, where he was in action during the Battle of Britain. Though not obliged to fly on operations, and indeed officially discouraged from doing so, he frequently flew with 257 Hurricane Squadron, and even added a couple of Ju87 kills to his tally. Later in the war, he'd become one of the RAF's first Spitfire Wing Leaders, at Hornchurch, where one of his three squadrons, flying sweeps over France, was 603.

His replacement was none other than George Pinkerton, and no sooner had he arrived than orders were received for 602 to move north, one Flight to Montrose, and the other to Dyce. Across the North Sea, the fighting in Norway was reaching its peak, and there were persistent rumours that 602 could be headed for Scandinavia. The news came of heroism, and retreat, in Narvik Fjord; by night and by day the Spitfires intercepted incoming aircraft which were all too often bombers returning damaged from low level raids.

It was an emotional time. 602 actually marked out a strip the size and shape of a carrier flight deck on the airfield at Dyce, and proved that they could, with a great deal of skill, land and fly off Spitfires without catapult or arrester gear; they pleaded to be allowed to go, but Dowding, conscious that a greater battle was coming, refused.

As May progressed, the news got worse; Hitler invaded Holland and Belgium, and the Luftwaffe struck at targets in Northern France. All of 602's leave was cancelled. The weather grew hotter and drier, but still they couldn't take on the enemy. They did blow up another Spitfire, though. At Montrose, a Miles Master, loaded with practice bombs, taxied into Hector MacLean's Spitfire. As both pilots ran for it, the aircraft gently wrote themselves off in a series of little 'Whoomps!'

Up at Dyce, they very nearly killed an MP. Ghandar Dowar, who'd built Dyce in the thirties, and who still occupied his office in the clubhouse, was sitting at his desk, as a 602 Spitfire was being lined up against ranging marks painted on the hangar door, in order to harmonise the guns. Suddenly, as an armourer accidentally touched the button, all eight Brownings barked. An airman working inside the hangar had his hat blown off as the fusillade went through the building, the wall, the kitchen beyond, and finally spent itself against the next wall – all except for one bullet, which got a little further, ending up, hot and flat, on Dowar's desk.

It may just have been coincidence that 602 were shortly moved back to Drem. If Dowar's nightmare had ended, Charles Keary's was beginning all over again.

*

As the Wehrmacht rolled towards Dunkirk, some of 'Glasgow's Own' were already involved. Douglas Farquhar wangled a number of flights over the armada of little ships, and Graeme was already in France, tangling with Messerschmitts in a 607 Squadron Hurricane. Marcus Robinson had taken command of another Auxiliary Squadron, No 616 (South Yorkshire) at Leconfield. When the British Expeditionary Force was taken off the beaches at Dunkirk, their Spitfires, operating from the forward base at Rochford, were overhead, fighting at the limit of their range, often outnumbered by three or four to one.

The day after 602 returned to Drem, the surviving Hurricanes of

605 Squadron, every one of them bearing the scars of battle, flew in. The Birmingham Auxiliaries, under their CO, Walter Churchill, had had a rough time in France, losing nine aircraft and four pilots in just six days, most of them to Messerschmitt 109s. The Glasgow boys eagerly seized the opportunity to talk to these men who had first-hand experience of fighter dogfighting. What were the 109's weak points, if any? Where was it most vulnerable? Was it as fast as the Spitfire? Above all, how could they best guarantee their survival? They found that the Hurricane pilots had learned the same lessons as the Scout pilots of the Great War. Never fly in a straight line for more than two seconds in combat. The pilot who has the height advantage controls the battle. Never follow your victim down – the chances are his wing man will nail you. Above all, 'Beware the Hun in the sun!'

Within three days, the Glasgow Spitfires sprouted rear view mirrors, mounted just above the canopy in streamlined casings designed by Sergeant Bert Simpson, who'd worked in Stevenson's the coachbuilders before the war. The fighter's worst blind spot was now less of a threat.

On 4th June, they nearly went. Ordered to Northolt to cover the last of the evacuation from the beaches off Dunkirk, they'd just finished loading two Bombays with equipment when the move was cancelled. That night, on the wireless, they listened to Winston Churchill announcing that the evacuation was complete. Britain stood alone.

New faces arrived – Pilot Officer Nigel Rose, together with Sergeants Sprague, Proctor, Elcombe and Whipps. Their operational training was carefully supervised by Findlay Boyd, determined that the rigid discipline they'd gained at Flying Training wouldn't lead them into danger in the hurly burly of aerial action. This was the second batch of Sergeant Pilot volunteers they'd acquired. In the first had been Harry Moody and Pat Lyall, who'd both now been commissioned, and McAdam and Bailey. John McAdam had been posted away; Bailey's first accident had been his last. Just before the turn of the year, in his first dusk flight, he'd killed himself flying K9977 into the ground.

At the end of June, Alastair Grant and 'Sprats' departed – Alastair to Training Command, where he'd teach the tyros how *not* to break Spitfires, and Sprats to become Birdie Saul's personal ADC. In turn, 602 gained Flying Officer C.J. 'Mickey' Mount, a charming Irishman who'd just been filling that same role, and who had an endearing stammer. What fascinated the pilots, though, what that it never appeared over the R/T.

Archie McKellar went, too – promoted to become a Flight Commander on 605. Churchill had particularly asked for him – in the Battle of Britain, the entire squadron would be grateful that he had. And, finally, Keary at last gave up the unequal struggle. He was replaced by Wing Commander R. L. R. 'Batchy' Atcherley – and no two men could have been more different. Batchy, and his twin brother David, were already an Air Force legend. Batchy had flown the Schneider Trophy seaplanes. At Hendon, long before the war, so the story went, David (or was it Dick) had been seen, resplendent in hunting pink, astride the tail of a Moth, flying by the reins. Dick (or was it David) had flown through the hangars and carved his initials in the snow with his wing tips. 602, no strangers to the business of establishing living legends, were delighted.

Sure enough, within two months of Atcherley's arrival, things really started to happen. The Spitfires and Hurricanes were redistributed all over the field, under cover of the trees, with bays hacked out by 602's volunteers, eagerly aided by the boys of some of Edinburgh's better known schools. Half the workforce of Tranent Council were appropriated to level an emergency landing field, and some bulldozers mysteriously appeared at Drem, to shove the mud and and trees around. After a couple of hazardous night landings, Atcherley, who never seemed to sleep and who was always first round at Dispersal to quiz the returning pilots, began to work out what would become the standard night landing system – 'Drem Lighting'. And, to the delight of the Auxiliaries, Keary's once-spotless, gleaming Humber was liberally daubed with mud-coloured camouflage paint.

On 25th June, as darkness fell, Pinkerton and Johnstone were on the 'night state'. Mid-evening, Pinkerton went off, only to return after a fruitless chase as aircraft were plotted, but missed by the searchlights. By midnight, Johnstone was in the air, and from his patrol line between Dalkeith and Musselburgh, its ends marked by coloured searchlight beams, he could see intense activity. Other searchlights lanced across the night sky; occasional flashes of ground fire sent tracer climbing after unseen intruders. Radio chatter gave evidence of a raid in progress – suddenly, three searchlight beams coned, and there, glinting, sat a Heinkel. Switching on his reflector sight, and dimming the ring until it was a soft orange glow, Sandy opened the throttle... not too fast, don't let the flames destroy the vision ... there it was, crawling into the ring. Overshooting rapidly, he got off a quick burst at near point-blank range, and was immediately rewarded with a shower of oil from one of the bomber's engines. His canopy smeared, he yanked the fighter away from a possible collision, and, pulse racing, collected himself again. There it was – still held by two of the beams, diving, trailing smoke now. Closing in a wide sweeping turn, he came in more carefully, his nostrils filled with the acrid stench of cordite from his own guns mixed with the smell of burning German oil seeping in somewhere. He thumbed the button, and this time clearly saw bits flying off the Heinkel. Pulling away, he was fascinated to see it descend, and, dipping below the searchlights, its landing lights came on, the intense white beams exploding in a glittering fountain as it ploughed into the sea. Then, the light became green, and finally purple, before vanishing in the depths forever.

Climbing to 2,000 feet, he fired off the colours of the day, two red Very lights, to attract possible rescue craft to the scene, before landing at Drem, where Corporal Burnett, his rigger, was waiting, with a mug of steaming cocoa at the ready. 'That was great, sir, we saw the whole thing, it was right over our heads!' The next morning, LO-Q sported her first little swastika under the cockpit coaming, and Johnstone and Atcherley were having the devil of a job pacifying two irate army officers who were wanting to know why the soldiery from Fife to the Borders had been forced to stand to, to repel an invasion force which never came, in response to the anti-invasion signal – two reds!

It was the first Spitfire night victory – and it triggered off a run of success for 602.

On 1st July, Paul Webb opened his score. Along with Johnstone, he sighted a Ju88 heading for Dunbar, dodging from cloud to cloud. After a chase, with only brief glimpses of their quarry, the two Spitfires were about to give up when it suddenly emerged off to one side. Pulling his fighter hard round, Webb got in a short, full-deflection shot from the beam; the most difficult shot of all at a fast-moving target, it didn't produce any results worth boasting about, though Webb claimed he'd seen smoke from one of the engines. The Junkers vanished in the mist. Back at Drem, a sceptical Intelligence Officer at first wouldn't even grant him a 'damaged', though eventually that was allowed. In fact, he'd killed the Junkers. Post-war checking confirms that it wandered right down the North Sea, instruments damaged, compass shot away and with one engine out, before crashing in northern France. Exactly a week later, Webb was wondering what he had to do to get a confirmed kill. This time, he hit a Heinkel at 20,000 feet off Crail, where it had unloaded five bombs which killed a cow, and he saw the port engine burst into flames, before the bomber did a wingover, and dropped into the clouds. They gave him a 'probable', but he was sure the Heinkel would never get back to its base. He was right. It didn't.

Findlay Boyd and Hector MacLean, meanwhile, had put another Ju88 into the sea off May Island. Since they both saw it crash, and the Navy did too, and pieces of it floated around for quite a while, they could hardly be denied their 'kill'. Findlay was quite pleased. A couple of days previously, he'd been in the act of taking off when a Dornier 17, which had sneaked in under the RDF net, came right over Drem at zero feet, machine guns hammering. It got clean away. Next day, Sandy Johnstone met another one – head on. He fired, the German gunner, equally startled, fired back. They both missed.

On the 9th, Dunlop Urie, who'd taken over from Robinson as 'A' Flight Commander, was up with Donald Jack, when they met two Ju88s east of Fife Ness. The Junkers, from KG30, Pohle's old unit, were minelayers, and so intent were they on their task that the two Spitfires surprised them. In a very fast action, Urie put one straight into the sea, while Jack severely damaged the other. He was awarded a 'damaged'. The Junkers certainly was – though it did get back to Westerland, it never flew again. 602 had by now brought 13 Group's total number of kills to over fifty. At the invitation of Birdie Saul, Sandy Johnstone found himself at a slap-up meal at the De Guise, and it wasn't just the half century he celebrated. The AOC announced that he'd just become CO of 602. George Pinkerton went to the Ops Room at Turnhouse.

Sergeant Andy McDowall got their last kill over the Forth – a Heinkel 111 brought down at night, in an action almost identical to Johnstone's. Through July and into August, things were hotting up over the English Channel. Before they got the call to the south, though, there was Batchy's Sunday Parade. With the promise of entertainment laid on for one and all afterwards from Sir Harry Lauder, no less, he got the station to turn out for a Church Parade. He also had the brilliant notion of getting the Padre to bless a Spitfire and a Hurricane. Some of the pilots thought this was a bit dubious, but nevertheless Walter Churchill wheeled out one of 605's cleaner Hurricanes, and 602 produced LO-N, which had more new parts than most of the others – it had been Alastair Grant's machine – and the ceremony duly took place.

Three days later, LO-N ended up in the boundary hedge, when Harry Moody overshot on landing in the mist. The next day, the 'holy Hurricane' plonked itself right down in the middle of the field. Neither aircraft flew again with their parent squadrons; the pilots were quite awestruck at the power of the men of God.

It was nearly midnight on 11th August, when Harry Moody and Pat Lyall, who'd been off duty, burst into the crew room in a state of great excitement. They'd been drinking in the Royal Hotel, where the barmaid passed on the rumour that 602 were just about to move south. Johnstone telephoned 13 Group. 'Yes, that's right', said the voice of officialdom, 'the signal's on its way to you right now. You're going to Tangmere the day after tomorrow.' They checked the calendar – yes, the thirteenth. Again. It seemed a good omen.

As the Spitfires wheeled into wind for the last time, Merlins snarling, exhausts popping, rudders and elevators flipping over with nervous little twitches, the pilots looked to Johnstone for the thumbs up. All sixteen fighters were there, the ground crews having slaved through the night. Batchy was there, too. His staff car drew up alongside the leading flight, and as the fighters rolled, the Humber went too, the Station Commander accelerating down the runway with Padre Sutherland hanging out of the back window belting out 'Lochaber No More' on his bagpipes. They roared aloft, wheeled over the little field, and, dipping their wings in salute, set course for the south.

CHAPTER SEVEN
'Their Finest Hour'

The Führer has ordered me to crush Britain with my Luftwaffe. By delivering a series of very heavy blows I plan to have this enemy, whose morale is already at its lowest, down on his knees so that our troops can land without any risk.

> *Reichsmarschall Hermann Goering, in a speech to his Air Fleet Commanders at The Hague, 2nd August.*

The big lick. . .the big lick. Very soon the big lick.
> *Gefreiter Ewald Schank, picked up dazed after his Me110 was blown apart over Manston, 14th August.*

August 13th: Weather – Fair. Early mist, slight drizzle. Channel cloudy.
'Adler Tag' (Eagle Day) finally launched. Luftwaffe fly 1,485 sorties.
Tangmere Hurricane squadrons (43, 601, 145) heavily engaged.

'Hey, come and meet 145 Squadron. Nice chaps – all two of them!' Paul Webb's greeting to Hector MacLean as they strolled into Woodcote House was hardly an exaggeration, either. Only four serviceable Hurricanes remained, grouped under the trees at the edge of the field at Westhampnett. A fifth lay on its back in the middle of the field. Its pilot, 145's CO Johnny Peel, his arm in a sling, came over to Sandy Johnstone. 'Glad to see you here. It's been getting pretty sticky, and we'll be glad of a breather. This is what I'm reduced to.' Within a couple of hours, the Hurricanes had taken off for Drem, and Peel had driven out of the gate single-handed – literally.

Thoughtfully now, the Glasgow boys examined their new home. There wasn't much to see. Three fields knocked together, the old hedge lines replaced by camouflage paint; a scattering of Nissens round the edges, and a grubby windsock hanging in one corner. Their parent station was Tangmere, from where they'd be controlled. The Senior Controller was none other than David Lloyd, who'd flown with 602 in the thirties. Tangmere's CO, Jack Boret,

drove up, and spelt it out to Sandy Johnstone: 'It's no sinecure.
You'll probably have to do between four and six sorties a day. Plus
night states at Tangmere every third night.'

Next day, they were scrambled seven times.

August 16th: Weather – Fair and warm: some haze over the Channel.
Heavy raids against 11 Group airfields. West Malling knocked
out.

12.58 hours: Urie, Boyd, MacLean and the others were stretched out
in the sunshine, on the lawn in front of the farmhouse that served as
their Mess. They'd been stood down, and wouldn't come on state
again until three. They were settling in, though there were problems – the airmen were billeted in a house surrounded by dog ken-
nels, on the road to Goodwood Racecourse. Sandy Johnstone had
been to inspect it that morning. He walked up to the farmhouse, his
nostrils still wrinkling. 'Fancy a beer, chaps?'

Mickey Mount opened a lazy eye. 'Y-yes, I-I don't m-mind if I d-
d-do. W-what's for l-lunch?'

They'd just settled down to spam and boiled potatoes, when the
ops telephone bell jangled. It was David Lloyd – 'For God's sake get
your squadron airborne – *now*! We have twenty plus approaching
from the south!'

'Villa squadron, *Scramble! Scramble!*'

Plates flew, pilots rushed out into the sunshine as the Tangmere
sirens moaned, ground crews, slamming tin hats on, hastily fired
the Merlins, pulled out the trolley accumulator leads, and helped
the pilots adjust their straps. From all corners of the field, the Spitfires leapt forward; miraculously, they all got off without a single
collision. Sandy Johnstone tried to collect his fighters – 'Villa
squadron, Villa squadron, orbit base, Angels 2'. Most of 'A' Flight
made it, the others were already scattered across the Sussex
countryside, as the air battle swept them up like a tidal wave.

As they lifted into the air, they'd seen the Stukas, in perfect formation, going over towards Tangmere. As the Spitfires climbed, the
Ju87s wheeled and dived, their rising banshee wail cutting through
the noise of sirens, racing engines, the *choomph! choomph!* of the
Bofors, and the *crump!* of the bombs which were already blowing
hangars and buildings apart. In one of them, David Lloyd kept his
cool – 'Come on, you chaps, do your best to clobber these blighters.
One of our walls is beginning to crack!' His words were the calm
centre in a seething turmoil of action, fear, and exultation. The

Hurricanes were in among the Junkers, the Me110s were lancing down, nose cannons barking.

'Jesus, I got one, I got one . . .'

'Look out, Blue Three, *look out. Break!*'

'Tallyho, Green Section, go for the bombers, go for the bombers, go for the bombers.'

'Two bandits, behind you, ten o'clock.'

'Behind *who*, for God's sake?'

'*Christ!* Oh Holy Christ, I'm hit, I'm hit.' An American accent.

'Hey, did you see that? He blew up.'

'. . . aircraft is hit, I'm putting her down.' Mickey Mount, without the slightest trace of a stammer.

All around, the kaleidoscope whirled. A Hurricane on fire, trailing smoke towards the sea; a Messerschmitt 110 flicking over, its canopy blown apart – Paul Webb would have no trouble in claiming this kill. A Spitfire, turning tightly, flaps still down, desperately trying to range on a dive bomber as it hedgehops towards the south.

Findlay Boyd, down below, had just tightened his straps and waved his fitter, Smithy, away. As he gunned the engine, the Spitfire raced across the field, and hardly had he felt the drumming of the wheels stop when a Ju87 appeared over the trees, having completed its dive on Tangmere. Findlay, his undercarriage only half pumped up, automatically corrected his aim as the Stuka curved across from the left. One burst put the dive bomber into the ground, almost intact, just at the side of the airfield. The Spitfire banked round, completed its circuit, dropped its wheels and landed; Boyd nipped over to the Ju87, and collected his first trophies of battle – a Luger, and a Leica. He'd been in the air for almost exactly a minute; surely the quickest 'kill' of the war.

Over his head, the rest of the squadron were discovering for the first time just how quickly the skies could clear – one minute, combat raging all around, the next, not an aircraft to be seen. One by one, the Spitfires, gun ports whistling like a set of pipes, rejoined the circuit and 'pancaked'. A knot of pilots gathered round Henry Grazebrook, the Intelligence Officer, at his little table over at 'A' Flight dispersal area, as the combat reports were filled in, the claims sifted, and a picture of the battle began to emerge. On the Flights, they had the panels off, the bowsers were pumping fuel into the Spitfires' tanks, and the Brownings were being reloaded.

The Germans had come towards the coast in strength. Over Portland, they'd separated. Five Stukas had hit the RDF station at Ventnor again; it would remain out of action for another week. Twelve Ju88s escorted by the Me110s had dived out of the sun on the Naval airfield at Gosport, with a second force hitting the neighbouring base of Lee-on-Solent. Johnstone, Urie and Webb had got among the escorts and hit at least six; three of these were definite kills. Boyd's Stuka was there for all to see. Andy McDowall and Nigel Rose had hit the 88s – at least one was down in the sea, with two others as probables.

It was only later that the cost became clear. Over at Tangmere, the columns of smoke rose, black and silent. Mickey Mount, thankfully, was all right. With a bullet through the coolant tank, he'd landed safely at Odiham, streaming a plume of white glycol vapour. His Spitfire would soon fly again. But four others wouldn't. They'd been hangared at the Sector Station – and now there just weren't any hangars left intact. Randall Phillips, who'd spent the afternoon under a table in the watch hut at Tangmere, came back and described some of the devastation. Sandy Johnstone drove over in the evening.

The station looked a shambles. People were still wandering around, dazed by the ferocity of the attack. Buildings were shattered, their contents strewn across the once-immaculate borders. Light, water, power and sanitation were all cut, the Tannoy out of action, the hangars, workshops, messes and even the sick bay destroyed. Broken aircraft lay everywhere – half a dozen Blenheims and seven Hurricanes hit by flying ordnance. And the remains of Billy Fiske's Hurricane, still gently burning in the middle of the field, its pilot slowly losing the struggle for his life in the station hospital. In the middle of it all, completing the air of bizarre unreality, Jack Boret, standing on the lawn, covered in grime, with his parrot, Percy, perched firmly on his shoulder screeching away in perfect imitation of a Stuka.

Johnstone told him of 602's efforts, and discovered that the Glasgow squadron's Medical Officer, Doc Willey, had proved to be one of Tangmere's heroes that day, rescuing and treating victims across the airfield. For his efforts, he'd be awarded the Military Cross. Boret was in surprisingly good humour. 'Good show, that, Johnstone. Percy, shut up, for Gawd's sake . . . oh, by the way, we got a signal in the middle of it all to say your move's been made permanent. The rest of your outfit should be down on Tuesday. Glad to welcome you on board.'

*

Two days later, the Stukas returned.

August 18th: Weather – clear at first; warm. Overcast later. Massed bomber formations return, hitting airfields.

13.25 hours: 602's pilots, after a quiet morning, are getting ready for lunch – they'll be released at 14.00. Overhead, there's a beautiful, straight condensation trail going north west from Portsmouth. Heads back, the Spitfire pilots gaze at it with some interest – it's clearly very high. The Hurricanes of 43 Squadron, scrambled to intercept 'Raid 47', won't get within 10,000 feet of the pressurized Junkers 86P reconnaissance machine. It sailed serenely on, at the edge of the stratosphere; a harbinger of battle.

A WAAF saw them first, on the screen at Poling RDF Station, near Littlehampton. A large group of hostiles, forming up over the coast of France. In the next room, Corporal Avis Hearn reported the sighting to Fighter Command Filter Room at Stanmore in Middlesex; they confirmed the plot. Across at Tangmere Sector, and along the coast, Fighter Controllers watched as the WAAFs moved the incoming raid symbols across the plotting tables with their long croupiers' rakes. At Poling, they watched as the screens glowed with the strongest echoes they'd yet recorded. This was a big raid – and it was coming straight for them.

In the Operations Room at Tangmere, David Lloyd watched the plots move, and agreed. He made his dispositions – ordering 601 into the air above the station itself; as the eleven Hurricanes roared off, 43 Squadron were ordered into their cockpits. Assistance was summoned from 10 Group to the west – and the Controller at Middle Wallop scrambled the Spitfires of 152 and 234 Squadrons. Eighty miles away, the Hurricanes of 213 lifted off from Exeter. By the time they would arrive, it would be nearly all over.

At Westhampnett, with Johnstone off, Dunlop Urie was in charge – and looking forward to his late lunch. With the whole squadron released, they were in the Mess. Urie had just taken a couple of sips from his pint of beer, when the ops telephone jangled. 'Villa Squadron return to readiness and scramble as soon as possible, please. A large formation is approaching Tangmere, and there are no other units available.' Urie set down his glass. He'd never get to finish it.

Convoy Patrol
A pair of 602 Spitfires over Methil Bay in the first winter of war.

Alastair Grant's Spitfire at readiness in a blast pen at Drem, 1940. Trolley acc plugged in, straps hanging clear.

In the Heat of Battle
Westhampnett, in the Battle of Britain. 'B' at 15 minutes readiness, parachute pack on tail-plane, engine warm, fitter and rigger even warmer.

'Villa Squadron – SCRAMBLE!'

Major Helmut Bode, in a Ju87 of the III Gruppe of Stuka Geschwader 77, was leading the largest formation of dive bombers assembled in the whole battle – all three Gruppen of StG77, eighty-seven aircraft in all, plus the twenty-two Stukas of 1/StG3. As they came out over the Channel, their escorts swung into place around and above – no less than 157 Messerschmitt 109s; 102 of them from Jagdgeschwadern 27 and 53 providing close escort, and fifty-five from JG2 out of Le Havre on a free-ranging sweep designed to flush out the RAF fighters.

Bode led them in over a slightly hazy Channel. Approaching Selsey Bill, the Gruppen peeled off one by one. Their targets – the naval air stations at Gosport, Thorney Island and Ford; Bode's own Gruppe were headed for Poling.

David Lloyd, watching the attack develop, and with the pattern of Friday's strike at Tangmere itself in his mind, directed the Hurricane squadrons against the force coming in just to the west of Bognor. As 1/StG77 started their attack on Thorney Island, the Hurricanes got in among them, and wreaked terrible devastation. Over the Isle of Wight, the Spitfires from 10 Group were locked in combat with the Me109s covering the Stukas – they were too late to prevent the attack on Gosport, but got at the Stukas as they headed out over the Channel.

Against the other fifty-nine Stukas, with their close escort of fifty Messerschmitts backed up by fifty-five more ranging in from the south-east, there were only the twelve Spitfires of 602 Squadron.

There had been quite a flap at Westhampnett after Lloyd's call. Across the field, fitters and riggers rushed back to the fighters, as their pilots, not exactly dressed for the occasion, ran for the helmets and parachutes, and made for the Spitfires. Some were serviceable; the 'stand down' meant that much needed maintenance could be carried out. Urie found his machine on jacks, its wheels off. Nearby was a brand-new Spitfire, delivered only that morning as a replacement for one of the four lost two days earlier. It hadn't yet had its guns harmonised, and bore no squadron letters. It would have to do. Swiftly, his gear was transferred, and Dunlop Urie led 602 into the air.

At Poling, the noise was deafening. Avis Hearn picked up the phone – it was Stanmore, with a new plot. A pause. Then, 'Hullo, Poling, that plot I have just given you is right overhead. . . .'

'You don't say!' Avis shouted back. 'The bombs are dropping on my head!'

'Are you all right?' the Stanmore voice kept enquiring: 'Yes, keep listening for my plot,' Avis replied. She stayed there, too, until the lines went dead, the doors blew in, and the dust engulfed the room.

As Bode's Stukas dived on the buildings below Poling's 350 foot towers, 'Ginger' Whall sighted the other Gruppe over Ford. He radioed Urie, who called Tangmere. 'Villa Squadron, tally ho! Bandits over Ford!' The first section of fourteen Ju87s were already in their dive. As Urie ordered Findlay Boyd to take 'B' Flight up to take on the Messerschmitts, and led 'A' Flight into the attack himself, the second formation of Stukas wheeled in the sky, and, in sections of three abreast, dived on the airfield. The six Spitfires came down the sky with them, catching them at the bottom of the dive and outpacing the chasing Me109s.

On the ground, men dived for cover as fuel tanks erupted in flames, aircraft disintegrated, and buildings blew apart. Urie only glimpsed the chaos as he raced after the bombers. Throttling back, he was still overtaking the Stukas at around fifty miles an hour; the Spitfire lanced right through the formation, firing at five before the hiss of compressed air and the clatter of empty breech blocks told Urie his ammunition was expended. The second Ju87 lurched under the impact of the bullets and fell to port, the fourth staggered, stalled, and went straight into the water.

Glancing in his rear view mirror, Urie pulled clear, as the Controller asked if they were engaged yet. He was just trying to think of a suitable reply, when his number two, as he thought, belched fire from both wings. It was a Messerschmitt! There was a tremendous crashing, rending noise from behind the seat armour, the stick jerked in Urie's hands, and then he was punched bodily forward as the cannon shells slammed into the bucket seat, the parachute pack, and both Urie's legs. A few seconds' respite, and a second salvo hit the Spitfire's tail. The 109 pulled away. Oberleutnant Baron Erbo von Kageneck reckoned he'd got his kill. He headed out to sea, after the retreating Stukas.

Just behind Urie, Ginger Whall had selected his target; a Ju87 of the second formation, heading out low over the streets of Bognor. Closing to fifty yards he fired four deliberate bursts along the fuselage. White chips flew from the Stuka around the cockpit. It banked into a gentle curve, recrossed the coastline, and gently descended to a near-perfect landing right up the sixteenth fairway on Ham Manor Golf Course, near Poling. Satisfied, Ginger climbed seawards, banged his throttle wide open, and set off in pursuit of Bode's Gruppe, heading out over the Channel after levelling the huts at the RDF station, where Avis Hearn was just discovering, to her relief, that she was still alive and more or less in one piece.

Picking out one of the tail enders, Sergeant Whall closed once again to 50 yards, and emptied the last of his ammunition into it, seeing strikes around the cockpit and engine. The Stuka caught fire, its wing tanks ruptured, and heeled over into the sea. Hastily checking his mirror, Ginger was surprised to see a trail of smoke. His own. The Spitfire had taken hits from the second Stuka's single rear gun. A glance at the instrument panel confirmed his fears – oil pressure zero, temperature rising rapidly. Carefully throttling back, Whall eased the wounded fighter round towards the shore.

High above, 'B' Flight were tangling with the Me109s of JG27 and JG53. The six Spitfires, outnumbered by some eight to one, were weaving, twisting, diving and rolling, turning ever tighter as they sought their targets and then sought escape.

'Villa Blue Leader, ten more at twelve o'clock. . .'

'Blue Three, *look out!* Break, *break*, you bloody fool. . . .'

'Jesus, he missed me. . . .'

'Come on, let's get down after them. . . .'

In a series of inconclusive combats, the Messerschmitts gradually forced the dogfight lower, and began to dive towards the Stukas, which were falling one by one to the guns of 'A' Flight. Suddenly, the sky was clear, and, miraculously, all six Spitfires had survived. Now the hunted became the hunters, as Findlay Boyd led them down. Fastening on to a diving Messerschmitt, he thumbed the button and watched without emotion as the German fighter took hits, and plunged straight into the sea. Racing towards the Stukas, he winged one, and then put a second down off Selsey Bill, 'Good. No survivors,' the other pilots heard over the R/T, as the Channel waters closed over Boyd's victim. Andy McDowall was locked in a tight circle with another Me109. Whoever broke first from this pattern was dead. Gradually, the Spitfire, with its tighter turning ability, hauled round on the German. Through the sight, McDowall saw his target creeping back, slowly, slowly. . . steady. . . and it was there. One burst was all it took.

But most of the Messerschmitts had broken through. They got among the Spitfires attacking the Ju87s, and hit four in quick succession. One was Urie's. Seconds later, Ian Ferguson, after firing at his third Stuka in line, felt the Spitfire shudder, as 20mm cannon shells hit the port wing, the elevator, and the petrol tank. The fighter was trailing vapour and becoming very sloppy on the controls. Unteroffizier Karl Born would claim a kill, but Ian wasn't dead yet. Preparing to bale out, he saw the streets of Littlehampton below, and changed his mind. Coming down towards open ground to the north of the town, a set of power lines suddenly appeared slap in front of him. With a flash, the propeller slashed through four of the six cables, each carrying 33,000 volts, before the Spitfire crash-landed beside Toddington Cemetery. Ferguson's rescuers found him standing beside the fighter, swearing volubly in what they reckoned was probably Polish. They were quite unable to converse with him. The gentle Ian's experiences of the last ten minutes had brought about a startling, but thankfully temporary, change of character . . . and a back injury which would take him out of the battle, but, ironically, almost certainly save his life many months later.

Harry Moody saw his Stuka roll right over onto its back and plunge into the Channel, but four Messerschmitts were already on his tail. One of them connected, and Harry rocketed down towards Ford in a desperate attempt to shake the others off. They let the Spitfire go, possibly assuming it was mortally hit. Moody, relieved, pulled out of his dive, and set his damaged aircraft down amid the devastation at Ford. One of his tyres was shot through, and X4161, another of the brand new replacement aircraft, ended up on her nose.

Mickey Mount didn't even get close enough to the Stukas to claim a hit, before the Me109s got him, too. With his controls stiff, his hydraulics leaking, and both wings shot through, he just made it back to Westhampnett, but L1005 would never fly again.

One by one, the surviving Spitfires arrived in the circuit. Every one had fired its guns, many had received hits. Hector MacLean and Sergeant Cyril Babbage had both hit the Stukas too, though, and 602 had come through their hardest day's fighting with honour. Dunlop Urie was the luckiest of them all.

After the Messerschmitts left him for dead, he gingerly felt for the controls and gently aileron-turned to the left, conscious that his tail section was badly hit. The rudder and elevator cables might well part at any minute, the radio was dead, and the pain in his legs made any action an effort of will. The fighter wouldn't climb, and in any case there was no question of baling out – the parachute pack was lacerated.

They all heard it when the Spitfire came in over the trees at

Westhampnett – the shell holes in the fuselage made the fighter sound like an organ with all the stops out. The undercarriage came down; the flaps didn't. The Spitfire bounced, sending shafts of pain up Urie's legs, and then shuddered across the field on two burst tyres. The brakes were gone, too, and it took a long run to slow the fighter down. As she settled for the last time, the fuselage visibly sagged. The ambulance, already alerted by the whine as the aircraft approached, raced out. Gently, Urie was lifted out and taken away. The fitters and riggers gazed in awe at the Spitfire. Cockpit shattered, radio in smithereens, half the tail surface shot away, cables shredded, and its back broken. There wasn't much left to salvage – X4110 had had a service life of just under twenty-five minutes.

Meanwhile, young Ginger Whall was picking his spot on the foreshore at Middleton-on-Sea. His engine gone, he couldn't climb to bale out. He'd decided to set her down in shallow water – that way, the impact would be cushioned, but the Spitfire wouldn't sink. Watchers on the shore saw the fighter level off, flaps down. It splashed twenty yards offshore, and then bounced high as the starboard wing hit an underwater obstruction. Spinning half round, it flopped back again, going backwards, and came to rest. Aided by eager hands, Ginger climbed out and waded ashore, completely uninjured.

Three of the Spitfires – Whall's, Urie's, and Mount's – were written off. The other two which had collected damage were repairable. Urie and Ferguson were both hospital-bound. But the 602 Spitfires, so heavily outnumbered, had given more than they got. They'd hit eight Stukas. Five were destroyed over the shore, two returned damaged to their bases, one with a wounded gunner, and the eighth crashed in France, at Argentan, killing both crew. In addition, they'd shot down two 109s – one of the close escort Gruppe, and one from the 'free hunt'. The other five squadrons, between them, accounted for a further ten Stukas, with more damaged, together with half a dozen Messerschmitts.

That night, the Commander of VIII Air Corps, Wolfram von Richthofen, cousin of the famous Red Baron, and the commander of the dive bombers, withdrew them from the battle. They would never again return in strength over southern England. In his diary, he wrote, 'A Stuka Gruppe has had its feathers well and truly plucked!'

One of the wounded birds had its tail feathers plucked in no uncertain manner. When a crew from Tangmere drove over to

Ginger Whall's first victim, to fly it off the golf course – it had landed virtually undamaged – they found they couldn't. Some souvenir hunters had already removed the entire tailplane!

The next day, amid scattered raiding along the coast, a group of Ju88s came back over Thorney Island. Johnstone led 602 into the bombers, and before the 109s came down to split them up, Glyn Ritchie got one – his first confirmed kill. Then the Messerschmitts arrived, and before the Spitfires could extricate themselves, Harry Moody found himself in trouble again. As the cockpit began to burn, flames coming back from the fuel tank which sat behind the engine, his hands were blistered. In some pain, he hauled back the canopy, and for the second time in two days baled out of a burning fighter. He landed, safely enough, in a back garden, breaking a couple of panes in a greenhouse before hitting the compost heap. The previous day, he'd landed on one side of a wall, with his parachute on the other. He was immediately surrounded by the pupils from the girls' school near Arundel where he'd fetched up, and, after recovering his composure, the handsome Pilot Officer was pestered from all sides for his autograph. Back at Westhampnett, he later received a letter from the School Captain, informing him that the girls had adopted him as their very own Spitfire pilot, and could he please write to them as often as possible with his tales of derring-do in the skies? In return, his fan mail was terrific – and the girls knitted him all manner of woollen items.

*

Even in the thick of battle, the Glasgow auxiliaries had a way of doing things in style. There were rumours of invasion. A squadron small arms muster was held, to check that the full fifty hand weapons were available to repel the invaders – mysteriously, eighty-five men paraded with their rifles. Just where they got the additional thirty-five, nobody knew.

And the tea ladies came. Virginia Gilliat and Barbie Wallace just turned up one day in a mobile canteen. It never failed to appear throughout the battle, manned – or rather womaned – by a variety of charming local ladies. After the worst of the fighting was over, late in the autumn, the official NAAFI turned up, insisting on their rights to the airmen's custom. There was nearly a revolt, but before the lads got around to doing what they threatened with the rifles that they weren't supposed to have, discretion proved the better part of valour – and they retained the tea waggon they weren't supposed to have either.

The officers' social life began to blossom. After the day's fighting was over, invitations began to come in; Johnstone, Mickey Mount, Findlay Boyd and the others frequently dined at Lavington, the home of Barbie Wallace and her husband Euan, who was Commissioner for London and a former Minister of Transport. They had their favourite watering holes, too. The Victoria Hotel, Bognor, where Hilda Godsmark was one of the attractions, the Old Ship Inn down at Bosham, where Sandy Johnstone found himself at the same table as the actor David Niven. It was a curious way to fight a war. One of the sergeant pilots, Alfie Eade, couldn't agree more. He'd flown Fairey Battles in France, and survived, which was more than most – then he'd converted to Spitfires, joined 266 'Rhodesia' Squadron, and seen his entire unit blown apart on the ground at Eastchurch during a heavy raid on the same day 602 arrived in the south. As the squadron pulled out to re-form, Alfie was posted to 602. He had a married sister living just a few miles from Westhampnett. He could take on the Luftwaffe by day, and return, emotionally spent, to his slippers by the fire in the evening.

On both sides of the Channel, the leaders of the opposing forces took stock. The Commander of 11 Group, Air Vice Marshal Keith Park, warned his squadrons to be prepared for more. In his Instructions to Controllers, he noted that the bombing was now concentrated on aerodromes, and directed that interceptions be kept over land where possible. Too many pilots were being lost in the sea. At Karinhall, at noon on the same day, Goering called his noon conference, and told his Air Fleet Commanders, 'I'm not at all pleased with the way things are going. Serious mistakes have led to unnecessary losses. We have entered the decisive phase of the battle. Everything depends on our beating the RAF. We must smash the RAF fighter force.'

On 24th August, they didn't hit 602's fighters at all, but as the Spitfires strained in vain to climb high enough to engage the Ju88s over Portsmouth, the bombs rained down across the town, hitting the docks, the railway station, and a picture house, which took a direct hit during a special matinee for schoolchildren. As the story spread round the mess that night, Findlay Boyd said, 'I just hope these bastards come back tomorrow.'

They did.

*

August 25th: Weather – Fair during morning; cloudy later on. The Battle enters its third, crucial, phase. Concentrated attacks on airfields and fighter defences, targets virtually unrestricted. Most Me109s transferred by this day to Pas de Calais.

They were beginning to wonder when they'd ever get their lunch in peace. That morning, 602 had been scrambled a couple of times, ending up playing tag with elusive plots out over the Channel, as the Germans teased Fighter Command with spoof raids. It wasn't until the late afternoon that the Glasgow squadron headed for the mess. They didn't make it, though. The RDF screens glowed bright as the bombers and their escorts formed up over St Malo, came out over Cherbourg, and picked up some of the few remaining 109s in the area at the Channel Islands. They tracked the raid in towards Weymouth.

Johnstone led 602's fourteen Spitfires west, climbing to over 15,000 feet. For once, they would have the advantage of height. They would need it. Boyd saw them first.

'Villa Red Leader, many bandits, eleven o'clock. Snappers (fighters) above and behind.'

'Villa Squadron, Tally Ho. Blue Leader, take on the fighters. Red and Yellow, follow me.'

As Findlay Boyd took seven Spitfires round in a sweeping climb, accelerating to fighting speed, Johnstone led the others west, before turning in to face the bombers – a mixed force of Ju88s and Heinkel 111s, with twin-engined Messerschmitts among them. There were around forty-five bombers; the escorts, mainly Me110s, numbered nearly two hundred. A few thousand feet below, the Hurricanes of 17 Squadron, drafted in to replace the badly-mauled 601, were climbing towards the bombers, and from the north, the Spitfires of 10 Group were racing in, in defence of their own fighter stations.

First to make contact as the Germans crossed the coast were 602. On their first firing pass, Johnstone's Spitfires split up the leading bomber formations. Some dived, others wheeled around seeking mutual protection, a few dropped their loads and turned tail. As the Spitfires came racing in, the Me110s which had eluded Boyd's attack dived on them, their formidable nose armament of two 20mm cannon and four machine guns blazing. Sergeant Sprague's Spitfire, trailing smoke, hauled off to one side, rolled, and fell clear. His parachute opened; he was later fished from the sea unhurt.

The rest of them, after that initial pass, found it almost impossible to get in among the bombers. From every side, the Me110s harried them. Their tactics were simple. Though fast and heavily armed, they were heavy and unwieldy. They would make their firing run, and then dive for home. If they couldn't escape, they'd form up into a defensive circle, protecting each other's tail. Donald Jack found himself tangling with five of them. He'd been told they were easy meat, but five weren't! Pulling the Spitfire as tightly as he could, he found himself turning inside the 110s' circle, just clear of their guns. In a few heart-stopping seconds, he fired at one, ducked back, and then, in a gut-wrenching turn, pulled round towards another 110. This one staggered under the impact of the Brownings, and fell out of the circle. Seizing his chance, Donald raced through the gap, and belted back to Westhampnett. His second 110 was a confirmed kill, but he wasn't caring. He went straight to bed, and slept like a baby, his nerves and body exhausted.

Boyd got the revenge he was seeking. By now the professional killer, his guns ranged to only 50 yards as opposed to the normal 250 or 400, he stalked the Messerschmitts in the upper skies. Closing from behind, he dipped the Spitfire just below the firing arc of the rear gunner, blasted the engines, hydraulics and radiators, and watched two of the big fighters spin into the waters below.

Behind him, Roger Coverley got the shock of his young life. As he ranged on a 110, one of the top-cover 109s hit him from the rear. His Spitfire took hits right along the fuselage; miraculously, Roger was uninjured, but the Spit was finished. As the engine burst into flames, he put her into a sideslip to the left, forcing the fire away from his escape route, and baled out to a safe landing.

Paul Webb, twisting and turning above the main battle, hit two 110s in quick succession – at least one would certainly never see France again. Down below, Johnstone blew the entire tail unit off a 110, but still couldn't get back to the bombers. Chasing a Ju88, he saw tracers zipping past his starboard wingtip; the 109s had arrived. He hauled back on the stick, the Messerschmitt zoomed after him, tracers flicking out again. Suddenly, the Spitfire stall-turned; the 109 pilot, taken by surprise, never stood a chance. As his fighter wavered in the turn, Johnstone's Spitfire came vertically down, blasted the cockpit apart, and the 109 spun down to crash in a sheet of flame in a spinney just south of Dorchester.

Cyril Babbage was the only one to get back to the bombers, though. After fighting through the Messerschmitt screen, hitting a

110 in the process, he destroyed a Junkers 88. Nigel Rose, locked in combat with the fighters, finally got through, to find his ammunition expended.

Back at Westhampnett, there was great excitement. In twos and threes, the Spitfires pancaked, and the ground crews greeted exhausted, but triumphant pilots, their nerves still taut. One sergeant jumped down from his fighter, and ran towards the 'B' Flight huts, doubled up. Concerned, Boyd's fitter, Smithy, asked if he was wounded – 'No, get out of my way, my back teeth are awash!' He just made it to the toilet, emerging later with a beatific smile. He'd lost his lunch, but much more importantly he'd lost his combat virginity too – and he was still in one piece.

The next day, the Commander of Luftflotte 3, Feldmarschall Hugo Sperrle, would launch his final daylight mass raid for some weeks. And 602 wouldn't get their lunch again either.

*

August 26th: Weather – Mainly cloudy, brighter patches along south coast.
Channel overcast.
Widespread activity. Airfields in Kent and Essex attacked during morning. Reconnaissance flight over Solent.

It was a perfect piece of controlling. As the fifty-two Heinkels of KG55, based around Villacoublay, came out over Le Havre, David Lloyd, mindful of the attack on Portsmouth two days previously, put up all his available units early. Altogether eight squadrons were in the air as the bomber force tracked in towards the town. Three of the fighter squadrons, including 602, found themselves above the Heinkels. 602 were in the best position of all, a thousand feet higher and up sun, with a perfect view of the bombers silhouetted against the cloud which covered the Channel. There was no sign of fighters nearby, and Johnstone led the Spitfires down in a classic interception. He sighted on the leading He111, and fired. Instantly, they all heard the agonised cry – *'Schpitfeuren! Schpitfeuren!'* By freak chance, the bombers were on the same radio frequency as the Spitfires. Now the air was filled with urgent cries in both languages, as the Heinkels sought escape, and the Spitfires fastened on to their targets. Within seconds, two Hurricane squadrons had joined in the rout. The bombers, wheeling and diving in confusion, now their warloads in the Channel; a few got as far as the outskirts of Portsmouth, but most turned tail and plunged into the clouds for home, their bombs falling harmlessly. There would be no repeat of the tragedy at the children's matinée this afternoon. Belatedly, the 109s came down from 26,000 feet to harry the Spitfires, but by then, three of the Heinkels had gone down. Ginger Whall had added to his tally, and young Pilot Officer Ellis Aries, who'd flown operationally for the first time on the day of the Tangmere raid, got a second for 602. He'd lived and learned a lot during the last ten days. Over Tangmere, he'd gasped in astonishment at the serried ranks of Ju87s and their escorts, and blurted out in surprise over the R/T, 'Why are they dangling little wires at me?', seeing the glinting lines curving down at his Spitfire. 'They're not wires, you bloody fool, that's tracer. *Break!*' Now, above Portsmouth, he saw the first silver flicker, and instantly broke left, down, and safely into cloud cover.

High above, Cyril Babbage was tangling with the wingman of Aries' attacker. He won the turning circle battle, and had just seen the Messerschmitt fall away, when another pair hit his Spitfire as it levelled out. Controls shot away, he had no option but to leap out as the fighter flicked over into a series of erratic rolls. The parachute blossomed, and his progress was tracked by a fishing boat below. They picked him up and delivered him safely ashore at Bognor, where he received hospital treatment for some shell splinters in his legs. Two days later, he was back, ready for more.

By now, the Heinkels were nose down for home, completely routed. Hector MacLean, his blood well and truly up, chased them, half his ammunition still intact. He closed in on a formation of about a dozen, and, following his own personal theory that only the German leaders were any good at navigation, flew right up the entire formation before opening fire on the leading Heinkel, as it approached the coast of France. He never saw the diving Me109 which hit him; but suddenly there was a series of bangs, just as his bomber spurted smoke. And instantly, the searing pain in his leg. The rudder bar jerked convulsively, the 109 shot past, too low on fuel to continue the attack, and Hector eased the wounded Spitfire into a gentle bank to starboard. Heading back over the Channel, he doubted if he'd make it. 'I remember thinking that the Spitfire was probably like myself – a goner. But the engine still answered the throttle. I pushed the stick gently forward – it felt like elastic.' He knew he was in serious trouble – the elevator cable was clearly only hanging together by a strand or two. If it parted, he was finished. He looked down. His right leg was a mess – the cannon shell had exploded right behind his shoe. His foot was almost completely severed, lying, still in the shoe, in a welter of blood and gore on the floor of the cockpit. The artery was pumping fresh, red blood. His scarf provided the tourniquet.

With the Spitfire in a gentle dive, he tried the rudder with his other foot. Nothing. The cable was completely shot away. Coming in over the Isle of Wight, his fighter was down to 500 feet, and sinking lower. The pain was as much as he could tolerate; consciousness was slipping away as the effect of the blood loss took hold. With what remained of his strength and will power, he brought the Spitfire straight in over the trees at Tangmere and crunched it down on its belly, right in the middle of the field. He was lucky. The fighter slewed round, bucked and jolted, but didn't catch fire. Hector was quietly, lucidly and comprehensively cursing as the ambulance crew lifted him gently out, minus one foot. As they laid him in the vehicle, he sent one of the orderlies back to collect his other shoe – it was a brand new pair – and the unfortunate man took one look at what was in the cockpit, and the shoe, before fainting on the spot.

They almost lost Donald Jack, too. High over the main battle, his oxygen supply packed up. As the Spitfire climbed through 20,000 feet, on through 23,000 and up to 26,000, he was fighting the weariness of oxygen-starved lungs, affecting muscles, heart, nerves. Lifting even one arm was agony; the cold intense. 27,000 feet – mental reaction slowing – and then they levelled off. Donald, with a supreme effort of willpower, drove into the 109s, sprayed his bullets round in a wide curve, and then dived steeply to where he could live without oxygen. He wouldn't claim a kill, but it was just another one of the heroic little moments in the daily struggle against the enemies both sides shared – weariness, and the elements themselves.

An hour later, he was up again, along with Paul Webb. This time, their target was interesting. They found it, low over the water, twenty miles south of St Catherine's Point; A Heinkel 59 floatplane. The ponderous, obsolete He59s were used by the Luftwaffe to rescue downed airmen in the Channel. Further up the coast, they flew in silver, with red crosses prominent – down in 602's sector, though, they were in full camouflage. But wherever they flew, they didn't just rescue survivors. They reported on shipping positions, and coastal installations – and they were escorted by Messerschmitts, which were very definitely not on errands of mercy. In a fast attack, Paul Webb put the Heinkel down for good, and the two Spitfires made their escape before the 109s could pounce.

Down on the farm, things were getting really civilised. The Glasgow boys were able to invite Frank Carey's 43 Squadron over for tea off some real china, before repairing to favourite haunts such as The Victoria, or The Dolphin in Chichester. The aircraftmen had their own watering holes – the Green Dragon in Chichester was one.

With a number of ex-bodybuilders and panel beaters on strength, transport was never a problem. One night, Sandy Johnstone, driving Virginia Gilliat over to Arundel to dine with the Duke and Duchess of Norfolk (how's that for Auxiliary style!) was blown into a ditch by a couple of bombs. Back at Westhampnett, Sergeant Bert Simpson and his lads soon had the Staff Humber back in shape. Just as well – as the official station car, it shouldn't have been off on such a jaunt anyway. Bert and his boys had their own old Humber, too, put together from the bits left over from previous bomb victims. But it wasn't enemy action that nearly ended their career – coming back one night in high spirits ('We were all half cut and we'd filled the tank with 100 octane for the Spitties') they encountered Dad's Army. The driver, amid yells of encouragement from the other six aboard, did the logical thing. He put his foot down, and crashed the roadblock. The local soldiery opened up as the Humber raced away in the gloom, swerving magnificently from side to side. In the morning, they found two neat little bullet holes – inches away from the petrol tank.

*

August 31st: Weather –fair over land, thick haze over Channel. The heaviest day's fighting. In concentrated raids. Fighter Command take their biggest losses – 39 fighters down, with fourteen pilots killed. Luftwaffe losses about even.

With Johnstone off flying on doctor's orders, Findlay Boyd led eleven Spitfires on patrol between Biggin Hill and Gravesend. As they approached Biggin Hill, they saw the bombers – two massed formations of KG2's Dornier 17Z 'Flying Pencils'. While lower squadrons climbed for the bombers, Findlay, catching a glimpse of a canopy flash momentarily in the sun high above, took 602 up towards the Me109s. There were a few Ju88s in the upper formation, too – rather curious, thought Findlay, as he split 602 into sections, and tore into the fighters. It was fast and furious.

Sergeant Proctor hit one of the twins, and watched it blow up. Dougie Elcombe, startled by a 109 with a green spinner flashing straight across his bows, let fly. The Messerschmitt vanished in a billowing cloud of glycol vapour. Harry Moody and Roger Coverley both connected briefly with 109s, and then, as if by magic, the sky was clear again, the Spitfires virtually unscathed. Boyd's protégés were certainly learning their trade. One the way back, Elcombe's Spitfire, which had been streaming a thin glycol trail, started to run rough as the temperature rose. He put it down safely at Ford.

That night across the Channel, a young Me109 pilot, Leutnant Hellmuth Ostermann, wrote in his diary:

> Utter exhaustion from the English operations has set in. Once more I lost contact with my squadron. The Spitfires showed themselves wonderfully manoeuvrable. Their aerobatics display – looping and rolling, opening fire in a climbing roll – filled us with amazement. I did no shooting but kept trying to get into position, meanwhile keeping a sharp watch on my tail.

At Westhampnett, Sandy Johnstone wrote in his:

> I have the Confidential Reports on the Officers to complete. At least I won't have to perjure myself overmuch, for they are, one and all, thundering good chaps.

*

During the next week, things began to build rapidly towards a climax. The 'big lick' was coming.

September 2nd: Severe raiding. On the biggest, six out of eleven squadrons scrambled, including 602, fail to make contact. Bombing has severely disrupted Fighter Control systems.

At Westhampnett, 602 welcomed Pilot Officer Glen Niven, who'd been about to train with them at the outbreak of war. Now they found that he'd been trained on Hurricanes and had never flown a Spitfire at all. After struggling with one for half an hour in the circuit, they arranged for him to be transferred to 601, which this day returned to Tangmere, to replace an already-exhausted 17 Squadron.

September 3rd: One year after the outbreak of war, the crisis was approaching. OKW (Army High Command) directs: 'Earliest date for invasion fleet's departure has been fixed for 20 September'. 1,900 barges, 1,600 escorts, 420 tugs assembling.

The first two Lysander pilots, 'Agony' Payne and 'Pedro' Hanbury, arrive. They have no experience of fighters. Boyd's instructions are explicit. 'Stick close to me. Do what I do. If you hesitate, you're dead. Don't question anything you see or hear. Oh, by the way, *that* is the gun button.'

September 4th: At Westhampnett, there are rumours that invasion is imminent. All leave cancelled.

13.00 hours: 602 scrambled with 601 and 43 out of Tangmere. Operating as a Wing, they climb for Beachy Head, and sight the incoming bomber formations, with Me109s and 110s stepped up above and behind.

South of Canterbury, Sandy Johnstone split 602, leading one flight towards a group of Me110s, while the Hurricanes, unmolested, set about the bombers. They'd climbed through freezing cloud, and Sandy fired a short burst just to check his Brownings hadn't frozen solid. Over a mile away, the leading 110 of the second group peeled off and dived straight down into the sea leaving an oily black vertical trail. No one else had fired – 'Seems a jammy way to notch up a victory', he noted in his diary.

Now the 110s went into their familiar defensive circle. 602 split it. Paul Webb and Roger Coverley both connected; as the 110s cleared the area, the Spitfires dived for the bombers, outpacing the vengeful 109s coming down from 28,000 feet. Harry Moody, humming to himself, (and at one point over the R/T when he thumbed the switch) sailed happily into battle, knocking chunks out of two bombers, and seeing one blow up as it flick rolled over the shore. A silent *whoof!* of flame-streaked smoke, and a few fluttering scraps gently fell. The leading 109, catching Findlay Boyd, was surprised by the speed of his reaction. A stall turn, a flick to the right, and the bewildered Luftwaffe pilot never knew what hit him. Dourly, Findlay turned back to the bombers, lashed a Dornier with the remainder of his ammunition, and collected his charges. The Spitfires were unscathed.

September 6th: Three main raids. 602 chased the second almost into France.

Some of them nearly didn't get back. Fed up with continually being vectored to where there was simply no 'custom', when they saw the retreating Heinkels and Me110s they went after them hell for leather. Racing towards Calais, they suddenly found the roles reversed – the incoming fighters could see the defending fighters – Me109s – rising up in defence of their bases. The Spitfires wheeled, but as Glyn Ritchie tried to squeeze off a quick burst at a departing bomber, his instrument panel disappeared in a welter of flying glass and metal, the canopy starred, and his legs were stung, then numbed, by hot shell splinters. His wingman, Sergeant Proctor, heeled round and shot the 109 out of the sky as it was turning to make sure of the kill. Pat Lyall had an inconclusive brush with another, but had to break off as the Spitfires put their noses down and roared for home.

The day started and finished in triumph for Findlay. As 'B' came on state in the morning, a certain pilot, unable to break the habit of a lifetime, yet again entered the little hut by the Nissens, complete with morning newspaper and toilet roll. Findlay taxied his Spitfire over, turned it tail on to the hut, and opened the throttle wide. The hut lifted clean away. . . .

That evening, though, the drinks were on Findlay. The news had come through of his DFC.

Two days earlier, at the Berlin Sportspalast, Hitler had whipped the audience once again into a frenzy. 'If people in England are asking today "Why doesn't he come?" I reply "Don't worry. He is coming".'

Four spies, caught on Romney Marshes, confessed they were to spy for the invasion units; moon and tides were right.

That night, the skies were still. 602 slept undisturbed.

CHAPTER EIGHT

'If London Can Take It'

We must prepare for heavier fighting in the month of September. The need of the enemy to obtain a decision is very great.

Winston S. Churchill, to the House of Commons, 5th September.

I personally have taken command of the attack . . . and have heard the roar of victorious German squadrons, which have for the first time struck the enemy right to the heart.

Reichsmarschall Hermann Goering, grabbing the microphone from the radio reporter as he stood at the Cap Gris Nez under the first waves of bombers returning from London, 7th September.

September 7th: Weather – fair, but a dense heat haze built up over much of the south coast.

14.00 hours: At Westhampnett, 602 called to readiness. So far, they've had nothing to do. A little later on, Jack Boret arrives with the VIP he'd warned them about – the Chief of Air Staff, Sir Cyril Newall. The pilots are a little tidier than usual.

16.10 hours: '*Scramble! Scramble!* Patrol Hawkinge, Angels 15.' Pedro Hanbury threw the phone down, and Sandy Johnstone hastily excused himself from the CAS. As the twelve Spitfires wheeled into formation, and climbed for the east, he glanced down at his watch. Under ninety seconds. 'Not bad. Hope the old boy was impressed.'

Boyd was wondering if they'd be too late again. Somehow the Controllers seemed slower these days. (They were – the communications network had been hard hit. But what they gave was now more accurate. Everyone was learning.) 'Villa Leader, hullo, Villa Leader. Many bandits approaching Dungeness, Angels 15 and above. Buster!'

Thin trails of smoke reached back from the exhaust ports. Down below, Newall noted the 'purposeful look of the aircraft as their engines roared and they sped towards the battle.'

In the Spitfires, they weren't feeling particularly heroic.

Johnstone, thinking tactics already. Should he add a couple of thousand feet to his directed height? Better to be a little too high, than caught in the murderous fire raining down from the 109s . . . Aries, rehearsing in his mind his first – and only – kill; a bomber nearly two weeks ago. Had it been a fluke? could he ever do it again? Ginger Whall with five to his credit, wondering if it was really true that you got the DFM for six kills . . . he switched on the reflector sight, and turned the knurled knob until the brightness was exactly right. By now a hardened veteran at 21, he knew what to expect. They were climbing higher; he set the bars to the wingspan of a 109. Pedro Hanbury, on his first operational sortie, checking every dial, every setting, again and again, practising the lifesaving tips he'd picked up from Boyd and the others. Get the head moving – check above, behind, to the beam . . . And Harry Moody, humming contentedly away in his cockpit again, adrenalin pumping already, senses alive. . .

'Jesus Christ, it's the whole of the Luftwaffe. . .'

Shimmering in the high sun of late afternoon, wave upon wave of bombers, driving for London. Stepped above and behind, the serried ranks of Messerschmitts. Covering mile upon mile of sky, as far as the eye could see. It was at once magnificent and terrible.

'Villa Squadron, aim for the bombers. Look out for snappers coming down . . . here they come . . . Villa, *break, break!*'

Suddenly, the sky dissolved into whirling confusion, the headphones filled with snatches of command, of exultation, of warning, of stark terror.

'He's a flamer . . . Jeez, that was close . . . *Hey, look out!*'

'Go for the bombers . . . more at two o'clock. . .'

'Hold on, Roger, I'm coming. Hold on!'

Momentarily, a flash of amusement – a portly German floating through the chaos on the end of a parachute, his arms held high in a gesture of surrender. 'Bloody hell, I've shot down Goering!'

Smiles behind oxygen masks; just as suddenly, they're wiped away by a thin, eerie scream. Mike switch pressed, a terrified youth shouts his agony to the world. His last, timeless seconds will live long in those who shared them.

This time, Aries would swear he broke left just *before* the tracer came – and he got his Dornier too. Then the Messerschmitts got him.

Proctor found himself jinking left, then right, as the tracer flashed past; suddenly, a twin reared up in his sights – long glasshouse, a 110. He let fly, saw little chips float off as the Messerschmitt completed its bunt. One damaged. He dived for the protection of the haze.

Sandy Johnstone was already there. Cautiously, he lifted the Spitfire up again, and was once again shocked by the sight of hundreds of black-crossed aircraft in unbroken phalanxes boring for London. What had all the sweat, the turmoil, the sacrifices of the last few minutes been for, he wondered. He squirted at a Heinkel, and sank below the haze as it flew solidly on. Heading east, he rose again, hoping to come in on the flank of the raid. Still they were there in dozens. By now quite alone, fuel low, he circled long enough to take in the sight of bombs raining down over the docks. Fires springing up from Tilbury, a vast white splash in the Thames Estuary. Probably one of our boys, he thought sourly. Now he swung for home, and three 109s slanted across from the right. Instinctively, he fired at the nearest; it rolled on to its back and dived away. He couldn't hang around to watch the results, with the other two whipping round to attack. Yellow noses – did that really mean a crack unit? – the thought was fleeting. He fired – the guns clattered briefly, then stopped. Time to go. He shoved the nose down, twisted, jinked, aileron turned, and all the time the 109s clung to the elusive Spitfire. These boys were really good. With the altimeter unwinding like a sweep second hand, he finally found sanctuary right down among the Slough balloon barrage, and threaded his way carefully to the west.

Back at Westhampnett, they found just six gallons of fuel left in LO-J's tank. Johnstone found Jack Boret and Sir Cyril Newall still there. The Chief of Air Staff got his first-hand account of London's first mass raid from 602's CO. Patiently, he listened, asked a few brief questions, and, looking grave, drove back to the capital in his staff car. The Blitz of London had begun in earnest.

At Westhampnett, they thought little of grand strategy. Their task was simply to fly, and fight, and survive in the burning skies over the city. And that night, for the first time, there were two who didn't return; Roger Coverley, quiet and dedicated, and Harry Moody, so handsome and reserved, who hummed contentedly into battle. Nobody saw them go down. Twenty-four hours might bring the news they hoped for – or the news they didn't want to hear.

Two others were down. Ellis Aries had crash-landed in a field near Maidstone. He was safe. So, too, was Pedro Hanbury, who'd been blooded in no uncertain terms. He'd damaged a Dornier before the Messerschmitts pounced.

Three new pilots arrived – Pilot Officers Fisher, Edy and Barthropp – and news came through of Paul Webb's promotion to Flight Lieutenant.

Johnstone noted that night in his diary, 'It has been a black day, and the threat of invasion hangs over us.'

The next day, Sunday, was quiet. There was no news of Harry Moody or Roger Coverley, and the fears became certainty. For the first time in the Battle, Sandy Johnstone would struggle for the right words – 'Dear Mrs & Mrs Coverley, . . .'

Many days later, Roger's body was discovered, in an orchard near Tunbridge Wells. There was no sign of his aircraft, and he had been terribly burned. To jump had been the quickest way.

To this day, nothing has ever been discovered of Harry Moody or his Spitfire. Sandy wondered about a second letter. But what on earth could he tell the young girls who now had lost their hero, and whose knitting was in vain?

That Sunday morning, two of Harry's colleagues sat in a little Sussex church. They didn't often go, but the text the vicar had chosen this day made them glad they had. From Psalm 63, in a gentle voice, he read,

'In the shadow of thy wings I sing for joy. My soul clings to thee; thy right hand upholds me. But those who seek to destroy my life shall go down into the depths of the earth; they shall be given over to the power of the sword, they shall be prey for jackals. But the king shall rejoice in God; all who swear by him shall glory; for the mouths of liars will be stopped.'

*

September 9th: – Weather – Scattered thundery showers. Channel fair.

The massed raids return over London.

Dowding begins to operate a 'stabilization scheme', labelling fighter squadrons as Category 'A' – in and around 11 Group, with the vast majority of experienced pilots left to him – Category 'B', a small operational reserve, and Category 'C', worn out units stripped of most experienced pilots, based away from the action to recover.

602 are Category 'A' – they will fight the rest of the battle. Both the Tangmere Hurricane squadrons are withdrawn. 601 have

already left for Exeter, replaced by 213, and today 43 swop places with Jimmy Vick's 607 (County of Durham).

16.35 hours: 602 scrambled as the plots of a big raid were tracked towards Mayfield. This time, with eight other squadrons, they had height, position, and the sun.

As Sandy Johnstone led them towards a fair sized force of Dornier 17s, they were just in time to watch a squadron of Hurricanes split them up in a beautifully executed head-on attack. What they couldn't know then was that it was Archie McKellar, newly arrived with 605 Squadron at Croydon, and itching to get back among the Germans. After the first pass, the Dorniers scattered in confusion. Like most of the bombers this afternoon, they wouldn't get as far as their designated targets.

As the Me109s came down from nearly 30,000 feet, 602 swept in to snap up the pickings. It was fast and furious. Johnstone and Lyall together swung on a Dornier – as the bullets crashed home, the bomber crew instantly baled out; 'Beginning to lose their nerve,' thought Sandy, as three parachutes blossomed. His own nerves were rattled a split second later, as a 109 appeared from nowhere, right on his tail. Just before the cannons found the Spitfire, though, Pat Lyall angled in, pulled off a beautiful piece of deflection shooting, and the 109 went straight down. But it was really Sergeants' Day. As the aircraft whirled crazily across the sky, Proctor got through to the bombers and knocked chunks out of a Dornier; Andy McDowall, cursing happily, blew a 109 to pieces, and Ginger Whall destroyed another bomber. As they flew west, he wondered if they gave you another DFM for the second six.

But it wasn't all one-sided. As the 109s made their first diving attack, they all saw a Spitfire pulling away, streaming smoke, and leaning into a gradually steepening dive. 'LO . . . one of ours,' thought Sandy. But he didn't see the 109s going after it.

Paul Webb reckoned he'd be lucky to get away this time. His engine missed, caught, and then started to smoke. As he dived, three Messerschmitts raced after him, taking it in turn to fire. Right down to ground level, the unequal contest went on, with Paul finding his options diminishing all the time. He couldn't climb, the engine wouldn't allow it. Now, his rudder control went, the cable and links shot through. After another series of shell strikes, even his aileron controls were badly damaged. He was virtually reduced to going in a straight line. Mercifully, the 109s, certain of their kill, hauled away. His thoughts were concentrated completely on his own survival. His chances weren't altogether good. Speed too high, no height to play with, no lateral control. He did the only thing he could – throttled back and aimed the aircraft straight ahead until the ground came up.

The Spitfire, still travelling fast, scythed into the treetops of a little copse. Leaves exploded around the cockpit as the propeller slashed into the upper branches – then, with idiot violence, both wings tore off at the roots. The fuselage battered on, breaking up. The tail section bounced, and tore away. The engine's weight dragged the nose assembly down into the soft floor of the little wood. Fifty yards further on, the cockpit section finally came to rest. As the inevitable little crowd ventured forward, they were amazed to see signs of life under the starred perspex hood.

They found Paul semi-conscious, cursing comprehensively, and miraculously suffering only a broken wrist, four broken fingers, and multiple lacerations to his head. He would have time now to get his new Flight Lieutenant's stripes – but he'd have to get somebody else to sew them on.

September 11th: Weather – Fine, with a few scattered showers. Cloudy over Channel.
London blitz continues – and the raiders return to Portsmouth. '*Seelöwe*' decision postponed.

14.45 hours: Smithy was relaxed in the cockpit, buried in his paperback. The canopy was closed; it had been raining, and if the Spitfire was going to climb five miles or more into the freezing reaches of the upper skies, the cockpit had to be kept dry. The sun was out now, though, and the place was beginning to feel like a greenhouse. He reached up and slid the hood back. It moved easily. 'Okay, Sid? She's nearly down to 40 . . . Better crank her up.'

Signs of movement under the wing. The diminutive figure of Sid Eveleigh, yawning, reappeared. He checked the trolley accumulator. 'Right. Ready when you are.'

Once again, the late summer peace of the Sussex countryside was shattered as the Merlin burst into life, and Smithy, the fitter, watched the gauges. The Spitfires had to be ready to go the instant there was a scramble – there would be no time to warm up, so whenever the oil temperature sank to 40°, they ran her up, checking the magnetos and pressure gauges.

The sound was so much a part of the daily routine, that nobody as much as raised an eyebrow in the 'B' Flight Nissen hut, hard by LO-K, Findlay Boyd's Spitfire. As Flight Commander, he had the privilege of the shortest sprint.

The Merlin stuttered into silence, and Smithy clambered out onto the port wing root, careful to rearrange the straps exactly as his pilot would want them. When it came to action, not a second would be lost. At the starboard wingtip, Sid once again arranged the parachute pack – shoulder straps hanging over the leading edge. Each Spitfire was prepared by a closely-knit team, the pilot totally dependent on his fitter and rigger, and they, in turn, taking an intensely professional pride in his performance. Armourers and wireless technicians were shared. The armourers had mixed feelings about 'Boydey' (or, 'Boyd the Bastard' as some called him). Findlay, by now the professional killer, had his guns tested every week, and harmonised to only fifty yards. If he came that close, the German in his sights would take the full weight of the eight Brownings at one concentrated spot. He insisted on a higher proportion of De Wilde explosive ammunition in his gunbelts – one De Wilde to every two of ball ammunition. The armourers called it a 'dirty' loading – the heavier De Wildes had a tendency to foul the barrels – but they were much more effective at destroying aircraft. Whenever Boyd was in combat, the barrels ended up in a mess and the armourers could weep. His last fifty rounds would contain tracers – a warning the guns were about to run out. But Boyd didn't usually need all his ammunition.

Smithy and Sid swore by him, though. They were proud of his 'gong' – he certainly got results. And he always spoke to them after he was down, before heading for the Intelligence Officer.

His cockpit check complete, Smithy carefully polished the perspex with clean cotton waste – perfect visibility was all-important – and took a rag over the insignia on 'K's' cockpit flap and cowling. Boyd's family crest – a gauntlet with the motto '*CON-FIDO*' – and the Wee Devil with the forked tail spearing a Messerschmitt with his trident. Above it, there was a row of seven little swastikas.

They'd had a quiet morning. Findlay hadn't been expected back. He was on leave in London, and there hadn't been much to do to help the other ground crews; after all, there were more crews than Spitfires now. But Boyd had arrived back that morning, recalled by his CO who was getting desperately short of experienced pilots too. He'd come over to the Spitfire, still grimy from a night helping the

ARP wardens put out incendiaries during an air raid on the capital, and said 'Get her ready, will you. I'll be flying today.'

They could hear the phone jangle – so even before the door burst open and the pilots ran for the Spitfires, they were in action. '*Scramble . . . scramble . . . start up!*'

Smithy dived for the cockpit, Sid belted round to the trolley acc; petrol cocks on, jab the starter button as the mag switches are flipped on, and the Merlin coughed blue smoke from the ports and fired. As the haze was whipped back by the slipstream, Smithy checked throttle and radiator flap settings, and climbed out of the cockpit.

Boyd was already under the starboard wing, hauling on the harness of his parachute pack as he ran round, jumped up on the port wing root, and into the cockpit. The parachute nestled in the bucket seat, with Findlay perched on top.

A quick check round, and he was on the R/T – 'Patrol Portsmouth, Angels 12 . . . let's go . . .'

Sid hauled the chocks away – the trolley acc was already out – and the Spitfire, on its awkward splayed legs, swung round, bounced over the rough grass, turned into wind, and raced skywards. Seven of them went up that afternoon, mainly from 'A' Flight, the ground crews watching critically, before settling down with cards, books, or tea and a wad; the ladies had the waggon in.

'Only bit of excitement today,' muttered Sid. 'At least we didn't get covered in mud.' That morning, they'd all had to help when a Spit had, unusually for Westhampnett, got bogged down in a corner. With 'erks' under both mainplanes, from undercarriage to wingtip, they'd heaved and sweated until, with engine racing, she'd lifted, and taxied on to firm ground. A dozen of them were sprayed with liquid mud.

Just over half an hour later, they heard the first of the fighters returning. 'Must have been close, Smithy.'

The Spitfires, in straggled formation, swung into the circuit. Two, then another on its own. Low over the trees, a fourth. The first pair, Mount and Babbage, throttled back on the approach. The sharper eyes on the ground had seen the blackened gun ports, now they all heard the whistle as the wind played through the gun bays. 'They've got something. Where's Boydey?'

'There! Look – over the trees.'

Like the other crews, they singled out their Spitfire, watched her flight, and tried to assess if she was wounded.

'She's okay, I think.'

'She's fired. Bloody good. Hope she got one.'

The others were counting. Five in the circuit. They'd all fired. There's a sixth, canted sideways, labouring to maintain height. 'Who's that?'

'Hang on. It's Rosie, I think.' The Spitfire lurched alarmingly, slipped twenty feet of precious height, then steadied.

The others were down, clearing the field to the Flights. Some holes, particularly on one of the 'A' Flight Spits. Now Nigel Rose made his approach, both wheels down, but obviously lacking control. The fighter bounced, slewed, careered across the field, but finally fetched up still in one piece. Rose was on the wing before they got to him. It would be some time before the Spitfire would fight again.

Only six.

'K' rolled up, turned in front of the Nissen, and Smithy leapt up to greet a smiling pilot. 'Get your brush out, Smithy, I got at least one. A 109. Right in the drink. She flew beautifully.'

The words were appreciated. 'K' was already submerged in a blue blanket, as the armourers descended, whipping the gun bay panels off, hauling out the boxes, feeding new belts in. The bowser rolled over, and she gulped 100 octane thirstily. Sid was checking all round for scars.

'Did everyone get back, Smithy? I saw somebody trailing smoke.'

'Rosie copped a packet, but he's down OK. The engine was all right. It couldn't have been him.'

'Right, I'd better get over there.'

Andy McDowall strode past, heading for Henry Grazebrook's little table, smiling. He only smiled when he'd scored.

'Sarge. Did you get one?'

'Yeah. A 110. Hit both engines. They started to climb out, but I wasn't having any of that. I went in again and hit those bastards right back in the cabin.'

Bert Simpson glanced up from the gun bay and his eyes caught Smithy's. He shrugged his shoulders. 'I suppose it gets to some people like that.'

'S'pose so, sarge. I just feel sorry for the poor sods in the 110.'

'Yeah, well, don't say so too loudly when Mac's about.'

Over at Grazebrook's table, the full picture was emerging.

They'd gone for the bombers, but a mixed force of 109s and 110s had hit them first. Babbage, Proctor and McDowall had all claimed victims, and Boyd had fought a desperate battle with two 109s all the way down from 22,000 feet to just 500. In a turning fight, the Spitfire had pulled harder, and as they came down the sky, she'd a bit more power to play with too. Findlay had put one victim into the sea; the other wavehopped for France trailing smoke.

But Sergeant Sprague hadn't come back. Nobody saw him go down, and there had been no reports from observers on the ground. 'Bloody shame ... and him just married two weeks ago.'

They could only post him as 'missing', but they all knew he wouldn't return. Strange how it didn't affect them the way Moody and Coverley's deaths had just four days earlier. The Reaper was just another enemy among many; the Luftwaffe, the weariness, the cold that froze your reactions six miles high.

But the sergeant's death wouldn't leave them alone. For the next three weeks, his young bride would sit in a car by the airfield, gazing for hours on end at the 'B' flight huts, waiting for the husband who could never return. No one could console her; she would not be moved from her vigil. Exactly a month after death had claimed him, the seas returned his body, washed up at Brighton. After the funeral, when he was buried with full military honours, she came back, just once, to remember – but not to accept.

That night, they drank to Sprague's memory – and to Sandy Johnstone's DFC. The next morning, they were down to five serviceable Spitfires. Smithy and Sid had found just one hole – where a 7.9mm German bullet had entered the leading edge of the starboard wing centre section, and when they opened the inspection panels, they found it had clobbered the main spar. 'K' was bound for the factory for a whole new wing.

*

September 15th: Weather – Fair with cloudy patches, clear by early evening.
Heavy raids on London, in which the Germans will incur their greatest losses since 18th August.

This time, in the carefully-orchestrated counter-attack, the morning's mass raid was intercepted by Spitfires over the coast, harried by Hurricane squadrons all the way in, and chased back out again by fresh pairs of squadrons. Park was able to keep some in reserve. 602 and 607, the last two ordered up, arrived over Mayfield too late to add to the rout, but young Paddy Barthropp saw enough to be convinced he was caught up in something historic. Landing after his first operational sortie, he wrote in his log book. 'Thousands of them.'

When the Germans came back, 602 would be among the first to hit them.

14.05 hours: After Jack Boret had rolled in with another VIP, this time the Under Secretary of State for Air, Harold Balfour, 602 scrambled in squadron strength. Their guest, a Great War scout pilot who'd been more appreciated than most, was treated, like Cyril Newall the week before, to the sight of the Spitfires racing into the sky, hauling round hard, and setting course to do battle over London.

14.12 hours: 602, together with the Hurricanes of 607, bound for Biggin Hill, sighted a formation of Dorniers over Edenbridge. For once, there were no escorting Messerschmitts, although Galland's 'free hunt' could be seen thousands of feet higher, streaming ice trails in the upper air. 'A piece of cake,' wrote Sandy Johnstone in his diary afterwards.

Hitting the higher of two groups of Dorniers, 602 went through them 'like a dose of salts' according to Johnstone. In the first pass, four went down; at least three were definite kills. The rest began to jettison their bombs short of the target, and put their noses down for home. Behind and below, the panic spread visibly through the second formation, like ripples on a huge pond. As 607 closed, the Dorniers broke, and Paddy Stephenson found two coming straight at him. He didn't even have time to fire. Like a boxer delivering a right and a left in quick succession, he aimed his Hurricane right at the narrowing gap between the bombers, and felt the *thump! thump!* as first one wing, then the other smashed into the Dorniers. Both bombers, short of a wing, crashed to destruction; Paddy found himself, somehow, in clear sky, with no wings at all. He managed to leap out, coming down safely (and appropriately, as they all claimed afterwards back at Tangmere) right beside a lunatic asylum.

Further on, the remainder of the Dorniers were scattered by a lone Hurricane in a head-on attack. Above, a 109 pilot, completely taken aback by what was happening around him, shot his own section leader down; then the Hurricane hooked round, and shot him down too. It was that kind of day. 602, racing down the bomber lines at over 350 mph, sent another one down and winged two more, completing the rout of Kesselring's leading formation.

It was all over in less than four minutes – just one small action in a vast battle which filled the skies as far as the eye could see, reaching back seventy miles to the French coast, spreading across a nine mile front, and stacked five miles high.

Back at Westhampnett, there wasn't a single scratch on any of the Spitfires – and 602 were amazed to hear the BBC announcing the biggest 'bag' of the entire Battle; 185 definitely down. It was, of course, an exaggeration; one of the biggest. The true score was sixty. But this was the day when they'd taken part in the defeat of the final massed daylight bomber force. Paddy Barthropp had an inkling of the grand scale of the day, though. Returning from the London skies, he'd opened his log book once again, and simply written, '*Still* thousands of them.'

A storm lashed the Channel for the next two days, during which Goering tore strips off his commanders, and told them the fighters must now bear the brunt of what was coming. One thing that wasn't coming, though, was the invasion. On the 17th, Hitler agreed with his Naval Staff that the RAF was 'still by no means defeated' and that invasion should be postponed 'till further notice'.

Over the next fortnight, the scrambles were frequent, the enemy decidedly nervy, but occasionally successful. They flattened the Spitfire factories at Southampton. They got Pilot Officer D.H. Gage twice, too. Two days in succession he came down minus his Spitfire, and each time ended up at the same railway station, asking to use the telephone to inform base that he was in one piece. Andy McDowall's DFM came through, and Boyd survived a direct cannon strike on his armoured windscreen. He landed at Westhampnett with his helmet looking like a hedgehog, sprouting tiny shards of toughened glass. The windscreen had disappeared. Miraculously, his face was unmarked. It had, of course, been right behind the gunsight at the time.

*

September 27th: Weather – Fair at Tangmere, cloudy over Channel. Rain over London.
Heavy attacks on London and Bristol. Germans lose 55 aircraft.

No 602 scrambled twice. In the morning, they were 'bounced' by high-flying 109s. Babbage only just saw them in time; his warning shout took the Spitfires sideways, and he got in a squirt at the tail-ender.

Thirsting for revenge, Boyd took them into the bombers over London. In a fast action, Paddy Barthropp opened his account with a half share in a Heinkel 111, John Willie Hopkin, newly arrived from 54 Squadron, got another, and so too did Cyril Babbage. Back at Westhampnett, as Smithy helped Boyd out of his new Spitfire, the pilot was animated. 'It was great, Smithy, you couldn't see the Channel for dead bodies.'

As Findlay sauntered off in search of tea and a smoke, Sid shrugged. 'I really don't think he likes Germans at all.'

Smithy was underneath the Spitfire, gazing at a mess of black oil which streaked right along the fuselage, across the wing roots, and which had penetrated into the cockpit floor. 'I don't think they're too keen on Boydey either.'

In fact, this time the Germans hadn't connected. The filter cap on the oil tank had come off as Boyd threw the Spitfire around the sky. Smithy and Sid had to pour a bucketful of petrol into the cockpit, after removing the seat and radio, and wash down the entire fuselage. They didn't smoke within thirty yards of her for the next couple of days . . . but when they suggested to their pilot that it might be in his own interests not to fire his guns, his response was just about hot enough to ignite the fumes anyway!

September 30th: Weather – Fair, scattered light cloud.
The last major daylight battle.

10.35 hours: Oberst Helmut Schwenhart looked out of his Ju88. To port, Richter's Junkers was keeping close station. The fifteen bombers of KG77 climbed steadily towards Cherbourg, from their base at Orleans/Bricy. Schwenhart was happy enough. Confident in his machine, one of the newer Ju88 A-5s, with better armour and a fifteen foot increase in its wingspan, he was setting off on his twenty-sixth operational sortie. A veteran who hadn't yet reached the age of twenty-one, he automatically fingered the orange scarf he habitually wore. The others in his Staffel were curious as to its origins. He let them wonder – it did his image no harm at all. Actually, it was a gift from his mother, and it had seen him through most of his first 'tour'. He thought about the fight that might lie ahead. They were headed towards Weymouth. They'd go in close to the Isle of Wight.

They'd had trouble there before – particularly from the Spitfires. At the morning's briefing, they'd been assured that the raids over London would have drawn the fighters away. They would have a top cover of 109s. Helmut glanced up. He hoped they were over the clouds. He certainly couldn't see them. KG77 levelled off at 12,000 feet, and droned on.

10.52 hours: Paddy Barthropp grabbed the ops phone. In the flight hut, dozing pilots who'd already flown two fruitless scrambles started awake. One headed straight for the door and vanished round the corner, doubling up, before Paddy shouted, 'Scramble. The Needles . . . Angels One Five.' He pressed the alarm. Across the field, the Merlins began to burst into vibrant life. In an avalanche of discarded books and papers, the pilots launched themselves from the hut. Over in the corner, one tired Spitfire was refusing point blank to co-operate. The other ten roared off.

Richter saw them coming first. He bellowed a warning to the rest of the Junkers, and looked up in despair for the escort that just wasn't there. The fifteen 88s scattered over Cowes. Behind them, on the same frequency, the bomb-carrying 110s did likewise. As they often did, Schwenhart and Richter stuck together, increasing the effect of their defensive firepower. It wasn't enough.

Sandy Johnstone led the Spitfires down from above the Ju88 formation. Selecting the leader of a pair which had stayed close, he closed to 100 yards, before firing. There were strikes around the cabin, and suddenly the port engine exploded. The wing tore off at the root, and as the doomed bomber lurched into its final, spinning dive, only one man got out. The parachute blossomed.

Just above, 602 were having a real field day. Pedro Hanbury, racing in just behind Johnstone, broke the other way, latched onto a second Junkers, and blazed away at it until, with both propellers windmilling, it went into an ever-steepening dive.

Pat Lyall, opting for quantity rather than quality, raced gleefully around the sky, taking potshots at a number of Germans, setting one engine alight here, knocking chunks off a rudder there. One probable, one damaged. (It certainly was – as it landed back in France, streaming a long feather of flame from an overheated engine, the tail fell apart. The crew got out alive, but very shaken indeed.)

Over St Catherine's Point, Ginger Whall and Andy McDowall were vying with each other. Between them, they got two more, and agreed the lion's share should go to Mac.

The Operations Book that night noted 'A good day's work'; and there was an unexpected sequel. Sandy Johnstone was dressing for dinner – at the Duke of Norfolk's castle, no less – when Jack Boret summoned him by telephone.

When Sandy finally turned up for his dinner engagement, he'd collected some souvenirs. A young German pilot, who'd baled out of an 88, had arrived at the Tangmere guardroom, and insisted on meeting his conqueror. When Sandy was introduced to him, he clicked his heels, smiled in a slightly embarrassed manner, and presented the victor with the spoils of war – a Luger, a flying helmet, a lifejacket . . . and an orange scarf.

October 1st: Weather – Generally overcast. Visibility only moderate.

10.45 hours: Scrambled and vectored towards Ventnor at 15,000 feet, Johnstone led 602 through broken cloud searching for '100 plus bandits approaching coast'. There were mostly 109s and 110s, many carrying bombs. The Controller's height estimation was wildly out. As the Spitfire pilots searched in vain, Paddy Barthropp saw a bunch of Me109s diving on them from behind a cloud. His warning came in the nick of time.

No 602 broke left together, and the Messerschmitts shot past. The Spitfires gave chase, and in a brief flurry of action, only John Willie Hopkin managed to range on a 109, with inconclusive results. Swiftly, the scudding clouds gathered up friend and foe alike, and Johnstone led them, thoroughly brassed off, back to Westhampnett.

It set the pattern for much of 'Messerschmitt Month', which saw the battle entering a new phase. Around 250 Me109s and 110s were converted to carry bombs, and throughout the month came in on a succession of nuisance raids, interspersed with fighter sweeps, and on occasions larger raids, composed of perhaps thirty bombers, escorted by up to 300 fighters. The problem facing the Controllers was knowing which plot contained the threat of bombs, and which could safely be left alone.

It was a strange, bitter autumn.

October 7th: Weather – Scattered cloud and squally showers. Widespread small-scale raiding.
The AOC, Keith Park, visits 602 for the first time.

15.30 hours: Lanky Donald Jack, just back from leave, squeezed himself hurriedly into the confines of the Spitfire's cockpit. As he gunned the engine and lifted into the grey sky, with Johnstone and Hanbury ahead to his port side, and Ginger Whall close behind to starboard, he wondered if he'd ever be really comfortable in a fighter. But even if he did have to use every available inch of the bulged canopy, he knew he wouldn't readily swop the Spitfire for anything. Over the last eighteen months, he'd come to feel real affection for her. She'd got him safely out of that vicious circle of five 110s; and when the oxygen packed up five miles over Southampton and he'd nearly lost control, she'd dived straight and true, and in the manner of her kind, dropped her tail as the speed increased – she actually helped you to pull her out.

He'd been grateful for the break. Now, ready again for action, he scanned the skies. Around him, 602 had eleven up, a magnificent sight as the sun dappled their camouflage paint, the fighters rising and falling gently relative to each other, ranged across the sky in pairs. Canopies closed now, pilots dropping their seats and grinning across at each other, making their inevitable gestures with fists or fingers.

Behind and below, twenty-four Hurricanes from Tangmere, squat and purposeful, as Jimmy Vick and Stuart MacDonald led 607 and 213 westwards. Just as the Spitfires eased out of the climb, Donald glanced down again at the Hurricanes, by now moving ahead at their lower altitude, and saw the two weavers at the rear sliding toward each other. Even a warning shout would be too late – the ether was silent as the two Hurricanes came together, locked in a deadly embrace for a long, long second, and then spun to earth. Only one parachute.

Silence on the headphones. Then, 'Green Two, move back and start weaving – and mind how you go, laddie.'

'Green Two, Roger.'

An omen? wondered Donald. Not the superstitious type, he quickly shoved the thought to the back of his mind. Keep checking those skies, come on, get back into that rhythm. Ahead, mirror, to port, mirror, to starboard, mirror, and start the cycle again. He hoped his reflexes would be sharp enough if it came to a fight.

Meanwhile, as the RDF stations plotted the enemy offshore, heading further and further west, the Wing was ordered to Portland. They circled to Weymouth, but saw nothing. Donald wondered idly if you could really get a whole Wing chasing itself in an

Ogo Pogo. Next, they were ordered back to Southampton, while the 10 Group fighters took over the stalk of the raid bound, as it turned out, for the Westland factory at Yeovil.

Back over Southampton, still nothing. Then, as they were wheeling to return to base, a solitary unidentified aircraft appeared near Brighton. 'Villa Leader, we have a bogey at Angels Ten over Brighton. Can we have a section on to it, please?'

'Villa Blue One from Villa Leader. Go on, Donald, have a crack at it.'

Together, Donald and Ginger Whall swung towards the seafront, accelerating slightly, as the rest of the fighters made for home.

Now, pulse accelerating with the rising note of the Merlin, the chase was on. There . . . just beyond that cloud . . . gone. No, there it is . . . 'Blue Two, bandit just below. Dornier. Let's go . . . Tally Ho.'

The two Spitfires raced across the intervening gap, and pounced on the unsuspecting Dornier 17. There was no return fire as Donald closed in, picked his spot, and lashed the wing root and starboard engine, pulling away at seventy yards. Behind him, Whall was already lining up, and made an accurate firing pass right across the bomber, 'walking' his fire over the centre section and cabin. The Dornier keeled over and went straight into the water.

'Good shooting, Blue Two. Let's go home.'

Ginger closed up on Donald's starboard side, and the two Spitfires curved round towards Westhampnett. Suddenly, without any warning at all, Donald was surprised to see Whall's Spitfire peeling away. 'Villa Blue Two, have you a problem?' Silence. 'Villa Blue Two, are you hit? Are you receiving me?' The Spitfire steepened its dive. 'Ginger, for God's sake, get out!'

The Spitfire flew straight into the ground near Arundel. Shaken, Donald returned to Westhampnett.

The others were already down, waiting for news of the successful combat – they'd heard his 'Tally Ho'. Palefaced, Donald climbed out and told them what he'd seen. Smithy and Sid were shattered. Whall had been flying Boyd's Spitfire. Their feelings were a strange mixture – anger that the young sergeant had written off their plane and yet the feeling, too, of personal loss.

Whall wasn't killed outright. He lingered for a few hours after admission to hospital. Donald Jack, who hadn't encountered any return fire from the Dornier, would always wonder if his first firing pass had killed the German gunner – or just woken him up.

New faces appeared regularly, to fill the gaps in the ranks – and 602 began to acquire a distinctly Canadian twang over the R/T. Jake Edy, rapidly working towards his DFC, had been joined by Pilot Officer J.S. Hart, and by 'Nuts' Niven, who had grumbled so long and hard on being relegated to flying Hurricanes with 601 that they'd finally sent him back to 602.

No 602 reflected on the changing patterns of their part in the battle. Aircraft serviceability was again becoming a problem, with the Spitfires scrambled so high and so often. Irritating, and sometimes downright dangerous, little faults developed. 'T' suffered a loss of brake pressure on landing one day, and investigation showed that the copper piping from the compressor on the engine had fatigued long before its time, and fractured. With daylight now much shorter, the repair was a torchlight job under a canvas cover, in order to ready the Spitfire for battle next morning. Various leaks appeared mysteriously in hydraulic systems; the HF radios began acting strangely when the autumn mists caressed the sleeping fighters at dawn. Sets which had been checked out the night before just packed up.

The pilots were being worn down, too – with day after day of 'Alert One', when they spent waking and sleeping hours in the readiness huts, and with frequent scrambles taking them on full oxygen climbs to 30,000 feet and more through freezing cloud that frosted the canopy inside and out, locked the guns solid, and left the Spitfire wallowing near the stall, they were sitting ducks for the 109s which ranged ever higher with their two-stage superchargers.

Next day, 602 thought they had another casualty. As the last of five Spitfires landed after a morning scramble, it taxied erratically round to 'A' Flight dispersal, pulled up a little short of the ground crew, and as the propeller flicked to a stop, they ran towards it. There were no signs of battle damage, but the pilot hadn't moved, his head slumped in the cockpit. When they got to him, he was snoring deeply and thankfully asleep. When they ribbed him about it afterwards, he couldn't remember a thing. Two hours later, he was five miles up, gulping oxygen to revive himself.

On the 12th, the strain was definitely showing. Intercepting a mixed force of 109s, some carrying bombs and some acting as escorts, the 602 pilots found themselves in a tight spot. As the bomb carriers dropped their loads early and turned for home, Babbage and Hart found they'd been attacking the wrong ones – their 109s didn't have bombs on, but they certainly had cannons! In a brief combat over Lewes, Hart's Spitfire was severely damaged, and Babbage was shot down, though he wasn't injured. To make matters worse, they couldn't even claim a 'damaged'. Two Spits out of action for no result was hardly 602's normal style, but Babbage cheered up somewhat in the afternoon, when, along with Fisher and Hart, he hit a Ju88 out over the Channel. They gave him a 'probable' for it. He was actually smiling again when he found they'd also given him the Distinguished Flying Medal. The celebrations in the Sergeants' Mess were echoed at Woodcote House, when confirmation came through of Boyd's second DFC.

It was around this time that Cuthbert Orde, an official war artist, arrived, commissioned by the Air Ministry to do sketches of some of the pilots. Johnstone, Jack, Boyd, McDowall and Mount were chosen. 'Well, it's my profile old boy, it's a classic.' 'See if you can get him to give you some hair back, Findlay, your top cover's hidden in the clouds.' 'Can't see why they picked you, Donald, old son. The canvas'll only come up to your neck . . . still, maybe it's better that way!'

And so it went on. But the real embarrassment was Mickey Mount's. A little later on, another war artist, Olive Snell, turned up, this time to do the complete job in oils. Mickey had to endure several sittings, and a barrage of pointed questions in the Mess. 'What have you got that we haven't then?'

'W-w-well, d-don't g-g-go sp-sp.'

'Want my fig leaf, old son?'

'N-no, I'm t-trying to s-say, d-don't go springing t-to conclusions, ch-chaps.'

'Course not. Is that paint on your cheek?'

'Wh-where?'

'No, the other cheek, you old devil.'

October 26th: Weather – Cool; cloudy with scattered showers. Fighter bomber raids across London and Kent.

For 602, it was one of the bitterest days. With the enemy plainly defeated by day, still the high-flying Me109 bomb carriers came over, and the squadron had its share of fruitless scrambles. Not once did they engage, as, from 10.30 onwards through the entire day, they were sent off section by section, climbing hard for London, circling at 28,000 feet or more with ice forming on the wings and canopies, and the pilots feeling first the numbness, then the pain as they descended westwards.

On one flight over London, they reached up to 31,000 feet, and were stooging around carefully, when one of the Spitfires gently put here nose down, and suddenly they all realised she wasn't coming up again. As they all stared down, they followed the dwindling shape of the fighter as it fell, steeper and steeper, arrow-straight for the ground. It was Sergeant Dougie Elcombe.

Despite repeated urgent calls on the R/T, there wasn't a trace of response. They gave up calling. The Spitfire took fully three minutes to fall. Then, crystal clear on the new VHF radios which had just been fitted, but very quietly, they heard the click and stillness of the carrier wave, and Elcombe's voice – 'I'm all right . . . I'm all right'. The Spitfire, forgiving in the screaming dive, had dipped her tail as the speed increased to nearly 500 mph in the denser air – and the young sergeant, probably the victim of oxygen starvation, had revived. 'I'm all right.' The last transmission clicked back to the hiss and crackle of static.

The rest of the Spitfires headed back to Westhampnett, a little uneasily.

Elcombe, levelling off under tremendous 'G' near the ground, must have found his fighter damaged by the stress of the dive – possibly with the engine torn apart by the racing propeller – because he tried to land her. He came in over the hop fields of Kent, and slid the fighter onto the ground. But the field was criss-crossed by wires, left up to foil any attempt by the Luftwaffe to effect a landing. They worked. They killed Elcombe.

Meanwhile, Sandy Johnstone, on ten days' leave in Glasgow, was still wondering which was harder – fighting Messerschmitts every day five miles high, or enduring the overflowing hospitality of 602's native city. Fêted right, left and centre, he spent the days at receptions, 'Spitfire Fund' rallies, and a luncheon at the City Chambers, where the guests included J.B. Priestley.

More importantly, the Lord Provost, Paddy Dollan, who took a personal pride in the squadron known as 'Glasgow's Own', helped to pull together enough in the way of interested parties to enable a Squadron Benevolent Fund to be permanently set up: there was no telling what hardships might befall the Auxiliaries or their dependents in the war – and the peace – that lay ahead. When Sandy returned to Westhampnett, he bought gifts from the City, the Provost, and the boys' families – and he also brought good news of Dunlop Urie and Paul Webb, both well on the mend, and Hector MacLean, now sporting a tin leg.

October 29th: Weather – Haze over Channel; fair but overcast inland.
The Luftwaffe's final daylight thrust in force.

12.20 hours: With Mickey Mount leading, the whole squadron scrambled and climbed for London. Throughout the morning, scattered raids had been coming in, increasing in scale; most of them were composed of bomb-carrying Me109s and 110s, escorted by umbrellas of 109 fighters. This time, the Controller got it absolutely right. Four squadrons were up as the Messerschmitts came in over the coast. Sighted by a section of Spitfires, the raiding force's height, direction and strength were radioed to Control, and the trap was laid.

Two Hurricane squadrons began to climb together, abeam of the Messerschmitts. No 222 Spitfire Squadron, out of Rochford, drove up hard, angling in from the rear of the fighter bombers – and sitting on top of the whole circus, 602's twelve Spitfires, already at nearly 30,000 feet, and just too low to leave any contrails. Slowly, the Spitfires wheeled in the blue vault, like hawks before the kill.

The 109s curved round to port, probably having seen the lower squadrons, and confident of their ability to race for home whenever the leading Spitfires climbed too close.

Mickey paused, savouring the moment, and without the slightest trace of a stammer, rapped out, 'Okay. Villa Squadron, Tally Ho. Let's get them.'

Now all the training paid off. Beating the Germans at their own game, the Spitfires came down the sky, pairing off, each wingman following his leader's every move, as they spread across the sky in the dive. Sergeant W.B. Smith, about to lose his combat virginity, tucked in behind Mount, Nuts Niven trailing Donald Jack, 'Wimpy' Whipps easing just out of Rose's slipstream.

As the roar of the Merlins rose in pitch, the Spitfires rocked, skidded gently and steadied, as each section leader picked his target; pilots crouched behind the reflector sights, thumbs covered the buttons, and suddenly there was a ripple of blue and yellow flame along the leading edges of Mount's Spitfire – then McDowall's – Lyall's – and then Jack's.

Noise. The reek of cordite. The cacophony, as hardened veterans and raw young tyros exulted in the perfect fighter attack.

'Jesus. I got him.'
'Look at that, he's baled out.'

'Take that, you blighter!' Good grief, thought Nuts Niven, he actually said that. Watching too many films. . .then an aircraft filled his sights. He fired.

Donald Jack felt the strikes. 'Green two, *break*, for God's sake!' The clattering stopped.

Across the sky, there was a whirling kaleidoscope of roundels, black crosses, and tracer. Mount, already through the Messerschmitts and climbing round the edge of the action, brought order from the developing chaos. 'Villa Squadron, they're breaking for home. Form up Angels 22. Angels 22.'

One by one, the Spitfires hauled up, using their superior speed gained in the dive, and they watched the first four 109s spinning down. Two parachutes . . . one fighter trailing oily smoke straight down, another flick rolling aimlessly, shorn of half a wing. They gave chase.

McDowall, his blood really up after one kill, pulled ahead, the exhaust stacks pumping out smoke as he broke the seal and went to Emergency Power. Of course, it broke the rules, too, but it would get him there faster. Still diving, his airspeed indicator crept round to 400 mph and a touch beyond. Tearing after his selected victim, the Brownings flashed for little more than a second. The 109 staggered, dropped a wing, and exposed the canopy. Mac's next burst blew it apart in a glittering shower. Belching white clouds of glycol, the German fighter went right down into the Channel.

Pat Lyall was off on another of his little personal flying circuses. Racing cheerfully around the sky as the Messerschmitts broke in confusion, he took potshots at two, seeing strikes on both, before latching onto his third, closing to forty yards, and emptying the Brownings into its soft, pale blue underbelly. A flicker of fire . . . then a long banner of flame streamed out, and the 109 fell like a firebrand. Over to starboard, one of the 109s had a bomb hung up. The pilot must have known what was coming; as the two Spitfires curved in, he didn't wait for the flash of the guns. He leapt straight out and fell like a stone for five thousand feet before the parachute blossomed. Maybe he'd heard about Mac.

Triumphantly, the Spitfires returned to Westhampnett. Ten had fired; nine had connected. And they claimed a dozen. Even after Henry Grazebrook had put his fine-tooth comb through the combat reports, it was obviously their finest show of all. Post-war research confirms at least eight, possibly nine, of the Messerschmitts – and the credits went to McDowall, Hart, Fisher, Jack, Lyall, Mount, W.B. Smith, Rose, and Whipps.

Two days later, the RAF decided to draw the line arbitrarily marking the end of the Battle of Britain. In truth, Hitler had drawn the line
already. The invasion wouldn't come now. . .and on the day of the
last major daylight operations, 602 had accounted for almost exactly
half of the Luftwaffe's total losses. And just as had happened a year
before, when they put Pohle's aircraft into the Forth, the telegrams
and signals came flooding in.

From HQ 11 Group:

> Group Commander sends warmest congratulations to 602 Sqn.
> on their magnificent combat at midday when they destroyed eight
> enemy fighters and shot down two others without loss of pilots or
> aircraft, creating a record for many months past.

And from Lord Provost P.J. Dollan: 'Glasgow sends you its gratitude
and admiration.'

One Spitfire, if the truth be told, was damaged that afternoon.
When the celebration began in the Mess, Donald Jack reckoned
'Nuts' owed him a double.

CHAPTER NINE

'One of the Few'

November 1st: Weather – cloudy; overcast inland. Early mist.

07.40 hours: Croydon satellite airfield. Hurricane V6979 scrambled on dawn patrol, ahead of a section of 605 Squadron. The wide undercarriage hooked into its belly, and the CO's aircraft droned up into the grey, forbidding skies. It disappeared into mist, climbing towards Kent.

07.50 hours: Distant sounds of machine gun fire heard above Mayfield. 'Aircraft heard diving, and zooming, for around two minutes.

07.52 hours: Above Woodlands Hall, a country mansion, a Hurricane suddenly burst from a bank of low cloud, flying inverted. Its spiral dive tightened into a crazy spin, until the machine plunged, still inverted, into flower beds in the grounds, with a dead hand on the stick.

As the echoes of the crash died away, a Messerschmitt 109 fell from the clouds half a mile away, and went straight in. Silence descended, as the mist shrouded the broken, twisted scatterings of aluminium and steel.

Evening: The tired Flight Lieutenant lifted up his pen, paused to rub his eyes, checked the date at the top of the Squadron Diary, and wrote:

> A sad day for the Squadron, as Squadron Leader McKellar was killed on the morning patrol. His charming personality, generosity, wit and vivacity will be much missed not only by the Squadron but by all with whom he came in contact.

He couldn't know it at the time, but his words were to be the sole official record of the passing of one of the battle's most outstanding fighters and leaders. The first of Fighter Command's pilots to be killed after the line which officialdom drew to mark the close of the Battle of Britain, his name would not appear on the Roll of Honour; the name of Archie McKellar, DSO, DFC and Bar.

Archie was born in Paisley, Renfrewshire, in 1912, the only son of John and Margaret McKellar. John, together with his brother, was building up a successful plastering business, and the family moved to Glasgow when Archie was three years old. He attended Shawlands Academy, in Glasgow's South Side, and though very small for his age (he stopped growing at a mere 5' 4"), Archie soon showed great promise on the sports field, betraying the quick eye, sharp reflexes, and excellent co-ordination which would later make him such a fine pilot.

He had an unlikely combination of ambitions as a youngster; one was to be a plasterer, following his father's trade, and the other was to fly. Met with stiff parental opposition to both, Archie persisted until his father at least relented on the question of him becoming a plasterer. But he wouldn't give an inch on the question of Archie flying. So Archie did the only thing he could. He learned on the quiet, at the Scottish Flying Club. It didn't take him long to gain his 'A' Licence, and he promptly celebrated by buzzing his home, waggling the wings of his DH Moth in triumph.

It was relatively easy for Archie to gain admission to the ranks of 602 Squadron – they rather liked his style. Archie, of course, revelled in the flying, as 602 flew ever more powerful machines, and when the Spitfires came, he found his ideal aircraft. He was born for air fighting.

He opened his shooting war with Pinkerton in the Forth raid, and a fortnight later his bullets brought down the first Heinkel over land. Through that first winter in 'Suicide Corner', he honed his skills in preparation for the coming battle. Within a year, he would establish himself as one of Fighter Command's most outstanding air fighters, winning the DSO, the DFC twice, and leading another Auxiliary Squadron, No 605 (County of Warwick) through the hardest days of the Battle of Britain.

He first met 605 at Drem, when they arrived in their battle-scarred Hurricanes to recover from the mauling they'd taken in the skies over Northern France and Dunkirk. McKellar lost no time in getting to know these men, to talk Messerschmitts and tactics with them. 605's CO, Walter Churchill, was impressed with Archie, and it came as no surprise when he was promoted and posted, on 21st June 1940, to become a Flight Commander on 605. When introduced to his Hurricane, the diminutive Archie noted at once its bulky, hump-backed fuselage and deep cockpit. He was undaunted. 'No problem. I'll fly it standing up!'

Within days, he had mastered the new fighter – and put on an unforgettable solo aerobatics performance one grey day over Drem after taking a Hurricane up on air test. Looping, rolling, and spinning above the airfield, he drew heads out of doors and windows as the song of the Merlin echoed over the rolling hills. His climax was superb. Blasting over 602's dispersal areas, condensation streaming from the Hurricane's wingtips, he pulled up at full throttle. Engine bellowing, the big fighter rose in an ever-steepening climb, and began to describe an upward roll – and, without wavering, followed with a second one. By now it was completely vertical, hanging on its propeller. With infinite care, McKellar half-rolled and curved the Hurricane into level flight without a tremor from the wings. It was the master at work.

When 602 went south on 13th August, McKellar was frustrated – he was desperate to get to grips with the enemy. But Dowding was playing his hand carefully, keeping a reserve of squadrons in the north. Two days later, it paid off, when, in an all-out offensive, the Luftwaffe launched all three Air Fleets against Britain. For the first time, Luftflotte 5, based on headquarters at Stavanger, came straight across the North Sea in force, the Heinkels and Ju88s escorted only by long-range Me110s; their targets were the great east coast bomber bases. 605 were ordered south, and at 13.10, Archie sighted two groups of He111s driving in towards Newcastle. Safety catches off, gunsights glowing, the Hurricanes closed in, ranging on the leading formation – about forty bombers.

Archie himself, curving his Hurricane gently to the right in his dive, opened fire on a Heinkel at 250 yards with an accurate three-second burst of fire, and saw the bomber falling off into a steep spiralling dive; levelling out, he saw glinting lines of tracer arcing over his starboard wing from Heinkels behind. He sideslipped left and suddenly zoomed, giving orders for his pilots to attack individually.

As he climbed, he opened up briefly – a long deflection shot at a soaring Heinkel; but the Hurricane shuddered, losing way in the climb with the recoil of the guns. He claimed no hits on this machine. Climbing into the sun again, he threw the Hurricane over into a slanting dive; the big fighter accelerated rapidly, and Archie found himself gaining on the leading Heinkel. He reefed the bulky fighter round and delivered a long and accurate beam attack, firing for over six seconds and closing to fifty yards. As smoke and flames shot from the engine nacelle, and its undercarriage swung down limply (a frequent occurrence with Heinkels), Archie swerved, 'walking' his fire onto the next machine, closing again to about fifty yards. Nothing happened, so he fired another quick burst from only twenty-five yards – again, he drew smoke and flames from an engine.

Within seconds he was in clear sky; he waggled his wings – nothing below; a glance in the mirror – clear; a check on engine pressure and temperature – normal; all control surfaces responding. Satisfied, he banked to port, and saw five twin-engined machines in their last dives. At least one, and probably two, were his. He tested his guns – no glinting tracer showing yet, he must have at least fifty rounds per gun left. He sighted a straggler from the second formation heading out to sea, and closed in easily. He emptied his guns into its fuselage and starboard wing from seventy yards. The burst lasted less than a second; with it, he probably killed the dorsal gunner, and caused the starboard engine to emit a thin stream of grey smoke. The Heinkel did not lose height, however, and shortage of fuel prevented Archie from following it anyway. He turned back, feeling very pleased with life at last, to discover that, altogether, 'B' Flight had scored four confirmed victories, and was to be awarded also four 'probables' and three 'damaged'.

Dowding's tactics had paid off, due in no small measure to the efficiency of McKellar & Co, whose grumblings noticeably diminished, finally to vanish altogether when they were ordered south to Croydon, in the thick of the battle, on 7th September. Before that, however, 605 held a notable celebration. This was occasioned not only by news of the impending move south, but also by the announcement at the end of August of the award of the DFC to McKellar in recognition of his service with 602 and 605 Squadrons.

On the very day they transferred to their new base, the Luftwaffe switched their daylight offensive from the fighter airfields to London itself. From Archie's point of view, of course, it was ideal. Croydon, one of the first areas inside London to be bombed, was right in the front line.

September 9th. 09.30 hours: The Croydon sirens pierced the silence and 605 scrambled. Ordered to rendezvous base at 20,000 feet, they climbed hard on a southerly track, and as they reached 15,000 feet over Maidstone, McKellar sighted the enemy formation – seventeen Heinkel 111s approaching at a higher level, with about fifty Me109s 4,000 feet above them and twenty Me110s on the flank.

It was a formidable force, opposed by a mere dozen Hurricanes with a height disadvantage. Squadron Leader Churchill turned the squadron, continuing to climb, with the object of approaching the enemy formation from out of the sun.

'A' Flight timed their attack to perfection, coming down in a power dive on the enemy's left flank. The Me110s streamed in to intercept with cannons blazing at 1,000 yards range, but they were two seconds too late – too late to engage the Hurricanes, but just in time to make them hesitate long enough to miss the bomber leader. Two Heinkels keeled out of the formation.

McKellar now came into his own, leading 'B' Flight. A gaggle of 109s made a belated attempt to intercept the Hurricanes, diving between them and their prizes. Archie was unperturbed. With perfect timing, he latched onto the tail of one Me109, and sent it down in flames after a brief burst of fire. Dourly, he re-formed his section, and returned to the task of attacking the bombers. He rapped out his orders. 'Green' Section were detailed to cover their comrades from the top-cover Me109s and they were thus in a position to observe the incredible events of the next half-minute. Just as McKellar was positioning 'Blue' Section for their attack, the bomber leader did an amazing, inexplicable thing – he wheeled his entire formation round, onto a head-on collision course with the Hurricanes. McKellar instantly and instinctively began to sight on the leading Heinkel as it thundered towards him, simultaneously calling his pilots: 'Right, lads, head-on attack. Each man pick his own target.' The gap closed at a frightening rate, but McKellar's Hurricane was rock-steady. Throttling back, to increase his firing time fractionally, he flew straight for the Heinkel leader in a slight dive. At 500 yards his guns flashed; the Heinkel shuddered, its perspex nose shattered into a thousand fragments, its leading edges taking fire. Archie saw a glow within its fuselage, and he swerved, 'walking' his fire onto the bomber on the leader's left. Simultaneously, three things happened. The left-hand bomber, Archie's second target, lost a wing, severed at the root; the centre machine exploded, clearly with its bombs still on board; and the right-hand machine burst into flames, turned on its back and dived uncontrollably earthwards. With a single four-second burst of fire, he had destroyed three twin-engined bombers! Seconds after opening fire, Archie flew straight through the patch of sky which had contained the Luftwaffe machines. There were only a few scraps of debris to impede his progress. McKellar finished his attacking pass by climbing and rolling away from a bunch of Me109s who seemed, hardly surprisingly, loth to offer much opposition to him.

He completed his patrol circling round a slowly-descending parachute, anxious to protect what he thought to be one of his pilots – he was much amused to discover later that his anxiety had been rather less than necessary. The parachutist was a German. It had been, he later wrote to Sandy Johnstone, 'lovely fun'.

For eight days after this action, Archie averaged one kill a day. The news of his performance spread through Fighter Command; he became known 'Killer McKellar'. The strain was beginning to tell on 605 Squadron, however. Despite a fair degree of success, morale was threatened by losses in men and machines. Since arriving at Croydon, one pilot had been killed and several injured, and the pilots were painfully aware that their sturdy Hurricanes were no match for the Me109s which always seemed to lurk in the sun.

It was in just such a situation that McKellar's qualities as a leader proved invaluable. His insistence that his men should take off on their dawn patrols shaved and clean, curiously enough, seemed to boost morale – it was certainly different! He led his flight, and frequently the whole squadron, with flair; on 11th September, for example, they succeeded in knocking down five of the enemy at no cost to themselves, one of these being claimed as 'frightened to death'! A young Luftwaffe pilot, observing the slaughter around him, had apparently panicked and flown his Messerschmitt into the ground.

McKellar himself was always able to 'show the lads how to do it'. On 15th September, he knocked down two Me109s over his own base, and also a Dornier 17 over Maidstone in a later patrol. He tended his flock like a careful shepherd – frequently, 605 pilots would hear the Kenley sector controller's voice in mounting irritation, 'Confirm that you are indeed on vector oh-nine-zero'. In fact McKellar, as always, was leading his men due west on the reciprocal course, steering 270° magnetic, seeking to gain valuable height before turning to face the stepped-up banks of German aircraft. Archie was equally valuable as a leader on the ground. On 11th September, for example, when the squadron ran the gauntlet of anti-aircraft debris in an open truck for a dinner party at the Greyhound Hotel, it was McKellar who led the merry-making, only too conscious that his pilots' minds had to be taken off one of the sights of the afternoon – a parachutist descending with smoke and flame curling up from his boots; gradually, the fire had crept up his back, finally burning through his harness, and the airman was still slapping at his body in agony as he hurtled downwards.

This was McKellar the leader. Usually first in most things, he achieved another notable success when he bagged 605's first night victory, in the early hours of 16th September. As he wrote to Sandy Johnstone, 'My night flying practice was very useful, I had the great luck to bag one of these Night Bastards shot down in flames.' He had spotted the He111 in a searchlight cone, and made no mistake with two short bursts from close range. It came as no surprise when McKellar was awarded a Bar to his DFC. The official citation concluded, 'He displays an excellent spirit, is a particularly brilliant tactician, and has led his squadron with skill and resource.' Archie had been to all intents and purposes leading 605 since 11th September, and this became permanent and official on 29th September.

Remarkable though his feats had been so far, McKellar's greatest day was yet to come. In mid-afternoon on 7th October, Archie was leading 605 at 18,000 feet over Sevenoaks, when they sighted fifteen bomb-carrying Me109s escorted by over fifty Me109 fighters layered above and behind. Undaunted by the odds, McKellar led his pilots into an up-sun position, ordered them into line astern, and then dived them onto the fighter-bombers below. 'I attacked the Number One,' his report ran, 'and saw a bomb being dropped from his machine. I fired and pieces fell off his wing and dense white smoke or vapour came from him as he went into a violent outside spin.' This machine was seen by others in the squadron to crash, and became Archie's first victim of the day. Archie, meanwhile, snatched a rapid glance in his mirror, just in time to see a Messerschmitt lining him up in its sights. He broke sharply to starboard, avoided the attack, and found himself just below and behind a second Me109 fighter-bomber, in a perfect firing position. Instinctively, he sighted, corrected his aim slightly, and triggered the firing-button all in one movement. His report stated, 'I opened fire and saw my De Wilde hitting the machine. It burst into flames and went down inverted east of Biggin Hill.' Victim Number Two.

By this time, the top-cover Messerschmitts had joined in the fray, and the sky was a tangled confusion of wheeling, twisting aircraft, most of which seemed to sport black crosses. Glimpsing yet another Messerschmitt on his tail, Archie surprised the German pilot by stalling sharply, and falling off in a spiral down to 15,000 feet. His pursuer shaken off, Archie looked around for another target. He sighted a Messerschmitt speeding towards the Channel, and instantly pulled his engine boost control. The Merlin bellowed, and the Hurricane leapt forward, closing steadily in a stern chase from slightly below. Archie reported:

> I gave a burst from dead astern and at once his radiator appeared to be hit as dense white vapour came back at me and my windscreen fogged up. This speedily cleared and I gave another burst and this machine burst into flames and fell into a wood with a quarry near it, west of Maidstone.

Victim Number Three, but McKellar wasn't finished yet. His blood was up, and it was one of these rare occasions when it seemed nothing could go wrong. Archie was a man inspired; pilot and aircraft were together striking a perfect harmony. As he climbed back towards the scene of the action, McKellar's quick eye caught a flicker of movement off to one side. He turned towards it, and glimpsed a Messerschmitt, dodging through broken cloud towards the coast. The Hurricane raced through scattered clouds in pursuit, as McKellar still had his boost pulled. As the two aircraft flashed from cloud to cloud, Archie brought off a classic piece of aerial stalking and interception, bringing his Hurricane once again into the perfect firing position, slightly below and astern. He fired, just once, from point blank range; the first inkling the Luftwaffe pilot had of what was happening came as Archie's explosive bullets crashed into his petrol tank, causing flames to belch from it instantly. Since in the Me109, the pilot sits on top of his fuel tank, the German airman's reaction was hardly surprising – he jettisoned his canopy and baled out.

Archie returned to Croydon jubilant. He had just achieved four confirmed kills within ten minutes – and all of them were 109s. Even for McKellar, it was outstanding, but his day was not yet finished. Leading 605 on patrol again ninety minutes later, he encountered another batch of Me109 fighter-bombers. In the short engagement which followed, he knocked down another Messerschmitt, and this gave him a total of five confirmed kills for one day, a feat seldom equalled in either of the world wars.

Throughout the rest of October, McKellar kept up his impressive rate of scoring. During a morning patrol with the squadron on the 20th, for example, he destroyed one Me109 and damaged a second

– 605's only success that day. His gun-camera films were an education to watch,* and his advice and example were followed by many of 605's pilots. His marksmanship was deadly, flying brilliant, his reactions like lightning. His Hurricane had never been seriously damaged in combat, and it hardly seemed feasible that the German Air Force would ever 'nail' him.

Time, however, was running out for McKellar. One by one he had seen his comrades killed or wounded. If the relentless, brutal arithmetic of losses was affecting him, he gave little outward sign of it, but nevertheless the strain was beginning to tell. More and more he became a man living on nervous energy. Writing to Sandy Johnstone, he said, 'Since last Sunday which was, as my Polish pilots would say, 'hot all over', I have spent my time leading the squadron away from enemy fighters, which, no matter how high I go, always seem to be 5,000 feet above us, my declared policy being for shooting at fighters only below 12,000 feet.' If the fighters were always getting on top of McKellar, so also was the pace – the never-ending tension which sent the heart racing and the stomach churning at the first jangle of telephone bells.

His eyesight, so vital for the fighter pilot, began to show signs of weakening under the strain; latterly, he was frequently to be found relaxed on his bunk, with pads of lotion-soaked cotton wool soothing and restoring his vision. He was a man nearing the limit of his resources, tempting fate again and again. On the last day of October, he was Mentioned in Dispatches by Dowding. The celebrations were short-lived, for within a few hours he was dead.

Characteristically, it was due to his warm-hearted, impulsive nature. Although not due to fly on the morning patrol on 1st November, Archie, while shaving, had discovered that another pilot just back from leave was on the duty roster. 'You can't go on patrol directly off leave. Wait here and I'll see you when I get back.'

No one seems to have seen that last fight – Archie was last heard calling his squadron to rendezvous near Maidstone, after they had been split up in a minor skirmish. It's thought that Archie, arriving at the rendezvous, sighted a formation of aircraft above, and automatically took up station ahead of what he took to be 605's

---

* Some of these are on public display in the RAF Room, Edinburgh Castle. They were taken during McKellar's combat of 15th October 1940 when he hit a Dornier 17 and a Messerschmitt 109.

18th August, 1940. Dunlop Urie's Spitfire had a short but action packed career. She fired at five Stukas, before a 109 punched these holes in her and broke her back. Urie went to hospital – X 4110 never flew again. Service life – 24 minutes.

The one they just couldn't get rid of –
The 'Flying Shithouse' (LO-A). The motto read 'Izal Get You'; she never did though. . .

Battle o'er.
'B' Flight Dispersal at Westhampnett, December, 1940

Outside officers' mess at Westhampnett, November 1940. Seated (left to right) Micky Mount; Findlay Boyd; Sandy Johnstone; Dunlop Urie; Donald Jack.

Hurricanes. But they were Messerschmitts – McKellar's overstrained vision had caused him to make a tragic, uncharacteristic error, and his overtaxed reflexes were unable, for once, to get him out of a desperate situation. He died fighting. He had not even had the time to collect his medals; only two days earlier he had been awarded the Distinguished Service Order, the citation for which referred to 'his outstanding courage and determination' and his 'magnificent inspiration to his fellow pilots'. He thus became the first of 'Glasgow's Own' to be awarded this decoration. Archie's father later received his son's awards from the hand of the King.

He was buried on 6th November, in New Eastwood Cemetery, Glasgow, in the family grave, the pallbearers including the Duke of Hamilton. Each year a group of 602 Squadron members would visit Archie's last resting place, to remember.

The grey marble, now weathered and moss-dappled reads:

"In glorious and happy memory of Squadron Leader Archibald Ashmore McKellar, AAF, DSO, DFC, with Bar. Beloved only son of John and Margaret McKellar. Killed in action 1st November 1940, aged 28 years, in the defence of London during the Battle of Britain. One of the few to whom so many owe so much.

CHAPTER TEN

Journeys and Encounters

We were visited by the new C-in-C Fighter Command today, Air Marshal Sholto Douglas, who talked to us about the possibility of going on the offensive soon. This is good news. . . .

Extract, Sandy Johnstone's diary, 28/11/40

We fused the shells for 12,000. I could see ours bursting below the bombers. As far as I know we never hit a single one. I found my mother's tenement flattened. She was OK, but I just remember feeling angry and helpless.

Gibby Fraser, A/A Gunner, Glasgow

November was a strange and bitter month. News of Archie's death cast a shadow over Westhampnett, and, as the snell winds swept in from the Channel and the afternoon skies darkened, the gloom lifted only gradually. Jack Boret threw an almighty party over at Tangmere, and the revelry included even Bud Flanagan, Chesney Allen and the Crazy Gang, complete with the Windmill Girls. The men who'd worked so hard at survival now worked harder at enjoying themselves – and 602 did have something to celebrate. Andy McDowall had knocked down a pair of Me109s over the Isle of Wight just a couple of days previously. As the Messerschmitts came over in individual raids, the big man was very definitely in his element. With his guns ranged to 50 yards, like Boyd's, he went fast, closed to point-blank range, and shot to kill. Ten days later, he took on five 109s single-handed, when 602 and 213 were bounced at 27,000 feet. As the first strikes hit the Spitfire, Mac nearly squeezed her inside out in the turn, and raced straight for the gaggle of German fighters. Ranging on the leader, he pressed the button; nothing happened! A single German bullet had smashed the compressed air bottle which powered the guns.

But now he was committed. Jinking, weaving, twisting and turning, he kept swinging back at the 109s, in mock attacking passes, keeping them at bay like a wolf among hounds. Gradually the 109s forced the fighter lower, but Mac was a hard man to nail. Suddenly, hauling to port to dodge a firing pass, he flew smack into another burst. One cannon shell came clean through his canopy and carried away the cushion behind his head. A second exploded on the armour plate behind the seat; the flying splinters wreaked havoc in the cramped confines of the cockpit, tearing at the instruments, and ripping his jaw open to the bone. A third blew half the tailplane away. But still they couldn't get him. In a last despairing effort, the Messerschmitt leader fired the last of his warload into the Spitfire that refused to play by the rules, and McDowall felt the explosions behind his seat again. The whole assembly crashed forward, jamming his face against the gunsight as his shoulder harness snapped. One arm, completely trapped, was useless. He flew the fighter practically blind, as blood ran into his eyes and pain clouded his brain, but his instincts never failed him. As the 109 passed him, its pilot staring impotently across, Mac used two of his fingers on the hand that still moved, in a gesture that needed no translation at all.

Unable to reach the undercarriage lever, he put the Spitfire down on her belly near Birdham, and emerged more or less in one piece. His jaw was stitched up, and for a few days he prowled the airfield, until they let him fly again. When he took a Spitfire up on air test, he went out very low. They didn't see him back for over an hour. When he landed, the lopsided little grin was back; but he'd left all his ammunition somewhere in France.

It wasn't for that kind of activity that they gave him a Bar to his DFM, of course. But even when he stuck to the rules, he was one of 602's supreme air fighters. In December, he gained his commission; and instantly suffered a little in terms of his image – 'Look, Andy, scar tissue or no scar tissue, you're an officer now, and a gentleman. And that means you don't come in this Mess without shaving. Every day!'

He was joined there by Cyril Babbage, also sporting his new purple and white ribbon, and a hacking cough, the result of an influenza bug which swept the squadron. One by one, they succumbed, and as the weather closed in, less and less flying was done. Perhaps they began to get rusty, but such combats as there were didn't produce much in the way of results as the month wore on. They just wore out (or broke) perfectly good Spitfires. Sergeant Cordell, on his very first flight, overturned on one landing. The gentle John Willie landed smack on top of Johnstone's just after a scramble – and wrote off one of the very few Spitfires fitted with metal ailerons; this machine was a vast improvement at higher speeds and altitudes than the standard fabric-aileroned types, and indeed 602 had been the first squadron to try them out operationally just a few days before. Now they'd proved they bent as easily as any.

There was one Spitty they thought they'd never get rid of, though. The 'Flying Shithouse' – a clapped out, rebuilt old Mark 1 which had already seen service with two other units, and which leaked oil, coughed and spluttered every morning on the first scramble, reeked of stale vomit, and, no matter how the erks struggled, invariably flew with one wing low, as sloppy on the controls as a lush on a bender. This ghastly lady was tarted up with a bit of inspired artwork – a lavatory pan and cistern with a pair of golden wings, together with a toilet roll bearing the motto 'Izal get you!'. She never did, though. Usually allocated, appropriately enough, to the 'arse-end Charlie', she would weave drunkenly from side to side behind the rest of them, like an ageing trollop, unable to rise to the occasion when summoned. Once – just once – she got close, when Nigel Rose urged her to the limit; and promptly got herself shot down. Nigel was unhurt, and they all breathed a sigh of relief when the lorries came and carried her away into oblivion.

Day after day, they flew up into the grey, overcast skies, seldom finding the enemy, and on a few occasions suffering the ignominy of being 'bounced'. As November ran out, came the bitterest blow of all. With Sholto Douglas visiting Tangmere, 602 were scrambled with Mickey Mount leading, and ordered up to 33,000 feet over the Isle of Wight. This was a stupid piece of fighter controlling; and 602 paid the price. The Spitfires were labouring at that height on about half power, their superchargers virtually useless, their controls sloppy and slow; as they emerged from cloud, the incoming Me109s, two thousand feet higher and already at fighting speed with their two-stage superchargers, easily outflew the Spitfires. Six were hit before the cloud at lower levels mercifully hid them from the German's gunsights. Closing down to low level on the approach, Pat Lyall's Spitfire suddenly leaned over into a gentle bank. They heard nothing on the R/T, but they all saw Pat baling out. He was far too low. The parachute had only started to develop when his body hit the ground. No last message, no explanations, no chance. He was the last to die in the south. When his funeral took place at Brighton Crematorium (his parents had wanted it to be close to his comrades) the whole squadron was stood down. The little chapel was packed.

Jake Edy nearly went too. Above Dover on 11th December, in the first action for many days, they were hit from above yet again.

Jake only just managed to get the Spitfire down in no more – it certainly wasn't in one piece. His crash-landing, with one wing already shortened by three feet, was highly dramatic. Going half sideways at around 130 mph, with wheels up, the Spitfire bounced, lost its wing completely, and made mincemeat of two unfortunate sheep.

It was time to pull out, and in the middle of December, they took their leave of Westhampnett, now occupied by a Polish Hurricane squadron. Heading north, they landed at Catterick for an unscheduled stop, and were amazed to find fuel waiting for the Spitfires and a slap-up lunch for the pilots. It was only as they were leaving that another sixteen Spitfires flew in, and George Denholm discovered that 602 had just snaffled the lunch he'd taken such trouble to arrange for 603 Squadron, en route for Turnhouse. Delighted with this unexpected coup, the Glasgow boys beat a hasty retreat, swopped aircraft with 610 Squadron at Acklington, and flew north in tired old fighters to Prestwick, relieved to be coming home for Christmas. All except Randall Phillips. As they dispersed the Spitfires near the old mill which would be home for the next few months, he'd already caught a glimpse of a lady he just didn't want to see. She was standing there waiting – the 'Flying Shithouse', magically restored by a Civilian Repair Unit to her former glory.

One by one, the old faces now disappeared. As the war spread around the globe, the original City of Glasgow veterans went with it, their experience now one of Fighter Command's most precious assets. Findlay Boyd took command of 54 Squadron, worked it up to fighting trim, and led it on the early fighter sweeps over France as the RAF went onto the offensive. 602 would meet him again in 1942.

Dunlop Urie had already left. After briefly returning to the fray at Westhampnett, when he shared in the destruction of a lone Ju88 with Boyd, he was posted as Chief Flying Instructor to an Operational Conversion Unit at Aston Down. Later, he'd be attached to Boyd's squadron, and to one led by Donald Jack, before taking command of 151 Wing – the first Hurricanes to be sent to Russia by carrier. He'd finish the war as a Wing Commander.

So would Donald Jack. Leaving 602 for a spell on the staff at 13 Group, he then formed 123 Squadron at Turnhouse, before going to the Middle East, where he eventually took command of the combined 80 and 33 Squadrons, becoming their thirteenth CO in 11 months. But the old 602 lucky thirteen kept working – Donald survived, to become, in the words of one of his pilots:

> The finest desert fighter leader I ever served under, and one of the greatest pilots never to win a medal. They should have given him the DSO. Later in the war some guys got it for a lot less in the way of accumulated experience. Donald may not have had a single moment of glory, but his courage and calmness through the campaign were an inspiration.

Andy McDowall, after gaining his commission, was promoted rapidly. He became Flight Commander on 245 Squadron in Northern Ireland, and went on to lead a squadron, then a wing, and finally, in 1944, became the first CO of the RAF's first operational jet squadron, No 616 (South Yorkshire) – another former Auxiliary unit. Their Meteors chased and caught the Flying Bombs as they came in over the Channel.

Mickey Mount and Jake Edy both went international; Mount left to command the newly-formed 317 'Wilno' Squadron – a Polish long-range photo-recce outfit, while Edy, who'd now acquired his DFC, went to try and exercise some kind of drawling, Canadian control over the Poles of 315 'Deblin' Fighter Squadron. Later, Mickey commanded a Desert Air Force fighter squadron, No 260, and then a bomber squadron, No 104. And he won his DSO in the desert.

Paddy Barthropp, 602's other Irishman, went back south to 91 Squadron at Biggin Hill. He'd win the DFC before Hauptmann Willius in a Focke-Wulf shot him down over France in 1942. He spent the rest of the war behind the wire.

Fisher, Gage, and Eade couldn't even get away from Westhampnett. They were posted to 610, who flew in to replace 602. Meanwhile, up at Prestwick, whole batches of Sergeants and Pilot Officers were posted in and out, as Fighter Command sorted itself out and prepared to go on the offensive. And wherever the war in the air went, the pre-war Glasgow Auxiliaries were to be found.

Some were instructing, like Marcus Robinson, who also led a Spitfire Wing on operations. Norman Stone, like Marcus, won the AFC, but he didn't survive the war. He slow rolled a Spitfire much too low; she dropped a wing just a fraction, and broke up. It was a tragic loss.

George Pinkerton, in between staff appointments, led the Speke Wing, and added to his score in the night skies over Liverpool.

Then, in January of 1942, he took command of the Merchant Ship Fighter Unit, that bunch of intrepid misfits and adventurers who were catapulted off merchant ships in Hurricanes, as convoy protection. Every flight out of range of land ended, in theory, with the Hurricane at the bottom of the ocean and the pilot, wet but safe, back on board the ship. Needless to say, it didn't always happen that way. Although George didn't fly the operations, morale on such a unit was all-important, as was training. The success of the MSFU during his sixteen months in command was testimony to his powers of leadership – so, too, was his subsequent promotion to acting Group Captain.

Paul Webb, the squadron humourist, tried a little bit of just about everything – after a spell instructing at Grangemouth he was posted as a Flight Commander to Donald Jack's 123 Squadron. Later he took command of a Canadian Spitfire Squadron – No 416 at Peterhead. Then it was off to the Western Desert, across the Mediterranean to Italy and then into Yugoslavia where he picked up a DFC in the air fighting above Tito's partisans. Post-war he was granted a permanent commission which took him to Canada, India, and for four years to Turkey as Air Attaché – in between which he commanded the Aberdeen Auxiliary Squadron, No 612.

Others, like Alastair Grant, went on controlling fighters – in his case, in the Western Desert, Madagascar and Burma, while Edward Howell, the Auxiliary who'd thrown over everything for a permanent commission in the RAF, found himself moving from staff post to staff post. When he finally got his command, it was to be the challenge of his life. He took over the combined 33 and 80 Squadrons, just after the death of 'Pat' Pattle – one of the very greatest of all air fighters, killed in a last, great air battle over Athens as the Germans ran riot through Greece, in the spring of 1941.

Howell remustered the remnants of the shattered Hurricane units in Egypt, and then took them into Crete, as the Luftwaffe prepared their airborne invasion. For a single, heroic week the five remaining Hurricanes of 33, together with four belonging to 112 Squadron, were the sole defence of Crete. One by one, they were shot down or knocked out on the ground. By 19th May, a single Hurricane was left. In it, Howell had brought down a Ju52 and a Stuka during the fight that took out all the other Hurricanes. This one was despatched to Egypt in the hands of a young sergeant. It was the last aircraft to get out of Crete before the invasion came. In

furious fighting, Howell was hit by a burst of machine gun fire, and
had both arms broken – one so badly that much of the bone simply
disappeared. In excruciating pain, and left for dead, he lay, drifting
in and out of consciousness before the Germans finally flew him
out to a military hospital in Athens. By the time they got to him his
body was a moving mass of flies – they'd laid their eggs in his
torn flesh.

For many months, he lingered between life and death, before
succeeding in recovering to such an extent that he was able to
escape. Still seriously hampered by his wounds, but by now guided
by a faith which had given him the power to lay hold on his own life,
he spent many more months in the hills of Macedonia, before successfully completing his escape after a hair-raising series of adven-
tures. Over a year later, the son of the manse finally came home to
St Andrews, broken and then re-made in body and in spirit, back to
the familiar grey stones, square towers, and the church bells pealing
the old Scots psalm tunes: 'Even as a bird, out of the fowler's snare,
escapes away, so is our soul set free.'

Ian Ferguson owed his life to the injuries he'd received in the battle
with the Stukas over Ford. Convalescing just across from the airfield at Westhampnett, he seemed totally recovered, except for a
nagging pain. He couldn't regain his flying category, though, as he
began to suffer periodic blackouts. The doctors could find nothing.
He was appointed ADC to the Duke of Kent, who'd got to know 602
quite well at Westhampnett, and who was serving in the RAF as a
Group Captain. The Duke sent Ian to his personal physician in
Harley Street, at his own expense, in an effort to track down the
problem. Eventually, in what was then a rare piece of X-ray
examination one single frame in a complete circular series round
the spine revealed a tiny fragment of shrapnel nestling between two
bones, right against the spinal column. The operation was tricky,
but successful. And while Ian was being treated, the Duke's Sun-
derland flew right into a hill in the north of Scotland, killing
everyone on board, including the Duke.

For the squadron, settling in at Prestwick, there wasn't much doing
in the air. On the ground it was a different story. David McIntyre,
delighted to have his old unit at Prestwick, was unstinting in his hospitality. Scottish Aviation laid on parties over the festive season, and
even helped mount the last full parade of the Pipe Band. McIntyre,
during one of the parties, had observed to Corporal Alec Reid that

it was a shame there wasn't a band any more for Church Parades, but, on discovering that most of the bandsmen were still there, and the instruments in store at Coplaw Street, he sent a van up to Glasgow, collected the gear, and 602's next parade was the most stylish of the war.

There was more than a touch of style around the officers' mess, too, with the Dukes of Hamilton and Kent dropping in, and with Amy Johnson forced by the weather to spend Christmas with them. Amy, who'd captured the headlines in 1930 with her epic solo flight to Australia, and the following year with a flight to Tokyo which included a nineteen-hour-leg from London to Moscow, captivated 602's young men with her startling blue eyes, confident, easy manner, and of course her tales of derring-do in the skies. She was serving with ATA, delivering aircraft around the country. What they couldn't know was that her next visit to Prestwick, early in January, would see her taking off on the last flight she'd ever make. Oxford V 3457 buzzed into overcast skies, and, after a refuelling stop at Squire's Gate, vanished, until, over four hours later, it came silently down into the Thames Estuary, its fuel spent. Amy had parachuted – a Royal Navy vessel got to within twenty yards of her as she struggled in her flying gear. The captain dived in. He was seen supporting her; then he was alone. Finally he, too, disappeared in the swirling, icy waters. The war was taking more than the front line pilots.

There were high spots too, of course. The weather provided one. As the Ops Book said on 4th January: 'P/O Babbage and P/O Rose arrived back from Tangmere in aircraft which they had collected. Bad weather had held them up but the time was put to good use as both came back engaged.' As things turned out, the weather nearly got its own back. Three months later, Nigel Rose got lost above cloud on a Ground Control calibration test flight. He landed over an hour late – and only just made the London train taking him to his wedding the next morning.

Sandy Johnstone became a radio personality. The BBC came to record some of his Battle of Britain experiences, and the talk was broadcast on 9th January, to the intense delight of the mess. 'Oooh, sir, can I have your autograph.' 'Oh, sir, you're wanted on the blower. Some guy called De Mille, from Hollywood.'

Actually, the whole squadron were destined for Hollywood, at least on film. When Twentieth Century Fox wanted some aerial scenes for their latest epic, *A Yank in the RAF!*, it was 602 who were chosen; the film unit moved into Prestwick for a month, and were delighted with the results. So were the pilots.

'Villa Squadron, scramble! Orbit base, Angels Two.'

'Oooh, Red One, just a moment, ducky, till I straighten my lashes.'

'Now then, darling, don't fuss so.'

'All Villa aircraft, please observe standard radio procedures, repeat standard radio procedures.'

'Well, my dear, whatever have I done to upset him?'

The Spitfires roared into the air, circled, and came in on a low pass. Round again, and this time a mock firing run on a Blenheim.

'Yippee! Take that, you goddam Hun.'

'My oh my, you're so handsome when you're roused.'

'Stay right there, honey, ah'm a-coming for you.'

'Ooooh, careful, darlin'. Be gentle . . . oooh!'

'Okay, cut it out, will you?'

On screen, of course, the flying looked superb – which may be the reason why the same scenes cropped up again and again; in *Mrs Miniver, Battle of Britain* and *Dangerous Moonlight.* And the lads discovered, years later, that if you look very closely in one scene, the film is the wrong way round, with the Spit's squadron letters reversed. They were a bit disappointed, though, when the director refused point-blank to film the 'Flying Shithouse' . . . from any angle.

When the King and Queen came to Glasgow, Sandy Johnstone was among the invited guests to lunch. He also went 'down to their place' – when his DFC investiture took place at the Palace. Paddy Dollan received his knighthood at the same time. Next month, it was Andy McDowall's turn. Receiving his DFM from the hands of the King, he chatted briefly in response to His Majesty's questions, took three steps back instead of two, and fell off the rostrum into the band. The squadron reckoned it was probably the only recorded case of Mac actually choking back the inevitable exclamation.

Through it all, the serious business of the war went on. The new pilots began their operational training, while the old guard, such of them as were left, kept up the readiness states, and the 'night states'. Much of the Luftwaffe's bombing was of course now under cover of darkness, and although some of the new night fighter squadrons, with their Defiants and big Beaufighters were working up, still the Spitfires with their makeshift blinkers had to cover. There were rumours that Glasgow might be on the Germans' target list. Rumours, too, of fifth column activities.

On 3rd February, the Admin buildings were gutted by fire. An accident, of course.

Exactly a week later, the officers' mess burned, and was extensively damaged. Coincidence?

The next policeman to appear wasn't from the local CID investigating the fires, but was a Detective Inspector from Scotland Yard, attached to MI5. And 602 found themselves wrapped up in one of the war's most intriguing, and worrying, stories, though at the time it was of course completely 'hushed up'.

Donald Fish was a detective specialising in aviation cases. This one had started when Ginger Whall's Spitfire was fished from the water off Bognor, after his forced landing on 18th August. It was a write-off, and after some parts had been salvaged, the airframe was dismantled and the engine, corroded by salt water, sent to be broken up by a small scrap metal firm at Belper in Derbyshire. As luck would have it, the firm was run by a couple of ex-miners, and as they were breaking up the main fuel trunk-pipe with their sledgehammers, they found, melted right along the inside of the pipe, and down into the flame traps, a substance they recognised from their days in the pits. Gelignite.

It hadn't exploded – and in fact it is quite normal for gelignite to melt, or burn, under high temperatures, unless it is detonated. But it clearly couldn't be ignored. Rolls-Royce engineers stripped the Merlin, and established that the equivalent of several full sticks of explosive had been loaded in the trunk-pipe.

At Prestwick, Fish questioned everyone he could. He couldn't question Ginger, who'd died later in the battle, and his investigations didn't take him much further. His next move was to Drem. Ginger's Spitfire had been delivered new to 602 before they went south – and there are a large number of mines and quarries near to Drem. The gelignite itself, an unusual size of ¾ inch stick, was traced to the Nobel Company, a subsidiary of ICI, and it was part of a special order manufactured in Ayrshire for some clandestine commando-style operations in Norway. After exhaustive searching, which led him as far as a Home Guard unit in Cornwall which still had 14 lbs of the stuff, Fish was no nearer solving the problem of how the gelignite had lodged itself in the Spitfire's trunking. But one thing was sure. She'd flown in the tracer-streaked skies over Sussex for nearly a week with seven pounds of gelignite sitting just ahead of the fuel tank and behind the flame traps. And somebody, somewhere in the east of Scotland, had tried to sabotage her, and kill her pilot.

The nastiest rumour of all circulated after the night of the Glasgow Blitz. On 13th March, the defence chiefs knew what was coming. The Luftwaffe's pathfinder unit, KG100, had specially-equipped Heinkels which could track in on intersecting radio beams, coned over the night's target. The incendiaries would light the way for the rest of the bomber stream, with high explosive and further incendiary loads. British scientists had succeeded in the past in intercepting and 'bending' the beams, but recently the Germans had switched to a new frequency.

During the day, they laid their beams over Glasgow. Unable to divert the bombers over open country, the Air Ministry decided that Glasgow would become the stage for the first 'Fighter Night'. The plan was simple. Up to a height of 12,000 feet, the A/A guns would have free rein. From 14,000 feet upwards, the fighters would patrol, without interference from the guns, with a 'buffer zone' in between. When the bombers came, the defences would fill the skies with steel.

All 602's night operational pilots were up in defence of their home city – Johnstone, Ritchie, who'd just returned from Drem, Andy McDowall and Pedro Hanbury. Two of them had already claimed night victories.

At 21.00, the sirens went in Glasgow and Clydebank. The Spitfires were already airborne, climbing to their allocated heights between 19,500 feet and 21,000 feet. There were Blenheims and Beaufighters up too, as the plots were tracked in and radioed to the pilots who gazed down on the darkened city as the first flickers of flak rippled across the sky way below, and the orange flashes and pinpoint fires of the incendiaries flickered into life, and began to spread.

Across the city, the searchlights lanced up through the haze, pencil-slim in the darkened vault, waving sliently, vainly, seeking their elusive targets. The Clyde shone dully, and slowly the silver-grey reflection took the colour of fire, as the incendiaries took hold. And now the anger flooded the airwaves.

'I see one. He's miles below. I see him, he's too far down.'

'I can see one too. Hell, he's gone.'

'Look over there to the west. Christ, can't I come down, they're all thousands of feet below me.'

'There's damn' all up here. For Christ's sake. . .'

The pleas were in vain. Down below, Gibby Fraser and his ack-ack crew knew the same frustration. Ranging on a Heinkel caught like a tiny silver fish in a searchlight cone, they saw their shells bursting at 12,000 feet, just below the bomber.

'Sarge, can't we shove it up two thou? We've got him right there.'

'No, you can't. We don't want to hit our own fighters.'

'What bloody fighters? There's nothing up there except bleeding Jerries.'

Across the city, ARP wardens struggled with their stirrup pumps against the growing fires. The sirens wailed their needless warning, the air was filled with the stink of explosion, grime, dust and fear. The tenements crumbled in Govanhill, Paisley Road, Hyndland, Scotstoun, Clydebank. John Cormack, lying in his bed, found himself buried, drifting in and out of consciousness. He stayed there for eight days before they found him.

And above the inferno, the Spitfire pilots fumed, cursed, and, with heavy hearts, returned in silence to Prestwick. The ack-ack boys got just one – a Heinkel which hit the Campsies. Another was put down way off course by Pilot Officer Denby of 600 Squadron. But over Glasgow itself, the solitary, fleeting contact was made by Pedro Hanbury, who deliberately came down to the buffer zone, and fired at a twin-engined shadow which vanished in the haze.

The entire raiding force had come across the city at 13,000 feet. It was the first, and last, 'Fighter Night' of the war.

Had someone talked?

CHAPTER ELEVEN

Rodeos, Circuses . . . and Clowns?

Welcome to the Kenley Wing. Tomorrow afternoon there'll be a briefing on the type of operations you can expect over France. Don't worry – you'll see plenty of action, but it might not all be to your liking.
John Peel, Wing Commander Flying, to 602 Squadron,
10th July 1941.

February 2nd 1942. 13.15 hours: Operations against Scharnhorst and Gneisenau. 7 pilots cannoned 1 transport. 3 a/c hit by flak.
Extract, 602 Sqn. Operations Record

You must take off immediately with your entire Wing. The Deputy Führer has gone mad and is flying to England in an Me110. He must be brought down.
Telephone call from Goering to fighter leader
Adolf Galland, 10th May 1941.

22.11 hours: In the Sector Operations Room at Turnhouse, Douglo Hamilton watched as the WAAF placed a new symbol on the Filter Board. Designated 'Raid 42', it had appeared first on the RDF screens on the Northumbrian coast, and was now being tracked in just south of the Farne Islands. The single aircraft was identified a few minutes later by the Observer Corps as a Messerschmitt 110. At Turnhouse, hoots of derision greeted this obvious error – the 110 just didn't have the range to get to Britain and back over that section of the North Sea. Over the last few days, they'd tracked a succession of single Heinkels and Ju88s over Scotland, and Raid 42 was clearly another. Hamilton watched as the aircraft's progress was traced. It swung towards the north-west at 22.20, and headed into Scotland; into his sector.

Now the doubts began to grow. A succession of Observer Corps posts reported it as a 110 – and the intruder, by now down to treetop height as it raced through the Borders going slightly north of west, was doing over 300 mph, impossible for a bomber, but very definitely possible for an Me110. It had already left a section of Hurricanes from Acklington well behind.

22.35 hours: As the 110 blasted right over Selkirk and vanished in the low, rolling hills, two Spitfires of 602 Squadron were scrambled from Heathfield (Ayr). Within ninety seconds, Flight Lieutenant Al Deere was in the air, vectored towards the last reported track of 'Raid 42'. A Defiant night fighter from Prestwick headed towards Kilmarnock on a projected interception course.

Deere now found himself on a wild goose chase. As the intermittent plots came in, from scattered Observer Corps posts, with the 110 well below radar sweeps, he found himself vectored all over the night skies around Ayrshire. At Turnhouse, it was decidedly embarrassing. Unable to keep an accurate check on their own fighters, crossing and recrossing their tracks, the intruder was lost for minutes at a time.

After forty-five minutes in the air, Deere was ordered back to Ayr. The Messerschmitt had blasted over Kilmarnock, turned south, and climbed over the Firth of Clyde. Heading back inland, it went up over the Fenwick Moor.

23.09 hours: Turnhouse Ops Room informed that the enemy aircraft had crashed south of Glasgow. They assumed the Defiant had shot it down. Hamilton went to bed. He wouldn't get much sleep over the next few days, though.

At Floors Farm, near Eaglesham, David McLean had heard the noise of the aircraft circling overhead, then zooming, climbing, and finally cutting out. As he left the buildings, the rising whistle of the final dive ended with a *whoomph!* as the Messerschmitt hit the ground, scattering itself across two fields, and catching fire. He ran towards the scene, and came across a single, hobbling figure. Challenging the flier, he asked if he was a German. 'Yes, I am Hauptmann Alfred Horn. I must get to Dungavel House. I have an important message for the Duke of Hamilton.' McLean couldn't believe his ears. He helped the German towards the Glasgow Road, having established that there was no-one else on board the aircraft. Horn was limping, having cracked a bone in one ankle and chipped a vertebra after parachuting, with some difficulty, from the Me110. His navigation, on a relatively light night, had been lousy. After flying almost directly over his target, the Duke's family home at Dungavel, on the westward journey, but failing utterly to locate it, he'd finally come down on his second attempt over twenty miles away.

He was taken to the Home Guard hut at Busby, on the southern outskirts of Glasgow. He was carrying no identification, just a few photographs, an assortment of drugs (including an elixir from a lamasery in Tibet), a couple of visiting cards from Albrecht and Karl Haushofer, and an envelope addressed to 'Hauptmann Alfred Horn, München 9'. While he waited for his interrogators to arrive, he surprised Dad's Army by lying flat out on the floor in a Yoga-style pose. He repeated his demand to see the Duke. He was taken to Maryhill Barracks in Glasgow, where his leg was treated, and continued to repeat his demands. By this time, at least two officers who'd seen him had begun to suspect his real identity.

The Duke was awakened at Turnhouse, and told that 'Horn' wanted to see him. During his stay in Germany in 1936, at the Berlin Olympics, Douglo had made a list of the Luftwaffe officers he'd met. He still had it; Horn wasn't on it. Early the next morning, he arrived at Maryhill, and entered the prisoner's room accompanied by the Interrogation Officer and the Guard Officer. The German at once said that he had seen Hamilton in Berlin in 1936, and that Hamilton had lunched in his house. 'I do not know if you recognise me, but I am Rudolf Hess.'

In broken English, the German started to lay out proposals. Hamilton, who had actually received two letters from the Hess/Haushofer camp via neutral Portugal (one of them mysteriously mislaid for months by the British Secret Service, the other one even more mysteriously never intercepted at all), soon broke off the conversation. Commandeering a 213 Squadron Hurricane, he flew south, and eventually reported directly to Churchill – but not until the Prime Minister had finished watching his film of the evening; ironically, it was the comedy, *The Marx Brothers Go West*.

Churchill, well aware that the German might be an impostor, sent Hamilton back north, this time with the BBC's Controller of European Services, Sir Ivone Kirkpatrick, who before the war had been First Secretary at the British Embassy in Berlin.

By this time, the prisoner had been taken to Buchanan Castle near Drymen. Just before interviewing him, Kirkpatrick had heard the German radio broadcast confirming that the Deputy Führer, 'took off from Augsburg on a flight from which he has not returned. A letter he left behind is so incoherent as to give evidence of a mental derangement.'

Kirkpatrick, knowing the real Hess was missing, knowing also that the man in captivity claimed to be Hess, and encountering him in a dimly-lit room at the end of an exhausting, unreal day, confirmed the identification. Hamilton spent the next two days travelling backwards and forwards between prisoner and Prime Minister,

F/Lt Findlay Boyd, DFC and Bar

S/Ldr Sandy Johnstone, DFC

F/Lt Mickey Mount, DFC

F/Lt Donald Jack

'602 – The Movie'.
Prestwick, 1941 – and note the A/C who nearly made the whole thing go with a bang beside 'R'.

602's All Stars?
There are a few real life heroes in here.

as one of the war's strangest stories developed. Once again, 602 were wrapped up in one of history's turning points.

The man who dropped in to see 602's former CO has, of course, been in captivity ever since; interrogated and examined by everyone from MI5 to psychiatrists in Britain, tried at Nuremberg, and for many years now the sole occupant of the echoing, damp halls of Spandau Prison, a pawn in the power struggles which have never ceased in Europe. His mission, realistically, never stood a chance of success. It came as a great shock to the Führer. So, too, to a British Government unable to turn it to any kind of political propaganda advantage. The Messerschmitt pilot, whoever he was, was always a pawn from the moment he took off. And there is real doubt as to his identity.

It is beyond any doubt that the real Rudolf Hess took off from Augsburg just before 18.00 hours on 10th May. It is equally certain that the aircraft which crashed near Eaglesham over five hours later couldn't have been the same machine. This one was from a front line fighter unit based in Denmark and southern Norway. The Hamilton-Haushofer connection was tenuous, but real enough. The 'identification' of Hess was hardly done under the most professional and favourable conditions. And the theories abound. Most people – and governments officially – suscribe to the theory that Hess really came to Scotland, and may well have been deranged. At least one writer maintains he was shot down over the North Sea and a double flew instead to Renfrewshire.

The motives for Hess's mission were clear – and real – enough. He was desperate to avoid war on two fronts. He knew the Russian invasion was coming. The motives behind the 'North Sea Substitution' plan, even with a devious mind like Heinrich Himmler's behind it, are much more difficult to pin down. And if Hess were sincere in his aims, why on earth did he take off in the first place from Augsburg in a machine which, *without external tanks*, couldn't possibly get him to Britain – and why would he run the risk of being shot down within a few miles of success?

Does the true answer lie somewhere between the two? Did Hess leave Augsburg intending to fly only to Denmark or Norway, whence the substitute pilot would fly to Britain, taking all the risks in the air, and be just convincing enough to persuade the British government to follow up the idea of a meeting with German envoys on neutral ground (say, Portugal), when the real Deputy Führer would emerge? And did the real Hess get the final shock of his life when, landing at some misty North Sea fighter base, he found himself hustled away by Himmler's heavies and quietly exterminated, leaving the way clear for his own ambitious deputy, Martin Bormann?

No 602 were amazed to read in the Glasgow *Daily Record* a few days later that Hess had been the pilot of the Messerschmitt. With the Deputy Führer on board, it had been one of the prize fighter targets of the whole war – and even if 'Horn' was a double, if they'd got him they'd have killed the story with the pilot. But, like every other aircraft up that night, they'd never even sighted their target. It gave the new CO, John Kilmartin, just the excuse he needed to inject a bit more life into the operational training they were doing, before going south to join in the fighter offensive now being mounted over France.

'Killy', who'd flown beside 602 as a Flight Commander on 43 Squadron at Tangmere, had just taken over from Sandy Johnstone, the last of the true pre-war Auxiliaries, who would go on to distinguish himself as a Wing Leader in Malta. The squadron had moved to a new, mud-splattered airfield at Heathfield, acquired new Mark II Spitfires ('same guns, same shape, a little more power, but cockpit heaters that worked, at last'), and taken on a distinctly cosmopolitan accent in the air. Glyn Ritchie was still there, by now 'A' Flight Commander, while Al Deere was his opposite number in charge of 'B' Flight. Stocky and with an infectious sense of humour, the man from Wanganui, New Zealand, had distinguished himself already with 54 Squadron over Dunkirk and in the Battle of Britain, in a series of hair-raising escapades. He would later write an autobiography called *Nine Lives*. By the time he joined 602, he'd used up about six of them, and he shortly added another.

When the engine on his new Spitfire II packed up far out over the water at 10,000 feet, he only just managed to stretch his glide far enough, scraping in over the Heads of Ayr by a matter of feet to pull off a dead-stick landing in a potato field. The Spitfire went right over onto its back, and Al only just managed to squeeze himself out. He walked some distance to a golf clubhouse, and went right in. A woman, somewhat startled, look him up and down. 'Good gracious, where did you spring from?'

Every inch the dashing hero, Al was level with the situation. 'I've just left my aircraft in that potato crop over there'. He switched on the smile. 'I'd love a drink, I feel a little shaken.'

'I'm sorry, all I can offer you is tea. The club is teetotal.'

The smile vanished.

Back at Heathfield, though, he finally got his drink. John Willie Hopkin, who'd served under him on 54, was delighted that Al was back to his old ways.

Preparing to fly on offensive operations at Wing strength, 602 settled down to a period of intense training, developing the tactics Boyd and Johnstone had worked on earlier, basing their combat flying on the pair, rather than the section of three aircraft. This had now become standard policy. Batches of Sergeants and Pilot Officers moved into the Nissens, and mastered the Spitfire IIs while a smattering of hardened veterans cajoled, encouraged, demonstrated and moulded them into fighting trim. Killy's gentle southern Irish tones were clipped and precise in the headphones; Al Deere's New Zealand twang full of authority laced with a dash of spicy humour. Nuts Niven drawled his cheerfully cynical way through all kinds of scrapes as only a Canadian could; 'Mitzi' Darling, newly-imported by Deere from 41 Squadron, was itching to get back to the fray.

As the new arrivals appeared, it was obvious who'd succeed in combat and who wouldn't. Critically, the 'romantic duet' (Deere and Darling) watched the Sergeants. One day, four arrived; Garden, Osborne, O'Connor and Willis. Three were good – O'Connor seemed to be the unlucky one. On his first landing approach, he overturned and it would take him five months before he damaged a German machine so severely.

Sergeants Niven and Nicholson arrived together. Niven would make their first 'kill' in the south, and go on to rapid promotion. Nicholson didn't go anywhere. Highly trained, but never with the natural gift of flying a fighter, he survived only three flights at Ayr. He was drowned in the Irish Channel.

Brown should have gone on to great things. On 6th May, he'd hit a bomber at night over Glasgow during the second 'Blitz', but three weeks later, practising synchronised diving attacks with John Willie, they'd collided. Hopkin got down safely, but Brown went straight into the sea.

They'd been doing a lot of training over the sea, and on 28th May, twelve of 602's Spitfires were detached to Limavady, Northern Ireland, and, in relays of four aircraft at a time, flew out over the Atlantic to provide continuous cover over the battleship *Prince of Wales*, returning with a destroyer escort from her encounter with the *Bismarck* and the *Prinz Eugen*. As Al Deere led in the first four fighters, the battle wagon looked a fine sight, her rakish bow sending plumes of spray high over the quadruple gun turrets, her fighting top rock steady above the swell. But as they flew past, dipping their wings, they saw the scars of battle; the ragged holes, the exposed armoured decking, the gun barrels that couldn't be centred, the evidence of the accuracy and the effects of *Bismarck's* 15 inch guns.

A month later, came news of their move. Kenley, right in the heart of 11 Group – they couldn't have asked for more. Killy wasn't going with them, though. To his disgust, he'd been posted first to 313 (Czech) Squadron, and then to West Africa. Pat Meagher had taken over 602.

On a glorious Thursday morning, they all lined up at Heathfield. Grinning across at each other, like a bunch of schoolboys on a spree, the pilots gave each other the 'thumbs up' – among other gestures – and waited for the signal to go. When it came, it found the CO with a dud engine. Thus it was that Al Deere, the chunky Battle of Britain veteran, led them south to battle again. The next day, they were over France.

July 11th 1941. Briefing 09.45. 602 close escort to 3 Stirlings bombing submarine repair yards at Le Trait, (Circus 43).
No trouble.
July 12th 1941. Circus 46. 09.30. Medium escort to 2 Stirlings bombing ship-lift on canal near St Omer.
12.30 – five pilots on fighter sweep.
July 14th 1941. Circus 48. 9 a/c off at 10.04 with W/C. Peel.
Patrol Le Touquet – Hardelot 18,000'. S/L Meagher shot down Me109.

Extracts 602 Sqn. Operations Record.

So it went on. Every day, they went up, sometimes twice or three times, taking the air war into northern France, on a variety of operations, usually operating as part of the full Kenley Wing. Johnny Peel – who they'd last seen heading out of Westhampnett in a cloud of dust driving his car one-armed, at the start of the Battle of Britain – had three squadrons under his command. With 602 at Kenley were 452 (Australian) Squadron, commanded by Bob Bungey, while at the satellite station, Redhill, was 485 (New Zealand) Squadron, commanded by Marcus Knight. One of 452's Flight Commanders was Brendan 'Paddy' Finucane, the southern Irishman who had opened 452's 'bag' on the day 602 arrived at Kenley, and who would later command the Glasgow squadron himself.

At their morning briefings, the pilots learnt the names of their game. A 'Circus', the largest type of operation, would involve a large number of fighters – sometimes 200 or more – escorting a small formation of bombers, the bait to lure the German fighters. A 'Rodeo' was simply a large-scale fighter sweep, in the pious hope that the Luftwaffe would be conned into sending up the fighters anyway. A 'Ramrod' was a straightforward bomber escort job, on a limited scale. 'Roadstead' meant an attack on coastal shipping targets, and 'Rhubarb' was a low-level sortie by two or four fighters, usually on a day when weather prevented anything else, against 'targets of opportunity' (locomotives, flak sites, Wehrmacht vehicles, marshalling yards, or anything else that moved.)

The operations themselves, usually meticulously planned by the desk-flyers, were a curious (and often dangerous) mix of lessons learned from the Germans during the Battle of Britain, and lessons ignored. The squadrons, sensibly, were now flying in formations based on the pair. But the battle veterans who'd pounced with glee on Me109s tied by orders to the labouring bomber formations over Kent, unable to work up to fighting speed, now found that they were ordered to stick to the Stirlings or Blenheims just as rigidly. Time and again the Spitfires found themselves bounced by fast-diving 109s – and 602 were unluckier than most. At a time when other Wings were re-equipping with the cannon-armed Spitfire VB, which had an improved all-round performance, the Kenley squadrons were still flying Mark IIs. The result? While the faster-flying VBs took on the top-cover and target-support roles, ranging free over the action, 602 were as often as not given the close-escort role, flying around the lumbering bombers. That's how they lost Glyn Ritchie.

21/7/41 They were up as dawn streaked the sky. Shivering, the pilots filed into the hut for their briefing. Another close escort, this time to Lille, with three Stirlings. As they had the day before, they were to refuel at North Weald, giving maximum endurance over the target. 'Right, chaps, 602 Squadron will stay with the bombers, 452 and 485 above and behind.' Groans around the room. Al Deere was to lead 602 for the first time, with Pat Meagher off operations due to a persistent stomach complaint. Paddy Finucane leaned over. 'I don't fancy your job, Al. Lille's a real hornets' nest. The Huns'll be buzzing around in droves. Rather you than me.'

Twenty miles into France, the Stirlings droned on, the Spitfires snaking gently to either side, pilots nervously scanning the skies. When it came, it was with shocking speed. A section of 109s went clean through John Gillan's North Weald Wing, and as the earphones erupted with the first urgent shouts of warning, it was already too late for Glyn. His Spitfire, streaming glycol, flicked over and down, spiralling and lurching ever steeper, her pilot shot through the head.

'Toddy Red, *break! Break!*'

'Toddy Leader, Yellow One's gone down. . . . Christ, look out, Red Two. . .'

'There's two more behind. Green One. *Break left!*'

Within seconds, the Messerschmitts had cleaved right through the ranks of Spitfires, and John Peel was on his way back home in a damaged aircraft. Behind Deere, his wingman, Sergeant Bell-Walker, had collected a cannon shell in his port wing, but carried on. Across the sky, above and around the bombers, pilots sweated, cursed, and tried desperately to avoid the snapping 109s, while maintaining station on the Stirlings, which, unmolested, dropped their token bombloads on the marshalling yards. It wouldn't alter the course of the war one little bit.

Back at Kenley, 602 counted the cost. Ritchie was dead. Three Spitfires were damaged. And the squadron couldn't claim a single Messerschmitt so much as scratched. Nuts Niven came into the dispersal hut and yanked his scarf off. The sweat ran from it as he wrung it out. 'I don't think much of that at all. That was bloody murder.' The others nodded in vigorous agreement. 'Hey, boss, when are we getting VBs?'

By the time they came, ten days later, Niven had been posted – to 603 Squadron at Hornchurch. He didn't appreciate it any more than he had his first posting to 601 during the Battle of Britain. After a week's intensive and pointed griping, they sent him back to 602. Much better, they thought, to direct his hate at the enemy.

He came back to find Al Deere in charge of the squadron, Meagher having been taken off flying due to his medical condition. Tommy Williams, a pre-war Auxiliary from 611 Squadron, had replaced Glyn Ritchie as 'A' Flight Commander. He was 611's last true Auxiliary – in a sense, Nuts was 602's. Though not operational, he'd joined the Glasgow squadron just before the war to train. But if they'd lost their Scots identity in the air, they certainly hadn't on the ground. Bert Simpson, Corporal Sweet, and the rest of the lads were

still there, working on the new Spitfire VBs which at last were beginning to appear. L/ACs Gibson, Douglas, Davis and Montgomery all
had over five years' service already – and Fitter Sergeant A.J. Mac-
Donald, who'd joined in 1929, was still going strong.

As far as the pilots were concerned, the turnover was nothing
short of startling. Each day as the enormous 'beehives' droned over
Northern France, the Messerschmitts would pounce, and a clutch
of Spitfires would go down. The veterans watched helplessly as the
fresh new pilots from the training schools, with twenty or thirty
hours on Spitfires neatly and proudly entered in their log books,
drove up in their second hand cars, unloaded their baggage, and set
off for Lille, or Le Touquet, or Abbeville, and fell prey to the
Messerschmitt they never saw.

After each day's Circus or Rodeo, the pilots would head for the
dim, smoky, familiar twilight of their favourite watering hole. At the
Valley Hotel, Caterham, and elsewhere, they talked tactics, survival, and voiced opinions of the Top Brass that weren't fit to print.
While Hitler pushed into Russia, the RAF Fighter Wings kept tying
down two of the Luftwaffe's crack Fighter Groups in the west. JG2
and JG26 – Galland's Schlageter Geschwader – were re-equipping
with a new version of the 109 – the 109F – which was at least a match
even for the Spitfire VB. And they had all the advantages. They were
free to find the height and position they needed; free to range across
the skies.

And any Spitfire seriously hit was lost to the RAF. Pilots were now
parachuting straight into captivity.

Some of them let off steam with the occasional 'Rhubarb', but
with the light flak growing in intensity and accuracy each week, even
that became less popular as a sideline. It was a war of attrition. Over
at Hornchurch, Findlay Boyd lost twenty-eight pilots in twenty-one
days, before his squadron was withdrawn. At Kenley, 602 found
themselves fighting the strangest of wars. With new pilots amply filling squadron rosters, there was plenty of leisure time in between
the desperate struggles in the angry skies. They could find themselves staring death in the face over Abbeville, and two hours later
be out on a '48', strolling down in a leafy lane in the warm August
sunshine, wondering at the reason and sanity behind it all.

There were a few good days. On 1st August, Deere had celebrated his promotion by getting his first confirmed 109, when 602,
for a change, bounced a formation of 109s as they rose up from
some heavy mist. Six days later, they got a couple more, but lost

Thornton. He was feared dead, but news came towards the end of the month that he'd survived, and was a prisoner. John Peel was shot down, too, into the Channel, but it was a British launch that got to him first. Taken off operations, he was replaced as Wing Commander Flying by Johnny Kent, a Canadian who'd already become something of a legend; this wasn't just for his successes in the air, it was more because he'd actually managed to whip the first Polish squadrons into some kind of disciplined order. Clearly a leader to be held in some awe! One of his first operations with the wing was also nearly his last – it certainly used up another of Al Deere's lives.

12/8/41. Briefing. 'Okay, chaps, it's back to close escort again today.' An uncomfortable shuffling of feet, a few coughs. 'Two Group are putting up half a dozen Blenheims. It's, ah, Lille again.'

'Aw, Christ, just when I was getting used to being alive again.'

Trust Nuts, thought Deere. He noticed, too, that Mitzi had gone deathly white.

'602 will stay with the bombers, 485 and 452 will cover from above and behind.'

Over North Weald, the Spitfires picked up the Target Support Wing, and headed south. Over the coast, still at low level to avoid German radar sweeps, the forces assembled. Once again, it was a nightmare of wheeling aircraft. One wing would arrive and orbit to port. Another would sweep in and begin a circuit to starboard, meeting the first three squadrons halfway round.

'I bet they've got that left-handed Wingco again.'

'Look out, here come the Poles.'

Straight as a ramrod, twenty-four Spitfires from Northolt carve right through the circling squadrons, expecting everyone else to get out the way. Belatedly, the Blenheims appear, and the whole formation sorts itself out and heads out over the Channel. A few miles from the French coast, the Blenheims start to reach for their bombing height. 602 climb with them, the other squadrons already rising above and behind, with Johnny Kent leading the Target Support Spitfires up to 25,000 feet.

In the Spitfires, rising and falling gently in the warm air, the sun striking tiny flashes from perspex and chipped camouflage paint, the pilots are alone with their thoughts. Deere, the professional fighter, checking mirror, gauges, reflector sight, making a last, infinitesimal trim adjustment; Norman 'Queenie' MacQueen, lowering his seat and smiling with his eyes across to Mitzi, still pale but with the adrenalin pumping strength and purpose; John Willie Hopkin, of the eternal schoolboy looks, hating the whole business of war, mentally screwing his rising fears firmly down, determination to do his duty written clearly across his furrowed forehead. Nuts Niven saw the dirty black puffs of 88 mm flak staining the sky ahead and below. The next bursts found the range. 'Wow, just smell those flowers.'

'Fairfax from Control, there are signs of heavy enemy activity in the St Omer area.' Cyril Raymond, well-known West End actor, now using his measured, clear tones to good effect as a fighter controller. The day is developing badly. The next voice is Johnny Kent's – and it's far from measured.

'Christ, Me109s diving through the clouds ahead of us!'

Around twenty 109Fs came down fast, wheeled to port, and curved in towards the bombers in pairs. Two slotted in behind Deere and his wingman, Bell-Walker. As they sighted, Deere reacted, 'Toddy Red, *break port!*' The Spitfires heeled into a gut-wrenching turn, as the 109s flashed past. Deere led them back to the bombers. They never saw the next attack – 'Break, Toddy Red, Break.' The shout came too late. Bell-Walker's Spitfire went down, trailing a long banner of flame.

Above, Kent was amazed to see another Spitfire curving across and opening fire on his number two, until he saw the black crosses and the square canopy of the Messerschmitt. His own number two had long since vanished, and the 109 pilot had been sitting there ever since they'd flown over Hazebrouck! Why he didn't fire will never be known – but once the young German found himself right in the middle of a formation of Spitfires, he probably just didn't know how to get out again without being shot down. As it was, he got away with it, but only just.

Re-forming 602, Deere once again formated on the Blenheims, and there was some respite from the fighters. Over the target, the 88s opened up, and although the Blenheims emerged unscathed, one of the Spitfires, hit in the radiator and oil cooler, went down.

On the return journey, the 109s came back. This time, nobody saw them in time. In the first attack, Booty went down, and Deere nearly did too. His canopy was shot off, a cannon shell had left a gaping hole in the port wing root, and as coolant leaked away in a dazzling white trail, the Merlin's temperature soared, and she began to run rough. Calling a 'Mayday', Al nursed his wounded machine back over the Channel, praying it would hold out long enough to give him the height he needed to get back in over the cliffs.

At Kenley, 602's Intelligence Officer, John Ozanne, was already piecing together the day's action. With most of the aircraft back, he knew they'd lost two. So had the Aussies. The pilots argued over just what had happened – 'I saw a bomber going down.' 'Nuts, they were all OK.'

'Did anybody see what happened to the boss?'

'Yeah, he was trailing glycol over the Channel.'

'Thank goodness for that!' The pilots stare at him – but the callousness is completely unconscious. Ozanne is simply pleased they all agree on at least something. He's called away to the phone, and returns smiling. 'Al's OK. He's down at Manston. They counted 37 bullet holes, plus a cannon shell in the wing and the coolant pipe severed. I reckon he's used up another life.'

On the debit side, 602 couldn't even claim a 'damaged' – the Wing, as a whole, lost five Spitfires, in return for three 109s. Three Spitfire pilots wouldn't fight again.

As the autumn closed in, things didn't get any easier. Day after day, the Close Escorts, Target Supports and Rhubarbs took their toll. Sergeants came and sergeants went – on Circus 100B, a raid on Abbeville, they lost 'Muddy' Brown and 'Banger' Squibb. Donald Jack had brought two of his 123 Squadron stalwarts to gain offensive experience, before they went into the front line. Both were Battle of Britain veterans – Flight Lieutenant T.S. Wade, one of his Flight Commanders, and Pilot Officer A.R. Tidman. Both were shot down on 17th September, on their fourth flight with 602.

Some of the old stagers were promoted out of the cauldron – Nigel Rose to become one of Findlay Boyd's Flight Commanders on 54 Squadron, and the gentle John Willie to an OTU to instruct. Among the newer pilots, a few began to make a name for themselves – Osborne, Willis, Johnny Niven, and Scorer, though before he could live up to his name, he had to live down rather an embarrassing episode in the middle of August. Coming back from a high-level sweep, he somehow managed to lose the rest of the squadron. As they landed, the controller was giving him a series of vectors over the R/T, but gradually Scorer passed right out of radio range, high over Occupied Europe. They suspected he was flying a reciprocal course on his compass, a classic boob. At any rate, he must have solved his problem, because he appeared over ½ hours later, descending from cloud over Martlesham. He landed safely – and proceeded to 'give himself up'. He thought he'd landed in Holland – and the windmills around Martlesham didn't help, either.

At least it gave them something to smile about; the frustration and tension of their operations is well illustrated by Al Deere's Combat Report from a single mission. This one was from Circus 108A, on 13th October. The combat, against around 100 Me109s, took place at 13.20, at a height of 16,000 feet fifteen miles north-west of St Omer – just one small action in a vast, running aerial battle.

I was leading 602 Squadron as close escort to 4 Blenheims. My section of 4 aircraft were on the port side and slightly above the bombers. Other than 452 Squadron there was absolutely no cover as protection to either the bombers or my section from the port side. We were attacked repeatedly, by pairs of Me109s, and had no alternative but to fight back. I was unable to warn Sgt Brayley, Red 2 (as my RT transmitter was U/S) that he was about to be attacked, and saw him go down with smoke and glycol coming from his machine. I also saw another Spitfire (I think Sgt Ford, Yellow 4) go down in a similar manner, and a 109 spinning out of control. I was by now alone, and had to ward off repeated attacks on my return. I managed a short burst at two 109Fs, the second from about 150 yards and above. I feel sure his hood disintegrated and caved in, as if hit by a cannon shell. (I cannot definitely confirm this). He then went onto his back and then vertically down from 13,000 feet.

Signed.

S/L A.C. Deere D.F.C.
602 Squadron

This had been quite a fight. Deere, Niven, Osborne, O'Connor and Scorer all claimed a 'damaged' apiece – and at least one of the 109s exploded into the ground – but Brayley and Ford were both dead. The day before, they'd lost Meredith too. Yet, through it all, they were building quite a reputation. 602, they said, rarely lost a bomber – and the statistics bear this out. Men who'd won their DFCs the hard way, like Deere and Tommy Williams, led by example.

There was one – just one – who came back.

Sunday, 21st September started much like any other day for Sergeant Patrick V. Bell. Recently posted in, he found himself briefed to fly in Deere's section, on a Circus. Once again, the 109s pounced, and in a running fight which saw 'Queenie' MacQueen damage a single Messerschmitt, 602's only success, Sergeants Hedger, Osborne and Bell all went down, and were posted missing. Hedger never came back at all; Osborne did, having scraped back over the Channel somehow or other and Pat Bell landed in France to begin four months of adventure.

He was lucky. Evading a Wehrmacht patrol by pure chance (they'd watched him come down, but were too slow off the mark) he was picked up instead by Resistance workers, and spirited away to a series of 'safe houses', around St Omer. He was amazed at the way in which 'The Organisation' moved him around under the noses of the Germans, in an area thick with airfields, flak sites and camps. He was in the hands of what by now was a highly professional organisation, which every week was passing airmen 'down the line', through France into spain, and back to Britain via Gibraltar – but it was in the process of infiltration by the Germans.

This escape line had first been organised by Captain Ian Garrow of the Seaforth Highlanders, who'd been left behind in France at St Valéry, when the Highlanders carried on the fighting as the BEF were evacuated from Dunkirk. The Germans were closing in on Garrow, however. A month after Pat Bell went through, they arrested him.

On 10th October, Pat was taken to the home of Fernand Salingue and his wife Elisa, in the village of Burbure, near Lille; there he was astonished to find a large group of escaping airmen, including Squadron Leader Henry Bufton and two of the crew of his 9 Squadron Wellington, and three other Spitfire pilots – Oscar Coen, an American, Belgian Alex Nitelet of 609 Squadron, nursing an injured eye, and George Barclay, a Flight Commander on 611 Squadron. The Salingues, who would later be awarded the Légion d'Honneur and the Croix de Guerre with Palme, had fifteen airmen and soldiers altogether in their house, right on the doorstep of the Luftwaffe. Two nights later, spotting what looked suspiciously like the Gestapo in front of the house in the twilight, the brave Fernand led them out, cool as you please, through the back door, and onto a country track to Lillers.

Pat spent the next couple of weeks in more safe houses, staying under cover in daylight, listening to the BBC in the evenings on clandestine wireless sets, and, incongruously, playing with his hostess's children. On the 29th, the whole party set off. With two Organisation guides, they boarded the Abbeville train – feigning sleep when anybody looked like striking up a conversation – and, with help from the famous Abbé Carpentier who produced forged papers, went on to Paris, where they had a good dinner, the food being carefully chosen (on some items, there was no rationing). Then, having just caught the train in no more, they travelled to Tours – and went to the cinema. Pat couldn't believe the sheer nerve of it all, but one of the guides pointed out, '*Ah, mon ami*, we are staying in ze dark, we are – how you say – invincible? *C'est bon?*'.

'No, Roland, you mean invisible' – but he was beginning to think Roland was maybe right the first time. After a two-hour train journey to Azai, they made a nervy crossing into Vichy France, at one point being rowed across a river right under a German-patrolled bridge. On the other side, they saw a couple of dog patrols, but stayed downwind, and eventually found shelter in a draughty barn.

More rail travel – to Toulouse, and overnight to Marseilles. The next stop, on 3rd November, was Perpignan, where, to Pat's amazement, they were actually put up in a hotel – the Hôtel du Loge – and on the night of the 5th they were driven to the foot of the Pyrenees. Then, on a bitterly cold night, a twenty mile hillwalk, through vineyards, forests, scrub and up to 3,000 feet. The wind shrieked across the pass into Spain, the moon shone coldly down. In pairs, they ducked and ran, collapsing exhausted among piles of dead leaves in the valley on the other side. After a few more days hiding by day and walking by night, they jumped a freight train to Barcelona, and leaped off in the wee small hours of the morning as the train slowed through the outskirts. They fetched up outside the British consulate grimy, bedraggled and absolutely exhausted. Now, the worst was over. Taken by diplomatic cars to the Embassy in Madrid, and welcomed by Sir Samuel Hoare, the Ambassador, they found themselves virtually prisoners until early December, when they finally made it by train to Gibraltar, arriving at half past four in the morning.

Pat turned up at Kenley on 8th January. He was luckier than he'd ever realise. His party – the largest ever passed 'down the line' by that particular organisation, which was masterminded by the

Belgian Albert-Marie Guérisse under the alias Pat O'Leary – was also the last for some time to remain intact. The notorious double agent 'Monsieur Paul' (Paul Cole) had infiltrated it. Later, Elisa Salingue was arrested and interrogated. Fernand, forewarned, only just escaped. There was a reward of 10,000 francs offered by the Germans for every airman handed over; the penalty for aiding escape was death.

The squadron, of course, were delighted to see him – not only had he added to the legend, but he'd done more than he would ever know to raise morale at a time when pilots saw their comrades going down almost every day. Pat's only regret was that he couldn't return to 602 – the rules about evaders just didn't permit them to fly over Occupied Europe again. He was probably fortunate. A new threat had just appeared in the skies over France, in the shape of the Focke-Wulf 190. First reported by pilots returning from Circus 101 – Bell's last flight – it was clearly in a different league from the Spitfire VB. Faster, with a much better rate of climb, greater acceleration in the dive, and possessed of a terrific rate of roll coupled with tremendous firepower, the little fighter with the stubby wings and big radial engine began to knock Spitfires down like ninepins. For the first time, 602 found themselves technically outclassed – and it was only the squadron's discipline and leadership – not to mention the pride they had in belonging to 'Glasgow's Own' – which kept them in the front line.

The weather continued to take its toll – two Canadians, Burke and Mackay, killed themselves flying blind at low level to Titsey Hill. But 602 flew and fought hard. The reputation was growing, through Fighter Command.

November 18th 1941. Ramrod to Hesdin Alcohol Distillery. Patrolling Hardelot – Dungeness, success. Sgt Garden, 1 kill, 1 probable. Sgt Willis, 1 probable, 1 damaged. P/O Niven, 1 probable. S/L Deere, 1 damaged. All Me109s. Niven returned minus starboard aileron.

But wearing a broad smile. . . .

In January, it was all change at the top. Kenley's new Station Commander was the legendary Victor Beamish, the oldest of the four Irish brothers who all served in the RAF, all won decorations, and all played rugby for their country. Victor was the man who, as Group Operations Officer, had been planning the Circuses and sweeps. Now, as often as not, he'd break the rules and tag along on operations, frequently with 602.

Al Deere's tour was over. He headed for America, to lecture on fighter tactics, and 602's next Commanding Officer was Paddy Finucane, whose activities were already celebrated by the Press. He'd just turned 21, and had got his 21st kill shortly before the celebrations. On the day of his birthday, came the news of the DSO to add to the three DFCs he'd already won; another Archie McKellar, they reckoned. 602 weren't in the least flattered – they just reckoned he'd come to the right unit at last. They also rather liked the way he'd received his last war wound – he'd fractured his ankle jumping over a low wall in the blackout!

And they got two new Wing Leaders – the first, Norman Ryder, was hardly installed in his office when the German flak got him, escorting a low-level Hurricane shipping strike. He went straight into a Stalag – and into his office at Kenley came none other than Findlay Boyd, by now sporting the DFC and Bar. It wasn't long, of course, before Boyd and Beamish started a private little war of their own. Whenever the weather prevented Wing operations, the pair of them would shut themselves in Findlay's office, pick a likely target, and then set out over the Channel at low level. On one of the first, they shot up the hotel which had thrown Findlay out in the summer of 1938. On the next one, they met more than they bargained for. . .

Thursday 12th February 1942. 10.28 hours:
Kapitän zur See Kurt Hoffman peered intently through the clear-view screen on the bridge of the *Scharnhorst*. The cloud was low – around 700 feet – and he couldn't see much of Galland's fighter umbrella. Ahead of the mighty 11 inch guns, the four mine-sweepers were toiling, gear out, to clear a path wide enough for the battleships, in a newly-sown minefield. The task was painfully slow. In broad daylight, approaching the narrowest part of the English Channel, speed was essential, but until the threat of mines was removed, they must follow at the sweepers' pace. Behind the *Scharnhorst*, her sister ship *Gneisenau* is rolling gently, a myriad of anti-aircraft gun barrels needle-sharp against the grey, sullen sky. Further astern, the heavy cruiser *Prinz Eugen* completes the convoy on their epic dash. Beside Hoffman, the unwelcome figure of the 'Black Czar', Admiral Otto Ciliax, whose flag is flying from *Scharnhorst's* halliards, and whose presence doesn't invite idle chatter.

They can't really believe their luck. Leaving Brest under cover of darkness, the breakout of the battle fleet, long-expected by the RAF and the Royal Navy, is still undetected. A combination of weather, technical problems on patrol aircraft, and sheer incompetence on the part of some commanders who really should have planned better has meant they're on the verge of pulling it off. A junior officer whispered nervously to the Navigator, 'It's incredible. It could be a training exercise on a shakedown cruise, for all the attention we're getting.'

That's when they saw the two Spitfires.

Kenley. 09.45 hours: 'Roight. Come on, Fin me boy, Oi reckon we're in for a quiet day. Oi'm thinkin' we could nip over the Ditch and stir things up just a touch. Are ye game?' Boyd needed no second bidding. Together with his Station Commander, he grabbed his flying gear, and telephoned Control with news of their Rhubarb. At 10.10, they climbed into their Spitfires and roared off towards the Somme Estuary. 'Always good for a flak ship or six!'

There are two other Spitfires in the air – Bobby Oxspring, CO of 91 'Jim Crow' Squadron, with Sergeant Beaumont, are flitting from cloud to cloud at 1,500 feet, warned by Control that 'something seems to be going on – but we're not sure what'.

10.30 hours: Findlay saw them first – two Me109s. 'Tally ho, Victor – look at these two beauties. One apiece. But I've got the leader.'

'Okay, me boy. Oi'm with you.'

The two Spitfires raced towards the Messerschmitts, which in turn climbed and swung around, seeking the cover of the massed fighters of the escort Wing over the battleships. At this point, a bank of cloud suddenly swirled aside. Oxspring, startled, saw the ships, broke radio silence, and radioed his sighting report. Nobody believed him. Then he saw Boyd and Beamish rocketing at very low level towards the *Scharnhorst*. On board, they saw the Spitfires, down to 400 feet, and travelling very fast indeed. After a timeless few seconds, the warships erupted in a welter of orange flashes as the guns opened up. The sky was filled with tracer of all colours, the larger guns throwing up enormous waterspouts. Ciliax turned to Hoffman and said, 'This is the start of it. We are now discovered.'

For Boyd, it was very nearly the finish. Diving through the curtain of flak at nearly 400 mph, the next few seconds were a series of flashing stills from a fast-running film; scenes which would live with him for the rest of his life. The sheer size of the grey monster belching fire, Victor's startled 'By Chroist, it's the whole of the Kriegsmarine', the bucking of the Spitfire, as a shell burst close, then the clatter of the spent fragments on the fuselage, and, incredibly, an eleven inch shell fired at maximum depression – he actually *saw* the shell strike the water, and ricochet across the swell like a skimming stone at the seaside. Then another landed below, and the Spitfire flew right through the waterspout.

Suddenly, they were clear, and they swung broadside to the ships, speeding down the line and taking in the details – the towering superstructures, rakish funnels, tripod masts – and then they fought their way through the escorts, putting long bursts of cannon fire into a couple of E-boats on the way. Findlay's pulled up, belching white clouds from its flanks.

They landed at Kenley just after 11.00, having maintained radio silence, unable to believe that nobody else had twigged what was going on. It was only Victor's urgent phone call, confirming Oxspring's sighting, that triggered the reaction. As history shows, it was doomed to failure. A VC would be won by the Fleet Air Arm's Eugene Esmonde, in an action which would see all the Swordfish biplanes brought down . . . and the RAF would spend the rest of the day in fruitless pursuit of the big ships, with torpedo bombers, heavy bombers and fighters flying raid after raid.

602 were over the ships twice, giving better than they got in a desperate attempt to clear the way for the Beauforts and Bostons – and with Findlay leading his old squadron against the flak ships. Although the day ended in fiasco, once again 602 had been there just when it counted most.

CHAPTER TWELVE

'Ace? . . . Which Ace?'

April 25th 1942 Circus 137 (Abbeville Marshalling Yards). Large number of E/A at Le Touquet. Lacey 2 FW 190s damaged. Gp/Capt. Corner (HQFC) flying with 602, hit – baled out too low over Channel – lost. Sgt. Green also lost. P/O Niven to Acting Flight Lieutenant.

Extract, 602 Sqn Operations Record.

06.15: Five miles from Ailly lighthouse in Sector 50. A large number of aircraft overhead.
06.20: A Spitfire crashed into the water 20 yards on our starboard bow.
07.10: Violent firing from shore batteries which got our range several times.

*Extract, log of Chasseur 43, Free French Navy,
landing commandos at Dieppe, 19/8/42.*

February 20th 1942. 'Wheezy Anna' eased over into a gentle bank, the hazy sun momentarily striking the green shamrock freshly painted on her side. The tracer lazily rose towards her, and then seemed to accelerate and whip past her starboard wing at lightning speed. Following his CO into the dive, Dick Lewis, one of 602's Australian contingent, ducked involuntarily in his cockpit. He checked the seat was as low as it would go. Paddy was leading him into yet another hairy situation. Already, he was becoming used to it – well, almost.

'See that juicy big transport, me boy?'

'Hullo, Red Leader, yes, I've got it.'

'Okay. Let's finish her cruising days. Tally ho!'

Together, the Spitfires came lancing down the sky, the Merlins rising in pitch. On board the ship, matelots and gunners heard them, froze for a split second, then dived for cover as the fighters, now low over the water and clocking around 380 mph, levelled out, blurred momentarily as they sighted, and then fired. The *choomph! choomph!* of the cannons mingled with the frantic, staccato rattling of the Brownings, and the snarling roar of the Merlins as the Spitfires, drawing steam from the flanks of the ship, leaped over it at masthead height, and climbed. That's when the Focke-Wulfs struck.

Racing out over the coast at Dunkirk, they converged on the Spitfires almost head on, and saw strikes on the leading machine. As the British fighters rolled away, still travelling very fast indeed, the 190s hauled round after them.

Finucane was conscious of a burning pain from his lower leg and thigh; every time he shoved on the rudder bar, the red-hot pokers attacked his nervous system. His arm was numb. 'Red Two, hullo, Red Two, return to base.'

Dick Lewis wasn't having any of it. 'Red Leader. Nuts to that. They're coming in again from the right. Ready to break starboard . . . Break . . . *now!*'

As the Focke-Wulfs opened fire, almost line abreast, the Spitfires suddenly vanished from their sights. As 'Wheezy Anna' stood on a wing and boomeranged round one way, Dick Lewis, pulling all the 'G' the airframe could stand, hooked round to port, and found the Focke-Wulf leader crawling back into his sight. He sighted, corrected, thumbed the button, and saw strikes sparking along the grey-green fuselage. He broke away, searched for Finucane, and saw him playing a deadly game of tag with the other 190. Racing across the wavetops, he loosed a sighting burst at the second Focke-Wulf, and closed up to 'Wheezy Anna' as the German broke left.

With Lewis calling the shots, the two Spitfires ducked and weaved their way across the Channel, but the Germans didn't give up. Eventually, the two 602 men conned them; Lewis pulled out to one side, throttling back slightly. Finucane, weak through loss of blood, shoved his throttle forward, and the Merlin belched black smoke from the exhaust ports.

Seeing the smoke, and completely fooled by the reason for it, the German leader closed in to complete his kill. Dick Lewis once again pulled all the 'G' he could, standing the VB on its wingtip and rolling in behind the 190. This time, the cannons must have struck control cables. After a short burst, the Focke-Wulf leapt like a salmon on the run, before plunging straight into the Channel. The other 190, thoroughly unnerved as Lewis came round again for him, abruptly turned and ran for home.

The two Spitfires rose over the white cliffs, and homed on Kenley. 602 were by now based at the satellite drome, Redhill, but with Paddy wounded, and his Spitfire shot up, the larger airfield was a safer bet. With Lewis circling, 'Wheezy Anna' made a perfect landing, and taxied up to Dispersal. But Paddy didn't get out. When they got to him, they found him slumped in the cockpit; he'd fainted from shock and loss of blood. Within a fortnight, though, he was back with his stick – and a week later was leading 602 into the air again.

The incident was something of a turning point; when Paddy joined 602, he was already becoming the subject of some notoriety. The Press had seized on him as a hero ('Top Scoring Fighter Ace to Lead Famous Squadron'), and he did seem to have shot down a surprising number of German aircraft, considering that, with 452, he'd frequently flown and fought in the same patch of sky as 602, when the Germans were killing more Spitfires than ever before. But now, after being wounded for the first time in his flying career, Paddy had proved his mettle. The Press continued to make him a very public hero – privately, he was totally different. Quiet and reserved, he was stiff and uncomfortable in the presence of the 'Top Brass'. His dreamy, clear hazel eyes, set wide apart, testified to the more romantic side of his Southern Irish character. He didn't make friends easily, but he won the respect of the squadron in the few months he led them. If they doubted his previous claims (and some of them certainly did) they never doubted that he'd win his place in The Legend.

Off duty, he was something of an enigma. There were persistent rumours that there were rare occasions when the other side of the Irish character had taken over, and he'd absolutely cut loose, wreaking havoc in a succession of pub rough-house brawls. He had, they said, even climbed half way up a church steeple in Croydon, and fallen asleep on a narrow ledge, until the Fire Brigade fetched him down. A couple of times, the lads tried to get him completely smashed, but their CO, his hazel eyes smiling quietly would stick to shandies, and watch his tempters slowly drink themselves under the table, before helping them up with a companionable, 'Now then, John, Oi think we'll be helpin' ye to yer room. Oi think we've had enough for one noight.'

His career with 602 was short, but eventful. On his first flight after recovering from his wounds, he led 602 into the air as Top Cover to Circus 114, bombing Hazebrouck. In a fast, running fight, at 23,000 feet over the target, Finucane shot the tail clean off a Focke-Wulf as it turned across his nose. As it spun down, he raced round in a curve, and closed on a second 190, which was diving furiously, unable to shake off Johnson's Spitfire. Together, the two 602 pilots attacked, and the 190, hit from both sides, went down trailing smoke, to crash near Hazebrouck. Johnny Niven, by now a Pilot Officer, got a 'probable' FW190, and John Dennehey opened his score with another 'damaged'. But it was Eric Bocock who emerged as the day's real hero. Sweating, cursing, and throwing his protesting Spitfire around the upper skies, he put down two of the agile Focke-Wulfs, earning himself the DFC. They returned minus Pilot Officer F.W. 'Backwards' Ferwarda, one of their Dutchmen, but four kills and three possibles made for a highly satisfactory balance sheet – and for a celebration in the Mess. Paddy was in good form. 'Now then, Eric, that was a creditable performance, y'know. But you mustn't keep tryin' too hard. Some of us have reputations to guard.'

Another with a reputation already well established was Ginger Lacey, who joined 602 as a Flight Commander at this time. Just after the Battle of Britain, the newspapers had published a list of Fighter Command's top-scoring 'aces'. It included, of course, Archie McKellar, Findlay Boyd and Al Deere – but Lacey was at the very top. Such publicity left him cold, but he was proud of his two DFMs – and pragmatic about his Commission. 'Well, you see, holders of the DFM were entitled to a cash bounty of £20 on leaving the service. And in order to take up a commission, you had to technically be discharged as an NCO. It seemed to me to be a sound financial move.' 602 took to him immediately. They appreciated him even more when he started hitting the Focke-Wulfs again. Though he didn't claim any definite kills, he certainly knocked chunks out of two or three. On 25th April, as they came over Hardelot as top cover, about 100 Focke-Wulfs rose up from Abbeville to take on the 35 Kenley Spitfires. 602, inevitably, led the charge. As Finucane took Red Section into the first group of German fighters, Ginger, leading Yellow Section, called out the warning as another section of 190s swung in behind. He was too late to stop Sergeant Green being hit, but as the rest of Finucane's section scattered, Lacey led his wingman down on a pair of Focke-Wulfs a thousand feet below. An instant before he fired, the Germans saw them, and heeled into a 45 degree dive, trailing white smoke and pulling away, boosters engaged. Ginger settled behind the sight, and, with throttle against the stop, the Spitfire vibrated, building up speed rapidly in the screaming dive. He peered through the orange ring on the angled glass, judging the long-range shot to perfection. A short burst made the Spitfire buck and shake, but it drew thickening brown jets of smoke from the German, whose dive steepened. Lacey pulled up, looked round, and saw two more 190s above and behind. Cheekily, he climbed right around them, as they wavered, their pilots looking this way and that. They'd obviously just been watching him in action. As he curved back towards them, they lost their nerve, and dived for home.

Turning towards Le Touquet, he found another pair, and reefed in to attack from the beam, seeing strikes on the rear fuselages of both before they, too, chickened out. Returning to base, he found an unexpected VIP had arrived; King George VI. They'd met before – when Ginger had picked up his double DFM at the Palace –but this time the King surprised him. He'd found out that it was Ginger who'd shot down the Heinkel which had bombed Buckingham Palace in the Battle of Britain. In the mess, after tea, His Majesty said thanks, and Ginger, in turn, said, 'Would you like a drink, sir?' The politeness was automatic. Perhaps the King's reply was, too – 'Yes, please'. So, too, were Ginger's next words – the words that came naturally to every fighter pilot. 'Two beers, please.'

The C-in-C Fighter Command frowned; the staff officers coughed quietly; but His Majesty drank his half pint without hesitation. It was only later that Ginger realised what he'd done. The King's later drinks were all sherries. But 602 were delighted.

This was the time when the 'aces' were gathering: Deere had gone, of course, but Finucane was on his way to equalling Sailor Malan's record 32 kills, and Lacey had 25; Bocock and Johnny Niven were off and running, and the next generation were learning their craft from the masters; Canadian Wally McLeod picked up the science of survival, and the art of air fighting, with 602, before going on to some remarkable deeds later in the war (on one occasion, in mid 1944, he shot down two FW190s with only 26 cannon shells – on another, he came so close that the German pilot baled out in sheer terror, before Wally had even fired a shot); Victor Beamish, who was to be seen first thing each morning, resplendent in shorts, hoofing around the perimeter track, and as often as not tagging on to 602 over France; on one occasion, he even shot down a 190 and claimed a 'probable' on a second. It was a sad day at Kenley when, after a fast running fight with the Focke-Wulfs over Le Havre, in which Finucane scored a 'double' – and 602 got another three – Beamish was shot down and killed. When he didn't come back, the whole squadron refuelled and volunteered to go back and search the

Channel, but, at the limit of their endurance, the Spitfires gave up without sighting Victor. They'd also lost their first Czech, Rudolf Ptacek.

Five days later, they nearly lost Findlay Boyd.

Findlay had taken up eleven 602 Spitfires on a sweep. It was a murky kind of day, and the Spitfires formed up low over the Channel, heading south-east right on the cloud base, slipping in and out of the curling tendrils of mist, guns armed, looking for anything that moved.

When it came, it was like lightning.

'Look out, 190s diving starboard, *break! Break!*'

'Christ, the boss is hit! Toddy Red, *go right!*'

The Spitfires, throttles hard on the stops, half-rolled, stood on their wings, and whipped viciously into steep dives, levelling out over the wavetops, three of them, going like the clappers for home, their pilots nervously scanning the skies . . . nothing. No, wait, over to starboard, about two miles distant, low over the water; a single fighter, trailing a thin stream of grey smoke, weaving gently. They swung towards the wounded Spitfire. RF-B. The Wingco's aircraft. Findlay, his radio out, gives the thumbs up – and returns to the job of struggling for height with his engine running roughly, his controls sloppy, and that dangerous elastic feel of the elevators – the cable hanging together by a strand. A strand that was stretching with every twitch of the torn aluminium.

Back at Kenley, they all heard the eerie whistle of the Spitfire in the circuit. Boyd tried to drop his undercarriage – no joy. No pressure. He wondered about hand cranking, but decided against it. Too risky. The legs might not lock, and there was no telling what the tyres and brakes might be like. The flaps didn't fully extend, either. . .

The Spitfire eased in over the boundary, travelling much too fast, and dropping her starboard wing alarmingly, but Boyd caught the swing, checked it instinctively, and with infinite care, throttled back as far as he dared, and thumped the Spitfire squarely down on the grass. She bucketed and slewed across the field; Findlay, thrown hard against the harness, bounced from one side of the cockpit to the other. After a final, rending ground loop, the Spitfire came to rest, and Findlay was up and out of her before anyone came close. She didn't burn.

Afterwards, in the mess, as they celebrated Findlay's escape – his fourth of the war – and Eric Bocock's DFC, the talk was centred on their clapped-out VBs. The real answer to the Focke-Wulf was the Spitfire IX – already rumoured to be coming off the production lines. But it was after this combat, that Findlay, always the individualist, got together with some of the ground 'erks', to see just how far they could improve on the performance of an operational VB. He air tested two or three possible replacements, selected one, and then set about cleaning it up.

The two outer wing Brownings were taken out, and the ports sealed. The weight loss was the main benefit. Findlay reckoned he wouldn't miss their firepower – he was getting close enough for the rest of the guns to make sure of his kills. Next, the external mirror went, replaced by one inside the bulged hood. The aerial stalk went, too; substituted by a razor-slim version, unofficially 'borrowed' from a high-flying PRU Spitfire. Next, the rivets were all filled, and the entire aircraft highly polished. It destroyed any vestige of camouflage – and indeed later Boyd actually had his Spitfire completely stripped of paint – and it was, of course, officially frowned on. With her red spinner the Spitty was a real eye catcher, and there were a few pointed comments about her pilot trying to re-live the days of the Red Baron who swept the skies over the trenches in his garish Fokkers.

In reality, though, it was Boyd the fighter leader carrying logic to the limit. Camouflage, he reasoned, was pointless, when 200 aircraft or more were flying each Circus. What was important was speed – and the new RF-B had gained some 30 mph with all the modifications. He was, of course, setting himself up as an obvious prime target – much in the way that the Spitfires sought out the Me109 with Mickey Mouse on the side in 1941, knowing it was Galland. But that suited Boyd down to the ground – confident in his superb VB, he was assured of targets queueing for a fight – and if he drew the fighters away from less experienced pilots, so much the better. 602, of course, approved – and it is a matter of record that, although Findlay kept up his rate of scoring, the Focke-Wulfs never again got near enough to the shining Spitfire to score hits.

Readers of the daily papers eagerly devoured stories of the 'aces' – and at Kenley, there were more than the usual. 602, of course, couldn't really care less, and never for a moment took the idea seriously. It was sufficient that they were now knocking down German fighters at a very favourable exchange rate – some three or four to one – so when the gentlemen of Fleet Street appeared looking for heroes, 602 enjoyed themselves.

'I've come to do a piece on your ace pilot.'

'Ace? Which ace?'

'You mean there's more than one?'

'Ah, you probably mean the Wingco. D'you know, the last time we were up, he ran out of ammo, and actually rammed a Jerry fighter?'

'Really! What happened?'

'Well, he found he'd knocked three feet off one wing, and the kite was flying a little shakily, so he rammed another with his other wing to even things up, and nipped back in time for lunch.'

'You're pulling my leg.' Surrounded by DFC ribbons, the unfortunate journalist was doubtful.

'Well, I lied about the second one. Actually, here's our real hero.'

A young sergeant in the dark blue of Australia steps forward, smiling modestly. 'This is Loop Shaefer. We were lucky to get him, y'know.' (Shaefer was a new arrival, straight from an OTU.)

'But – he's not wearing any medal ribbons.'

Aarebrot, the silent Norwegian, leaned forward, and whispered earnestly, 'It is so. Bot, som tings are so . . . ah . . . underhand, is not possible to give medal. Loop vill talk . . . but only if da tonge is – ah – looser.'

The journalist sighed, and ordered yet another round of drinks for the pirates of 602 Squadron. He never did print the story. Who'd have believed it anyway?

The real fighting was hard.

April 13th 1942: 'Rodeo' Hastings – Le Touquet – Desvres – Sangatte – Deal.
Airborne 14.15

At 23,000 feet 10mls E. of Calais, CO saw about 15 FW190s below.

602 dived to attack. As soon as attack started CO saw 20 – 30 E/A about to dive on 602. He immediately ordered a defensive circle to be formed. E/A made numerous attacks – position became so serious that CO asked W/C Boyd for help. E/A made repeated attacks for about 15 minutes as defensive circle gradually wove into a decreasing spiral, losing height in a series of steep turns, and unbroken by E/A. Reaching 10,000 feet Sqn. dived one by one for the Channel, which they crossed at only 50 feet, followed by E/A to 3 miles off Dover. P/O Niven 1 kill, P/O de la Poype 1 Me109F

damaged, F/Sgt Willis 1 FW190 damaged. Casualties, surprisingly, nil.

And the real stories are as stirring as any.

May 17th 1942: Over Beachy Head, the incoming Spitfire Wings milled around at 500 feet, sidestepping one another in the circuit as the twelve Bostons swept in, in a tight formation, and set course for France. The mission was to bomb shore installations at Boulogne – 'Ramrod' 33. The Kenley Wing were flying High Cover, and 602 were detailed as Top Cover squadron – the highest of the Spitfires as the beehive formed up and headed for France. Finucane led them in a steep climb, the Merlin 46s using their superchargers to the full, thin streams of grey smoke whipping back along the fuselages. Visibility was fair, the Channel a hard grey-blue beneath the camouflaged wings. Each pilot completed his checks – oxygen on, seat down, radiator flap set, trim adjusted for optimum climb, gunsight on.

At 25,000 feet, they crossed the coastline, sweeping the skies, and trailing their coats to the Focke-Wulfs. The sun burned into the tiny cockpits, the adrenalin started to flow in tense young pilots. The twelve Spitfires, fanning out across the sky, twitched and gently weaved, as numbed feet and hands massaged controls. Keith Hodson, for once, beat Paddy to it. 'Red Leader, Blue One. 15 bandits high at ten o'clock. They're not reacting.'

'Roger, got them, Keith. Keep your eyes peeled, chaps.' The Spitfires swept on. 'Red leader from Blue Four' – Joe Kistruck, the sergeant with the far-seeing clear eyes. 'Ten 190s ahead to starboard, two thousand feet down.' He'd spotted the flashes of light from the angled canopies – and then the dappled grey/green cruciform shapes flickering against the chequered pattern of the countryside. Finucane acknowledged, and led them down. As the Spitfires dived, the higher 190s came after them.

Again, the whirling kaleidoscope of aircraft. Young Tait saw a 190 rising in his windshield, and clinically compared it to the recognition silhouettes he'd burned into his brain in preparation for this moment. The radial engine, the square wingtips, the long bubble canopy. But what no picture could convey was the startling mottled green and yellow warpaint, the stark black cross – the blurring of the wings as the German fired at some unseen target, the cascade of spent cartridge cases from the wing chutes. Suddenly, Tait woke up, sighted, and fired. He had a glimpse of his shells sparking on the camouflage, and a fleeting vision of the canopy flying off. The 190 dropped like a stone. Startled, he pulled up, half rolled, and dived, seeing his victim falling away in a sweeping curve. He'd just told himself not to follow it down when the glinting tracer flashed over his canopy, bending away into infinity, and he threw the Spitfire right over into a screaming dive. His unseen assailant vanished.

In the first pass, Finucane knocked down a 190. With a long burst of cannon fire, he shot its port wing clean off. It was his 32nd confirmed kill. Nobody else had done better.

The Spitfires dived for the coast, re-forming over Cap Gris Nez. As Yellow Section extricated themselves from the mêlée, a section of Focke-Wulfs jumped them, and sent Flight Lieutenant Major down, trailing glycol. The three remaining Spitfires were racing for the coast when they saw three 190s diving down past them, then to their amazement, about eight shiny, whitish-yellow balloons rose up fast towards the Spitfires. One pilot swerved violently, and suddenly the balloons, which didn't appear to be trailing wires, were gone.

The last attack came over Cap Gris Nez. As Blue Section raced out over the coast, they were heavily engaged by a fresh swarm of Focke-Wulfs. Keith Hodson closed to point blank range on one; infuriatingly, it just kept on flying. Kistruck, twisting and turning, just managed to scrape out over the water, but he'd seen Willis going out below him, chased by a 190. Willis didn't return.

The final drama was being played out over the water. Major went into the sea off Cap Gris Nez, and as they circled, they saw him waving. There was no sign of the dinghy, though. John Dennehey went down low and slow, and dropped his, while the rest of the squadron formed a covering screen. Major never reached it. The water was bitterly cold – when the Air Sea Rescue launch got to him, he was long dead.

The Spitfires, by now very low indeed on fuel after circling for so long over Major, turned for Britain. Four of them made it back to Kenley, three landed at Hawkinge, and three at Manston, just over the white cliffs.

It was Paddy's last kill – and it equalled the famous Sailor Malan's 32. He was soon after promoted to become the RAF's youngest Wing Commander – at 21 – and left to lead the Hornchurch Wing. But not before he'd pulled off a remarkable piece of airmanship. On one of his last flights with 602, out over the Channel, he'd found himself turning his Spitfire through Strudwick's slipstream, when 'Wheezy Anna', thrown by the turbulent air, actually put a wing into the water. It should have been certain death, but Paddy, with lightning-fast reactions and exercising all his considerable strength, hauled her out and returned safely. His next brush with the Channel was his last. Leading his Wing over Le Touquet, he collected a stray bullet. The Merlin, deprived of coolant, seized. Paddy, too low to bale out, was resigned to his fate. His soft Irish voice came calmly across the airwaves. 'This is it, Butch'. The Spitfire was a terrible aircraft to ditch. Before you even laid the wings on the water, the radiator and oil coolers would dig in, gulping seawater. 'Wheezy Anna' never gave her pilot a chance. Together, they went straight down. 602 grieved; Paddy had earned their respect, no mean achievement. A silver cigarette case they'd had inscribed would never be delivered. Instead, they presented it to his father.

No 602's days at Kenley were numbered. Paddy was replaced by another Battle of Britain veteran, Pete Brothers, who had knocked down a dozen or so already, and fitted the 602 mould rather well. Findlay Boyd completed his tour at Kenley with the award of the DSO. Later, he'd head east, where he started shooting down Japanese Zekes and Bettys over Rangoon, ending the war with a score of 28, a DSO, two DFCs, and the Air Efficiency Award – and a hatred of Germans which thirty years later still made him growl when a group of tourists pulled up outside his little hotel – the Ferry Inn – in Uig at the north end of Skye. The Mercedes had German plates.

Brothers took them north, to Peterhead, where they swopped aircraft with Paul Webb's 416 Squadron. They didn't languish long, though. In the middle of August, with rumours flying that something big was in the offing, they were ordered to the most famous fighter station of them all – Biggin Hill. It was from there that they'd lead the five Spitfire squadrons over Dieppe. On the 18th, they got in some practice escorting a 'Rodeo', and Brothers shot down a 190. That evening, along with the station's other units, which included a USAAF fighter squadron, the 307th Pursuit, flying Spitfires with the American Star on the fuselages, they attended a briefing by the Station CO, Group Captain Hallings-Pott. And they went early to bed, knowing that the morning would see the first ever large scale invasion of 'Fortress Europe'. 602, by now boasting Belgian, Dutch, Norwegian, Polish, Czech and French pilots, were keyed up as never before.

03.15 hours: The corporals and batmen went the rounds, shaking and cajoling the pilots into wakefulness. Many of them, slightly self-consciously, got out their best blues; all the Free French certainly did. They washed, shaved (a miracle for some of 602's scruffier types) and put away their 'operational' breakfasts amid an excited, low hum of nervous chatter.

As they walked out to the dispersals, Lord Lovat was already leading his Commandos ashore in France, and the battle was joined. With dawn streaking the eastern skies, they climbed into the Spitfires with the Lion Rampant crests, and one by one the Merlins fired, the blue and yellow flames from the exhausts bright in the misty grey dawn. As the engines ran up, the Spitfires shivered, as though chilled by the north-easterly, the dew which had gently covered them through the night blown back. Their flanks streaming, canopies steely in the half-light, the twelve City of Glasgow Spitfires eased out of their bays, and led the thundering procession to the head of the runway. A ragged cheer came from some of the ground crews, a few hats waved in the cold morning air. There seemed to be an extraordinary number of people who'd found some reason to be up and about that Wednesday morning.

05.50 hours: With a silent little explosion, a green Very light rose from the control tower, and arced over the waiting airfield. Brothers flicked his rudder and elevators briefly, grinned across at Eric Bocock, and moved his fist. Together, the Spitfires accelerated across the field, in three groups of four, rising into their element from the famous Bump, their wheels lifting into their bellies, their exhausts flickering bright in the gloom, the sound of their flight echoing across the rolling countryside and the sleeping bungalows. Three minutes later, 222 Squadron took off, followed by the Americans. The fighters swung south into dead grey skies, to pick up 133 and 401 over Lympne. With 602 leading, the Biggin Hill Wing set course direct for Dieppe, the Spitfires hugging the still waters of the Channel.

06.05 hours: 602 climbed hard over the destroyers, reaching for height in the hazy skies. Below, the gloom was stabbed repeatedly by the muzzle flashes of the 4 inch guns, targeted on coastal batteries. Smoke was drifting out from the town itself, the legacy of an early Boston raid. The Canadian sergeants, all too aware that 5,000 of their countrymen were fighting for their lives on the beaches, pleaded to be allowed to go down and have a go at the coastal batteries. Then the Focke-Wulfs appeared, racing across out of the haze. Sampson saw them first, called the angles to Brothers, and promptly shot a straggling 190 down. Brothers, his Spitfire straining at full throttle, whipped round at a second, and saw strikes. Below, a large transport blew up. Off to port, twenty-four Flying Fortresses droned on towards Abbeville – only the second American daylight raid of the war, and a useful diversion. 602, finding no more action, went back to Biggin Hill, landing some minutes ahead of the 307th Pursuit, who were cock-a-hoop with their first ever kill. 602, who'd got one too, together with a 'damaged', were brassed off. They'd come to fight.

'First show a walkover. Sampson – 1 FW190 kill, CO 1 FW190 damaged. Second round. Off at 10.15, back at 12.35. 3 kills, 1 probable, 8 damaged. Very good show this, for they milled round in the thick of it.'

10.30 hours: As they approached Dieppe, with 602 again leading at 10,000 feet, the scene had been magically, horrendously changed. The haze over the Channel had cleared – against the blue water they could see the twisting white trails of the little ships dodging the heavy shells; the fighters trailing smoke and heading for home; the obscene yellow stain spreading as a downed pilot cut open his pack of fluorescent dye. A pall of smoke covered the target area. Their headphones filled with the cacophony of battle – and ahead, a vast, running air battle filled the skies. 'Hullo, Grass Seed. Toddy Red Leader. Many bandits over target, Angels Nine and above. Attacking. Tally Ho!' Pete Brothers led 602 in a sweeping curve to port, seeing a gaggle of unescorted Dornier 217s heading out to bomb the transports which were now labouring to take the shattered remnants of the land forces out of the cauldron of battle.

The Spitfires pounced like hawks. Eric Bocock sighted on a Dornier, and destroyed it with two well-aimed bursts. As he wheeled to confirm its destruction, he heard Marryshow's urgent yell –'Blue One, *break port*, man!' He reacted instantly, and the tracer flashed through the patch of sky his Spitfire had just occupied. Marryshow sailed past after the 190, cannons hammering. A second Focke-Wulf was slanting in, drawing a bead on the Spitfire, so Bocock hooked round and struck again, lashing the German fighter's tail surfaces. It leaped like a startled deer, and flicked away. Suddenly, he was in clear skies.

Down below, Sergeant Hauser saw his shells striking a Dornier right across the cabin; it went into a sickening dive, and, with pieces breaking off, plunged straight into the sea, narrowly missing a transport.

Attacking behind Blue Section, Bill Loud's blood was up. Climbing straight up the back end of a Dornier, he watched as Caldecott's shells sparked along its fuselage. Bill fired, briefly. The Dornier went into its final dive, trailing smoke and glycol. Something detached itself and spun clear – the parachute streamed, but didn't develop. The German airman took long seconds to die. Loud raced across to a second Dornier. As he closed to fifty yards in a quarter attack, one engine burst into flames, and the Dornier captain let his bombs go, seeking to escape. Bill left him to it. With no bombs, he couldn't do any damage. Caldecott got another, too.

In ten furious minutes, they accounted for three Dorniers, probably a fourth, and damaged at least eight others. By any standards, it was remarkably good air fighting. When the Germans gave up and abandoned the unequal fight in disarray, Brothers reformed the squadron. Off to one side, a section of Focke-Wulfs hovered, indecisively. When the Spitfires turned towards them, they lost their nerve, and turned tail.

'Aw, hell, somebody's been talking, Boss. They know we're back.'

'Shut up, Blue Three, or I'll have a double off you.'

Eleven came back. They'd lost Goodchap.

13.00 hours: Third round. Squadron went off again almost on empty stomachs. Gave them sandwiches and lemonade. Wonder what they'd do on beer and oysters? Eleven came back. F/Lt Niven DFC is in the sea. Reports say he has been picked up. Sqn. had a shaky do and only claim is a destroyed by P/O Sampson who sent a FW190 straight into the sea. Cold luncheon revived the boys and they are ready for more fun – such as it is. Score to date: 4 destroyed and 10 damaged for loss of 2 pilots and 2 planes.

Last patrol took place at 16.50 hours and all came back at 18.10 hours. Nothing seen. Sqn. then released and had plenty of beer –and what was more important, *sleep.*

At the end of the day which had seen disaster on the beaches, and over 100 RAF aircraft shot down for only 48 Germans, the Biggin Hill Wing's total was reckoned as 5 kills, 7 'probables' and 29 'damaged' – and the startling fact is that 602's share was 4 kills, 1 'probable' and 11 'damaged'. In fact, they'd done better than they thought. Next day, they flew back up to Peterhead minus four Spitfires and three pilots. One of them, though, was safe. Johnny Niven had been picked up, with both ankles injured, and delivered to Brighton Municipal Hospital. He'd even sent a telegram to Peterhead to tell them the good news, on the 20th. Three days later, it still hadn't arrived. The Diary records – 'The GPO has apparently never heard of Peterhead. We're not surprised!'

To crown it all, one of their 'damaged' was later raised to a 'kill', on the evidence of another Spitfire pilot, who'd watched their second fight from the deck of the destroyer which had fished him out of the Channel. He wasn't in the least surprised to discover he'd been watching 602 at work.

CHAPTER THIRTEEN

'Rest? . . . What Rest?'

December 30th 1942: Since arriving in 14 Group 3 officers have left us to command Flights. We have lost the CO and both Flight Commanders and had over 24 pilots posted from us. One wonders why we were sent up here for a 'rest?'

January 12th 1943: F/O Pringle posted to Mediterranean. Wrecked the Mess, good job too.

January 13th 1943: AOC visits – news of a move south at the end of the month. All personnel shed years of worry and looked much brighter, younger and happier.

Extracts, 602 Sqn Operations Record.

September 16th 1942: As the rain streaked the perspex canopy, whipping back on the outside and dribbling through the worn seals to drip annoyingly on his leg, Joe Kistruck reflected on war's changing fortunes. A month before, he'd been tangling with the Focke-Wulfs over the Pas de Calais, well on the way to becoming a hero, in the crackerjack squadron they all wanted to join. Now, he was getting cold, wet, and thoroughly brassed off in a tired old Spitfire somewhere near Fair Isle.

Fair Isle!

There's nothing fair about it, he thought sourly. 602 had arrived at Peterhead, and promptly been ordered further north. One Flight was at Skeabrae, defending the Orkney Islands against the might of the Luftwaffe, the other was even closer to the Arctic Circle – at Sumburgh in the Shetland Islands. They'd forsaken their war-weary VBs for even more clapped-out VAs, which didn't even have cannons. Now, Joe was on patrol between the two island groups, with Gerry Eames, the new Canadian Sergeant who was completing his operational training.

'Dalmat Blue Two, close up. Come on, Gerry, I don't want to lose you in this muck.'

'Dalmat Blue One, okay.'

'That's Roger, Gerry . . . er, Blue Two.' He wasn't trying too hard.

'Roger, Joe, okay!' Neither was Gerry.

The two Spitfires swung round, back towards the island. Suddenly, miracle of miracles, it happened.

'Dalmat Blue One from Control, Bandit over Fair Isle. He's just dropped some bombs. Vector one one zero. Buster!'

You'll be lucky, thought Joe, as he pushed the throttle forward, and the old lady began to shake and rattle. She nearly rolled, too, but Joe was an old hand – he caught the inevitable drop of the port wing as the speed increased.

The Spitfires, now just below the cloud base, came in from the north-west, and caught sight of the Heinkel low over the water, racing for home. They closed in, lined up behind the bomber, one on each side, and stole up to 150 yards before the sleeping German rear gunner cottoned on to what was happening. Kistruck fired a long burst, which silenced the gunner, and Eames followed up, hitting one engine. Just before they lost it in cloud, with an engine out and only twenty feet above the waves, they both found they'd exhausted all their ammunition. Oh, for a pair of cannons, thought Joe, as they headed back with their tale of woe.

It wasn't just the Fives they hated. They'd also inherited half a dozen Spitfire VIs. These machines had pressure cabins, to enable them to get up into the stratosphere. They also had a highly undesirable feature – the ground crew bolted the canopy down once the pilot was strapped in. Escape in flight was next to impossible.

September 25th 1942: P/O Gray took Spitfire VI Scatsta – Skeabrae. Got lost, landed at Grimsetter. Took off, flew into storm, got lost again, and lost R/T contact with *Natal*. Flew round to west coast, belly landed at Gairloch, Ross-shire. A/C Category B. Pilot unhurt.

When they went south again at the end of January, it was with a newer batch of VBs, but it was without Johnny Niven, who'd been rested, Eric Bocock, who was having the time of his life in the USA on a goodwill visit, and Pete Brothers, who'd taken over the Tangmere Wing. His replacement was Mike Beytagh, a Battle of Britain veteran who'd also flown in the Western Desert. Shot down over Tobruk, he'd lain helplesss in the hospital as the Germans unloaded several tons of bombs on it. He was long overdue a DFC – but despite his experiences, his sense of humour was intact, his blue eyes and even white teeth smiling from a fair, youthful face.

His control was magnificent. It was only on close examination you could see the shadows under the eyes, and the habitual twitch of the left hand as it crumpled his forage cap. He would lead 602 for a year.

They landed at Perranporth in Cornwall, and found they faced every fighter pilot's nightmare – long trips over the sea. As often as not, they slung long-range slipper tanks under the Spitfires' bellies, and ranged right down into the Bay of Biscay. Even Rhubarbs and fighter sweeps over France meant eighty miles over hostile water. On one of the first, Eames and Smith collided. Eames survived, but Smith went straight in. Eames, as events were to prove, was one of the great survivors of all time. On 11th April, on a shipping reconnaissance, he was lost – or so they thought. But nearly two weeks later, he was picked up from his one-man dinghy, still alive, still conscious, and with a few scraps of carefully-preserved aircrew rations left. By many days, it was a record . . . and Gerry reckoned he'd never be seasick again.

The days lengthened into weeks at Perranporth, with the squadron engaged on an endless round of convoy escorts (standing patrols, usually of four Spitfires, at the limit of their range, relieved in shifts), weather patrols ('If you can't see your nose, it's mist, if you can't see your compass, it's heavy mist') and bomber escort missions to Brest and St Nazaire. Time and again, the Bostons or Marauders would go in at around 10,000 feet, and the Spitfires would be thrown around the tracer-streaked skies by the flak bursts. When the fighters came near, the VBs would strain to catch them, pilots cursing, Merlins thrashing at maximum power – but the old ladies just didn't have it in them. 'Struddy' Strudwick was particularly vexed. 'Look, you guys, I reckoned when I came to 602 I was headed for a real war. Tell you what. The clouds are pretty low. Who wants to come over to France? If we can't get the Focke-Wulfs, maybe we can get the Focke-tanks.' Or words to that effect.

Struddy was not to be denied. He did score the first strikes on a 190, over Brest – and he certainly did his bit to add to The Legend. Returning from a Rhubarb in mid-February, he noticed his engine was overheating slightly. He was a bit puzzled. He hadn't noticed any flak at all, and the Spitfire seemed to be intact. The ground crew pointed out the cause of the trouble. He'd come back with bits of French evergreen wedged in the radiator and oil cooler. They were rather proud of him. On the same trip, Bob Gourlay had gone out even lower. Six miles off The Lizard, he'd actually hit the sea with his propeller. The blades shattered and spun away, and Gourlay instinctively hauled the stick back into his stomach. The Spitfire managed to reach 400 feet before running out of airspeed; just high enough for Bob to bale out and get his canopy to open. He had no dinghy, but the boys had an accurate fix on his position, and he was picked up an hour later by an ASR Walrus amphibian. When he thawed out, he was a bit put out to find that it wasn't the Navy who'd fished him out. The amphibian didn't carry any rum. Back at Perranporth, he reported to Beytagh.

'Now look, Sergeant, I'm not at all happy about the loss of this aircraft. Not at all happy.' Mike kept a perfectly straight face.

'I'm very sorry, sir. But you told us to go in under the Jerries' radar net.'

'Yes, Sergeant, but not under their bloody sonar as well.'

One by one, the VBs went, on too many occasions taking their pilots with them. In March, three Canadians arrived – Willis, Guy and Robson. Within a couple of months, only Robson was left. Willis had his tail sliced off by a Mustang during an Army co-operation exercise, and the Focke-Wulfs got Guy over Abbeville. Baggett managed to write off his Spitfire without injury, after his engine had cut clean out over the water. Gliding back over the coast, he ripped a wing off in the subsequent forced landing, and broke the Spitfire's back.

By this time, they'd moved three times, as the 2nd Tactical Air Force mustered its resources prior to softening up 'Fortress Europe' for the invasion. First, they went to Lasham, where they practised for hours at low level against tanks, troop convoys, and as artillery spotters. Then it was to Fairlop, in Essex, where they went on bomber escorts and sweeps into France, Belgium and Holland. Through it all, spirits were kept remarkably high, a tribute to Beytagh's leadership, and if the tensions were ever present in the skies over Europe, they were certainly relieved in all kinds of ways on the ground:

March 23rd 1943: F/Lt Freeborn and P/O Strudwick went shooting rabbits. Rabbits were never in any danger. Score Nil.
March 24th 1943: Following telegram was sent to F/O Yates (the Piltdown Prune): 'Yates, Lime Grove, Marsland Road, Sale, Manchester. Arrived Perranporth today found you on leave STOP Jimmie now ten months old STOP coming to see you STOP arrive Manchester 2.32 Thursday via London STOP I still love you.

Enid.' That ought to stir something – and it did.

March 25th 1943: Last night P/O Piltdown Prune's father telephoned the station and asked that 'Enid' should be prevented from going to Manchester. Following telegram was sent this morning. 'Sorry STOP The joke fell flat STOP The boys'. Hope it patches things up.

Various pilots read interesting book on sex life. Future contact with females should be more satisfying. Most of them are going of a nurses' dance tonight anyway.

Extracts, 602 Sqn Operations Record (!)

In June, they went to Bognor, to Number 122 Airfield, spending the days escorting the endless Marauders, Mitchells and Bostons on their medium level raids, and the nights roughing it under canvas. A new batch of pilots arrived from Down Under – McKenzie and Morgan from New Zealand, and Finnie and Dumbrell from Australia. Towards the end of the month, the Spitfires all went to Cranfield, to have their supercharger blades cropped. When they came back, the pilots found that the low-level performance had slightly improved, but it was nothing startling. The fighters also ran out of puff at around 12,000 feet. Struddy was philosophical. 'Oh, well, I was getting bored with heavy flak. I guess I'll just have to settle for light stuff now.'

Next month, the 'light stuff' got him.

June 15th 1943: 602 were flying as Close Escort to some Bostons, bombing Poix. About fifty enemy fighters, mostly FW190s, rose up to fight, careening in through some sleepy Escort Cover Spitfires. For once, the 602 boys got the chance to mix it, and in a furious five minute action, Bill Loud, by now a Flight Lieutenant and 'A' Flight Commander, got one, and Robbie Robson another. But there was no celebration back at their new base, Kingsnorth, although they were 602's first definite kills since Dieppe, nearly a year before. As the 190s came in, the 'B' Flight Spitfires were taken by surprise. Four were missing. The Canadian, Tysowski, had gone down in flames; McKenzie's Spitfire, its tail completely shot off, spun uncontrollably, and blew apart as it hit the ground. Struddy, by now also a Flight Lieutenant, leading 'B' Flight, had dived hard, trailed by Flight Sergeant George Hannah, the squadron's only Glaswegian pilot.

They'd dodged the 190s, but flew straight into a hail of 20 mm flak. The squadron were shocked. Hannah's loss was particularly poignant. He'd been a fitter in 602 before the war. When war broke out, he'd volunteered for pilot training. When they posted him back to 'Glasgow's Own' at Perranporth, there wasn't a prouder or happier pilot in the whole of the Air Force.

Strudwick was replaced by the man who would end up leading the squadron for much of the rest of the war – Flight Lieutenant R.A. 'Max' Sutherland, veteran of seven fighter squadrons, and former boxing champion. Posted in from 222 Squadron at Hornchurch, one of the most comfortable fighter bases of the lot, his introduction to Kingsnorth was, to say the least, disconcerting. The driver who'd picked him up from the station took him over a little bridge, turned sharply right and left, and through a gateway. Ahead, a sea of mud, stretching for nearly a mile in any direction. The van skidded, slithered, and finally bounced onto some metal openwork trackway oozing with mud.

'Home from home, sir,' came the driver's cheery voice.

'You mean, this is it?'

'Yessir.'

'Where are the hangars?'

'There aren't any, sir.'

'Where are the living quarters?'

'There aren't any, sir.'

'Don't keep saying, "There aren't any". Look, what *is* there?'

'Well, sir, there's these two trackways. That's the runways. Then there's tents to sleep in, and another one for the Adj, and a big one to eat in. And the Spitfires are under camouflage netting – look, there's one over there.'

As it turned out, Max did get a room in a real building – rank has its privileges – it was a derelict little cottage down by a piggery. His ears, and his nose, left him in no doubt that the piggery still functioned.

There were three squadrons down on the farm, Tommy Maggs explained: 'Well, we're here to find the best ways to ensure operations can go ahead from newly-prepared airstrips after the first landings in France. We're also finding what – ah – doesn't work too well. By the way, I thought I ought to tell you, before anyone else does. Since the beginning of the year, we haven't had a Flight Commander who's lasted more than two months.'

'Thanks a whole bunch, Tommy.'

Niven, who'd been rested, Freeborn, who'd taken over 118 Squadron after winning the DFC and Bar, and Gibson, De Naeyer, and Strudwick, who'd all gone down to the flak or the Focke-Wulfs.

But Max would prove exceptional – in all kinds of ways.

*

In August, they moved to 125 Airfield, on the sandy spit of Dungeness, sharing the site with another Spitfire unit, No 132 'City of Bombay' Squadron, and a rocket-firing Hurricane Squadron, No 184. The work was just the same – living under canvas, pilots learning to service their own machines 'in the field', interspersed with the inevitable medium bomber escorts. On one of the first, the Americans confirmed everyone's suspicions about their airmanship – and Max proved his mettle.

The Marauders crossed into France at 10,000 feet over Boulogne, in clear skies, with 602 close in on either flank, rocked by a few flak bursts. Their target was Merville airfield, but long before they reached it the ground became obscured by cloud. The Marauder leader started to tack across the sky, evidently completely lost. With a discipline that defies description, his crews started wandering every which way, in smaller and smaller groups, as the flak, and the bomber navigators, directed them all over the sky. Deeper and deeper into France they wandered, while the Spitfires' fuel gauges wound down. One by one, 602's pilots radioed their intention to turn for home.

Max found himself alone; the sole protection to six Marauders which had stayed together and were still heading deep into France. He was only too conscious that at 10,000 feet, just above the white cloud layer, their dark camouflage paint had exactly the opposite effect. Deciding he'd had enough, he dived on the leading bomber, and streaked round right across its nose. The Yank gave him a fairly rude gesture. Max repeated the manoeuvre. He'd just spotted the first gaggle of Focke-Wulfs 5,000 feet up-sun. This time, the bomber leader cottoned on, and turned his idiot charges onto the compass course that was easiest of the lot – due north.

Max swung in behind the bombers, and climbed a little, weaving gently. The sun was at their backs now; so was the threat of the German fighters. He pulled his tinted goggles down, and started the systematic search of the skies, mouth dry, pulse beginning to race. Suddenly, right above the bombers, a red ball of smoke mushroomed. Marker-flak! Somebody was calling in the fighters. Max felt the tightening of the stomach muscles, the watery feeling deep in his bowels.

As they approached Abbeville, he caught the first tiny sparkles of light, reflected on the fringe of the sun's aura. As he wheeled the Spitfire, the sparkles lengthened into long white vapour trails as the Messerschmitts dived. He forced himself to count them. Forty. Jesus!

The 109s careened over the bombers, and four peeled off, streaking in line astern, closing on the Spitfire's tail. Max held them in the mirror, judging his turn to the last split second. As the leading edges of the first 109 flashed, he hooked round viciously to the left, quarter-rolled, and then stood the Spitfire on a wing. Levelling off, he whipped into a reverse turn, and let fly at the third and fourth Messerschmitts. The last one dropped sideways, like a shot partridge. Tracer flashed over the Spitfire's port wing and Max slammed the joystick into the right side of the cockpit. He saw, out of the corner of a sweat-filled eye, four more fighters diving on the Marauder leader.

As the 109 leader levelled off, he was startled by the lone Spitfire, coming straight at him, head-on, like a bat out of hell. At a closing speed of some 750 mph, the fighters rocketed towards each other. At the very last second, it was the German's heart which failed him, and he pulled up, exposing an oil-streaked belly to the Spitfire's guns. In a split second, he collected a couple of shells, and almost knocked the aerial off the Spitfire. Max blinked, and gasped for breath, his throat constricted in a spasm. The Spitfire shuddered in the 109's propwash. The relief was fleeting.

Four Messerschmitts were attacking the bombers from the rear; four more swept in on the port flank in a diving pass. Max threw the protesting Spitfire at the second group, only to find two more on his tail, firing steadily. He half rolled, levelled, skidded to starboard, whipped into a climbing turn, and finally lost them off the top of a loop. Suddenly, a second Spitfire appeared, firing continuously in a slanting dive at four more 109s harrying the tail-end Marauder.

Max was by now surrounded by five Messerschmitts – three on his tail, and two diving on him from up-sun. He fired at one as it approached, and saw strikes right along the fuselage. It spun. He sighted on a second, and blew bits of its tailplane off, just as more shells exploded ahead of the Spitfire's cockpit. He stall-turned, caught the 109 briefly in his sights, and saw his ammunition strike home just aft of the cockpit. The guns wheezed into silence. Max shouted with rage; the tears of frustration running down his cheeks. Saturated with perspiration, shivering violently, he watched the last of the 109s diving for home, thoroughly unnerved. He closed on the other Spitfire – Tommy.

Resuming station above the bombers, he counted them. Still six, one laying a trail of oily smoke across the sky. As they came down to 1,000 feet over the coast of England, Max doubled up and vomited. Completely creased, he came over Hythe Beach. Bathers waved towels cheerfully up at the Spitfires.

Together, they eased down towards home.

*

The autumn went in a succession of bomber escorts, the targets frequently being airfields, where the flak at 10,000 feet was murderous; St Omer, where the gunners raked Wing Commander Bobby Yule's Spitfire – he often led his Wing flying with 602; Amiens-Vendeville, where Beytagh hit a 190 and big Bill Loud sailed right into about a dozen German fighters, emerging safely at the other side, and landing with his gap-toothed grin wider than ever; Courtrai Marshalling Yards, where Max Sutherland's swashbuckling nearly ended prematurely. Throttled back to only 200 mph, the Spitfires went right across the target with the American Marauders. Suddenly, there was a tremendous explosion right underneath Max's machine, and he felt the stick being thrown against his right thigh as the world turned upside down, and then spun into inky blackness. Recovering, he found the Spitfire screaming vertically down, whipping to the right in a vicious spin, and with the airspeed indicator reading 500 mph. Hauling with all his strength on the stick, he blacked out again as the fighter screwed herself out of the dive, and rocketed skywards again. Dodging the chasing streams of tracer, Max weaved out over the coast, and climbed towards the fight which was still going on above. He peered through an oil-flecked windscreen, and was startled by some tracer flashing straight at him. Ducking instinctively, he felt, rather than saw, the Messerschmitt blasting right over him. Recovering, he watched, fascinated, as a Focke-Wulf came right across his sights, with a 602 Spitfire in hot pursuit, only fifty yards behind, and firing continuously. The machine guns sparked on the leading edges, the cannons belched black smoke, and the German fighter, as though in a slow motion film, rolled onto its back, and leaned into a steepening dive. Snatches of garbled R/T chatter filled Max's headphones, then, through it all, came that rich, slow drawl from Pincher Creek, Alberta. 'Ah've hit him. Okay, now let's git just a li'l closer.'

Frank Sorge.

Max watched the Focke-Wulf. Flickers of flame appeared round the cockpit as the dive steepened. The Spitfire closed to only twenty-five yards or so, firing steadily, and raced down the sky, thumping cannon shells into the 190 until it was an inchoate, flaming mass hurtling earthwards. The R/T fell silent, and they all saw the flash as the Focke-Wulf struck.

'Ah've got him, fellas.'

As Max closed on the last of the 190s, he found he wasn't alone. Bruce 'The Bombshell' Dumbrell had appeared from nowhere. Together, they broke up the remaining eight Germans. Back at Newchurch, they didn't even bother to claim any. As The Bombshell pointed out, 'Now, if you want to talk about a real kill, just ask Frank. . .' Actually, Frank was a trifle abashed. In his excitement, he forgot to lower his wheels as he landed. He figured he'd cancelled out his Focke-Wulf.

Next month, they finally got their long-awaited Spitfire IXBs. With its two-stage supercharger, ejector exhausts, slightly altered nose and polished surfaces, it was the most finely balanced Spitfire of the lot. Well over 400 mph straight and level, and a performance at least equal to the latest Focke-Wulfs, meant that in 602's hands it was a devastating machine.

October 8th 1943: RIGHT EAR reported 12 E/A 25 miles west of our position. Nothing was seen of them however, and they were later reported to have turned away to the west, obviously having discovered that 602 had been equipped with IXBs, and a distant glimpse of the 'LION GULES' (sic) must have been sufficient.

A few days later, on an escort mission to a dozen Mitchells bombing Schiphol Airfield at Amsterdam, Sorge repeated his daredevil tactics as they came out over the sea. With the rest of the squadron watching interestedly, he bounced a pair of Messerschmitt 109s, firing all the way down. One went straight into the water; the other, completely unnerved, ran for home. There was a third – piloted by a German who was either crazy, inexperienced, or possibly both. He came in 3,000 feet above the bombers, went down in a dive at full throttle, firing from over a mile away. He missed completely, and rocketed on down to about 2,000 feet above the waves. Calmly, Max led 602 down in line astern, and they took up position 3,000 feet higher. Every time the 109 turned for the coast, the Spitfires circled over his escape route, gradually forcing him lower. By now he was just over the wavetops, turning tightly, his wingtips pulling white trails in the damp sky. Finally, Sutherland dived, and as the Spitfire flicked its wings and angled down, the young Luftwaffe pilot pulled too hard, stalled, and went straight into the sea in an explosion of foam. Not a bullet had been fired. The cynical, amused tones of Robbie Robinson pronounced, 'One Messerschmitt destroyed – one German frightened to death.' And so it actually appeared on their Record Book.

They finally gave Mike Beytagh a DFC. It was about a year too late, and a source of continual wonderment to the pilots that the commander who'd come to be respected, and even loved, by the doughtiest bunch of air fighters ever assembled in the Air Force should be so ignored by a Command which perhaps didn't appreciate his attitude to red tape and pomposity. He was, by now, almost literally past caring himself; on many occasions the boys watched anxiously, nerves stretched to breaking point, as Beytagh flew dead straight through the fiercest flak, nursing scared American bomber crews on the twitchiest of operations. When he left in October, the diary noted, 'His period of leadership has been a happy and successful one, and he has been for over a year not only CO, but a friend and inspiration to every man in the squadron.'

Max became The Boss, and shortly afterwards found himself in Glasgow, where for three days he was fêted, overwhelmed by hospitality from Paddy Dollan, Rolls-Royce workers at Hillington where they made the Merlins, and the parents of Pat Lyall and Glyn Ritchie. With him on the trip were many of the Scottish pilots and ground crew. They were left in no doubt at all of the pride the city took in 'Glasgow's Own'. Sutherland was so moved, that he promised his hosts that he'd do them one very special favour. He'd take the 602 Crest into the centre of Hitler's Berlin, and fly it right up the Wilhelmstrasse.

Before that could happen, there was the little matter of getting into Europe. 602 moved to permanent accommodation over the winter at Detling, near Maidstone, and kept up their constant series of operations over France. Joe Kistruck notched up his century of ops, and kept going. Ken Charney picked up a DFC, command of Sutherland's old Flight, and some rather nasty bits of flesh and bone in his radiators and leading edges coming out of France after escorting some Hurribombers on a low-level attack at Hesdin.

'Ken, the Hurricane leader says you escorted him right into the target, firing all the way at a flak post.'

'Yes, that's about right.'

'Ken, he says you were *below* him on the way in.'

'Oh, really, sir?'

'Don't call me "sir". So what happened, did you hit a flock of birds on the way out?'

'Well, to tell you the truth, I'm not sure whether they were birds or rabbits.'

Hoots of approval in the background – and a shout of 'Get the Line Book!'

Spirits were high – in more ways than one. Wing Commander Yule got permission to change the call-signs. He now became simply 'Bob' – Sutherland was 'Max', and 132's CO, Count Colloredo-Mansfield, was 'Colly'. The two 132 Flights became 'Gin' and 'Lime', instead of 'A' and 'B', and 602 adopted 'Beer' and 'Skittles'. One afternoon over Amiens, the R/T chatter went something like this:

'Hullo, Bob to Max and Colly. Huns coming in from Port quarter. Beer and Skittles attack from starboard. We'll have Gin and Lime to follow.'

'Oh goody.'

'Beer and Skittles going down.'

'Gin going down. . .'

'Lime following. . .'

'Goodness me. What a mixture' – unidentified falsetto voice.

'Oh, I *am* a silly girl' – Canadian falsetto.

'Shut up.' Bob Yule, sounding a bit serious.

'Shan't. I feel giggly.' Probably 'Moose' Manson.

A brief diving pass at twenty or so Me109s, which scatter in confusion. The Spitfires, carried by their momentum, haul up and out of the mêlée.

'Beer coming up. Five o'clock.'

'Gin coming up. Six o'clock.'

'Lime coming up to. . .'

'Oh, dear me. *hic!*' – trailing off into a rather rude noise.

*

There were no spirits higher than those of Les Enfants Terrible –
two irrepressible French subalterns by the names of Jacques
Remlinger and Pierre Clostermann. They'd trained together, and
Remlinger had joined 602 direct. Pierre had gone to the Free
French 341 Squadron at Biggin Hill, where he was fast establishing
a reputation as a daredevil in the air. 'Rem' had teamed up with the
Belgian, Jean Oste, and with Jimmy Kelly, the Englishman who
raged whenever anyone spoke French, and was more or less kept in
check by 602's senior Frenchman, Capitaine Pierre 'White Shirt Or
Else' Aubertin. But when 'Closet' came to 602, the fastidious
Aubertin found his patience sorely tried. Sometimes 'Mon
Capitaine' would go silent, brow furrowed, and anxious pilots
would ask the reason for the trouble.

'Sair, I come from France, where since ten years, I am troubled
wiv jeune subalterns. Since one year I com 'ere. I 'ave no big troubles. I am 'appy. I 'ave ze little troubles, wiv ze Garman, but me I
like zese little troubles. Maintenant, two naughty French subalterns
arrive 'ere. Now, I 'ave ze big troubles.'

Of course, 602 were rather proud of all three. 'Rem' and 'Closet'
kept wearing their outrageous technicolour scarves, trying Aubertin's patience, and generally keeping their end up rather well.
Remlinger went off one day to play rugby for the RAF against the
Army, and emerged the hero of the piece, with two tries. Clostermann, who 'probably knew more about aircraft than any other two
pilots', according to Sutherland, carried all before him on the
romantic scene, looking like Charles Boyer and turning on the
accent with his dazzling smile. And, of course, they did some very
nasty things to the Germans.

So, too, did Jonssen, the big blond Norwegian, who rarely said
much, but who had now made 602 his home. After all, he didn't
have another any more.

These were the men who longed for the day when they'd go into
France. Instead, they found themselves bound for Orkney and
Shetland again, for another 'rest'. It was far from that. Brassed off at
leaving their IXBs behind, and inheriting some very tired old LFVs,
which had clipped wings, and shortened supercharger blades
('Clipped, cropped and clapped', as Tommy Thomerson put it suc-
cinctly), they forsook the air whenever they could for the ground.
Max organised an 'initiative test'. The pilots were blindfolded, told
they had baled out over enemy territory, and had to make their way
into the airfield at Skeabrae and gain entry to the Control Tower.

The Army, the RAF, and the local police would be the opposition. They were deposited at various points by a lorry. Within an hour, the island was in uproar, as 602's pirates ran riot. Sentries found themselves bound and gagged, their loaded rifles stolen; a motor cyclist had his machine taken by 'a young maniac brandishing a revolver'; lorries were hijacked; a couple of 602's scruffiest types raided an officers' mess and made off with about enough food for four days; another pair almost stole a plane. They actually had the engine of the Fleet Air Arm Roc turning when the Navy woke up to what was happening. The best effort was Danny Morgan's.

The stocky New Zealander crashed his 'borrowed' lorry through the barriers at the Main Gate, screeched to a standstill at the foot of the Control Tower, fought his way past three armed guards, and burst into the Flying Control area beaming: 'How's that, sir. Do I win?'

Occasionally, the Germans did come over. Max and The Bombshell were just about to open fire on a daring Ju88 one misty day, when the flak gunners shot it right out of their sights. But they did make one spectacular kill, which drew the newshounds from all over the country.

February 20th 1944: Ian Blair, who'd already won the DFM on Blenheims, sat in the cockpit of the magnificent, shining Spitfire VII. 602 had a pair of them at readiness for high-flying intruders. The VII, known to some as the 'Strato-Spit', was special. With its pointed tailfin, and its extended, elfin-like wingtips, it was designed for the stratosphere. It had a pressurised cabin, and like the earlier Sixes, the canopy had to be bolted down. Across in the other machine, Bennetts moved his gloved hand in a rude gesture.

'Pandor to Dalmat Red One. Bandit approaching Scapa, Angels 35. Vector 090 degrees magnetic'.

The Spitfire shuddered as the supercharged Merlin fired. The two machines were off within a minute, climbing hard to the east. As they went through 30,000 feet, Ian saw the white trail forming, a few thousand feet higher, arrow-straight towards him. Pulse racing, he set the sight, drew the last ounce of power from the thundering Merlin, and felt the long, slender wings lift him higher, higher with every minute.

As the silvery dot grew, he was astonished to see it was a Messerschmitt 109, with long-range tanks under its square wings. Still, he hadn't been seen – or else the pilot of the Messerschmitt reckoned there was nothing that could touch him. He was coming over the islands close to 38,000 feet.

The shape grew in Ian's sight. A 109G, shimmering in the deep blue of the upper air. He glanced at the altimeter. 37,000. Ahead now, the 109 curved round over Scapa Flow, exposing film and eased into a dive, sweeping past Bennetts to port. Ian, numb with cold, slapped his frozen wrist against his thigh, and pushed the Spitfire gently into a turn, closing the angles. The 109 pilot must have got the shock of his life. Suddenly, he saw the Spitfires arcing across the sky, streaming ice trails. He shoved his machine into a much steeper dive.

Ian knew he'd got his man. The thoroughbred Spitfire careened into the dive, accelerating to nearly 500 mph, and relentlessly overhauling the 109. There was no possibility of escape. At that speed, the German pilot couldn't attempt to manoeuvre – he'd rip the wings off.

As they went down through 15,000 feet, Ian's cannons thumped, briefly. Flashes studded the 109, and a wing peeled right off, to flutter down crazily, as the rest of the fighter blew apart. Ian felt the clatter of wreckage on his Spitfire, and then blacked out as he strained against the stick to pull her out. He recovered from the blackout to find himself back up near 20,000 feet. He landed, slightly shaken, on a nearby island, all in one piece.

The combat broke all records, and the newspapers flocked to Skeabrae. Ian became famous all over again – his was the face of the blond fighter pilot who'd already appeared on the 'CARELESS TALK COSTS LIVES' posters. Now, he'd not only won himself the DFC, he'd done something much more important. He'd written himself into The Legend.

Their last week in the north was a mix of tragedy and comedy. Tragedy, when Moose Manson flew to Abbotsinch with Penny in a Dominie. The aircraft hit a hill in Renfrewshire, as they circled in fog, and Moose was terribly burned. At Hairmyres Hospital, they told him he'd never fly again. Moose told them he would. . .

And there was comedy, too:

March 7th 1944: F/O Bruce Oliver had his fair share of fun in these dear old aircraft. He took off to patrol at dawn, and was half way round the circuit when an oil pipe burst. He managed to get down safely before anything else gave way, and took off in another aircraft, noted for its ability to do an automatic roll to the right. This aircraft flew quite successfully for about 40 minutes, but then the dear old lady called it a day – the engine made most disconcerting noises, and then petered out. Luckily, the Isle of Shapinsay was close enough for the pilot to make a perfect forced landing on soft ground from 1,000 feet. Any traces of constipation remaining after the first episode were, by this time, completely eliminated.

Four days later, they went back to their beloved IXBs at Detling.

Kenley, 1942.
Ginger Lacey in doorway, Paddy Finucane (with pipe), Keith Hodson (with tan) . . . the rest
without a seat.

'Pull the other one, boss. . .'
    As Paddy Finucane demonstrates a point, Max Charlesworth has obvious doubts! L-R,
Bocock, Niven, Strudwick, Finucane, Charlesworth, Caterall, Tait, Thorne.

Merlin thundering, control surfaces coming alive, 'P-Popsie' is waved out from her dispersal bay at Ford, for a Ranger mission over France. 27th April 1944.

602 loved their IXbs: 400 mph straight and level, superbly balanced, 20mm Hispano cannon close-ranged, and two-stage superchargers to take them into the Focke-Wulfs in the upper skies. Who could ask more?

(*Left*) 'They winged me . . .'
Nuts Niven survived this cannon strike on the port aileron of X 4603, during the Battle of Britain, 29th October 1940.

(*Right*) 'They winged me too . . .'
Johnny Niven's VB AB 848 LO-F), Nov. 18th 1941.
And they still said the Focke-Wulf 190 was a figment of the imagination. . . .

CHAPTER FOURTEEN

Right up the Wilhelmstrasse

Highlight of Fighter Command's week's work was on Wednesday, when Spitfire bombers led by S/Ldr R.A. 'Max' Sutherland DFC of Orpington, Kent, dived through a storm of flak to score direct hits upon a V2 site erected for safety in the shadow of the 'House in the Woods', a former Royal Palace in The Hague.
National daily paper, quoting Air Ministry release.

June 5th 1944: Evening – special briefing. *The Show* would soon be on, and those who knew were very excited and like cats on hot bricks. The change in the faces was amazing – at last their dreams were coming true, and they were ready.
Extract, 602 Sqn Operations Record.

April 13th. 11.00 hours: 'Okay, open your legs, chaps – I can't hear myself think for the sound of bone knocking against bone.' A ripple of nervous laughter went round the briefing room as Bruce Dumbrell entered, just ahead of The Boss. That morning, each of the thirty-six Spitfires lurking in the camouflaged dispersals at Detling had a 500 pound bomb slung on the shackles under its belly, and as the pilots went to be briefed for the first ever Spitfire dive-bombing mission in Northern Europe, the sweating armourers had called to them, urging them to knock the Huns for six. Most of the pilots were sweating, too, thinking of the murderous flak that they'd dive through. It had been hairy enough the week before at Llanbedr, on the North Wales coast, where 602 and 132 had pioneered the technique of dive-bombing with the nimble IXBs. There was a lot of trial – and a little error, too. 602 had demonstrated their new-found art to the 'top-brass' – and, coming down at over 400 mph, 'The Bombshell' had dropped his bomb right on top of Fox, who only just baled out in time. Then McConachie, the Scot from Armadale, found his bomb hung up. As he shot past at low level to show the watchers his plight, it came free, exploding close to the bigwigs and showering them with mud.

'Look, it's not the flak that worries me, Bruce, so much as where you guys are gonna lay your eggs.' The Aussies of 453 didn't miss a chance. A hush descended as Max entered. Today, he'd lead the Wing; he was the natural choice. Just as 602, on the thirteenth again, would lead the bombing.

'The target, gentlemen, is a No-ball, twelve miles south of Le Tréport. As you know, the Jerries are still putting in these launching ramps faster than the bombers can hit them. Now we're going to show them what Spitfires can do. I will fly with 602, who will bomb first, followed by 132 and then 453. We will attack south to north, coming down with the sun at our backs. We will stay together in the dive, with only forty yards between aircraft. That way, we should saturate the defences. That's the theory, anyway. . . .'

12.55 hours: 'Kenway to Max Leader. Thirty plus bandits at Angels 20 over St Omer.'

'Max Leader to Kenway – Roger. Keep your eyes open, chaps.' He prayed the fighters wouldn't show. If they did, the Spitfires would have to drop their 500 pounders and fight. With Le Tréport two miles ahead, the first dirty black puffs stained the sky, and the Spitfires were tossed by the bursts which quickly found the range. In thirty-six sun-warmed cockpits, the sweat flowed, ice cold, down the spine.

12.59 hours: 'All Max aircraft, target three o'clock below. Max going down in five seconds.'

In the forest, the excavated VI site showed clearly against the darker tones of the woods. Max caressed the controls of the Spitfire to bring his target along the outline of the starboard cannon barrel, under the wing, and as soon as it reappeared behind the trailing edge, just inboard from the aileron, launched the attack.

'Max diving now, *go!*'

Already clocking over 350 mph in its shallow dive, the Spitfire stood on its wingtip and rolled over into a 75° dive, as Max shoved the stick over and forced the throttle wide open. One by one, the others followed – Dumbrell, Oliver, 'Rem' and 'Closet', Aubertin, Jimmy Kelly, Jonssen. . . .

It seemed as though the Spitfire was vertical. Max, hanging from the straps over the gunsight, felt the speed build up, heard the crescendo of noise as the Merlin howled and the slipstream wailed. The ground leapt up to meet him as the aircraft hurled itself madly down.

'Christ, the flak!'

In split seconds, Max sighted on the generator building – as clear as it had been in the recce photographs delivered only yesterday –

he was only vaguely aware that the flak was lighter, but more intense, like long grasping tentacles seeking the Spitfire as she screamed across the sky. A quick glance at the altimeter – Jesus, 2,000 already. Ease the stick back, and just as the target slips down the rings and the black veil descends over the vision, press the tit . . . a lurch, as the bomb went. The blackout came, the stick was shoved right into the stomach and held there, and then came Denny Morgan's voice, 'You've hit it Max – what a beauty!' Easing the stick gently forward, Max found his vision clearing as the Spit rocketed skywards. A long line of flak burst across his path – he slammed over to port, and saw his protégés descending like a waterfall on the VI site, by now obliterated. One by one, they emerged from the smoke and flame, and weaved their way out to the coast. All thirty-six of them.

On the next mission, the Germans were ready. As the Spitfires dived, Bob Yarra of 453 collected a 37mm shell between the radiators. The Spitfire's wings folded, and the whole flaming mass went straight down to blow itself apart right on the launching ramp.

As the build up to the Big Show went on, the Wing moved to Ford, between Littlehampton and Bognor, where they shared the airfield with another nine squadrons. They went back to escorting the Mitchells and Marauders on medium level raids which would see several hundred bombs failing to knock out more 'No-balls'. Max pleaded to be allowed to dive bomb some more. 'No, you've got to escort the bombers,' came the answer. 'Okay', said The Boss, 'then can we escort them with a 500 pounder on each Spitfire too?' The Operations Planning Officer finally gave up. 'Okay, you bloodthirsty blighters. Do your worst.'

So they did.

On 9th May, they hit the Mirville railway viaduct – a vital link on the Le Havre-Paris route, which had so far been comprehensively missed by all the bombers. An official press release, in unusually lurid prose, described how the 'Spitfire squadrons dived through a "wall of flak" to attack the great railway viaduct, of 39 spans. The Spitfires scored direct hits on the centre and at one end. This attack was the highlight of the day's cross-Channel offensive, which again went on from dawn to dusk.'

They were averaging three trips a day. The next day was a bit special, too. Max led them in Group Captain Jamie Rankin's Spitfire, his own being flak damaged – again. At extreme range, they escorted some Marauders all over the skies until they found their targets.

With only forty gallons remaining in each of the Spitfires' tanks over Neufchatel, they began shepherding their charges back towards the coast, when the Focke-Wulfs pounced. As they came down, Max judged the break to perfection; 'Max to Joystick aircraft . . . hold it, hold it . . . *break port. Go!*'

The Spitfires vanished, as one, from the sights of the leading 190s. While Frank Woolley led six Spitfires back over the bombers, Max took Remlinger, Thomerson and Dumbrell into the circling Focke-Wulfs. In a frantic action, they put two down, and possibly a third, but they all heard someone's agonised cry. . .

'Joystick Leader to Blue 1. You okay, Frank?'

'Yes, boss, but I've lost one.'

'Beer 2 okay, sir.'

'Beer 3 okay, sir.'

'Joystick Leader to Beer 4.'

No reply. Bill Frith, the new boy.

The next problem was fuel. Calling a Mayday to Control, requesting a priority straight-in approach to Ford, Max led them carefully down in the most economic glide. As he landed, he found himself sighing with relief. Just as the Spitfire turned off onto the perimeter track, the Merlin coughed, spluttered and ran silent. Two other Glasgow Spitfires stayed where they were after braking. It had been that close.

Two hours later, they slung their 500 pounders at a VI site at Bellevue, and returned in time to make a recording for the BBC of their morning's combat. The reporter wished he'd had his machine running as the pilots jumped down from the Spitfires and made for debriefing –

'Why so glum, Al? I thought that was pretty good.'

Robson was deadpdan. 'Aw, shucks, I'm losing my touch. I could swear I put that bomb two feet too far to the right.'

Moose Manson came back, against all the odds. He'd been unconscious when they carried him, terribly burned, from the wreckage on the Renfrewshire hillside. How he persuaded the civilian doctor to let him back is a mystery. How he persuaded the Scots doctor at Ford to give him a flying category is even more mysterious. But he wasn't going to miss the Big Show. As June broke, they knew it couldn't be far away. On the fourth, they bombed a coastal radar station in Spitfires which had just acquired black and white zebra stripes. The next morning, they packed the briefing room as Jamie Rankin in his clear Inverness accent broke the news.

That night, as they tried to sleep, the skies were filled with the cease-less rumble of the four-engined transports carrying the airborne troops who'd be the first to set foot in France.

They'd moved their beds from the tents to the crew room, where they slept en masse. The Adjutant, Hank Boyle, woke them at 5.30 on the morning of the 6th, and passed round steaming mugs of coffee. The room was silent.

'This is it. It's today, Max. It's on.'

An uproar broke out. Pilots gathered round The Boss, laughing, ribbing each other, firing questions, animated as never before – except for Mon Capitaine. He simply sat there, the tears unashamedly rolling down his cheeks. Just this once, he didn't care who noticed.

*

June 6th. D-Day. 08.15 hours: The Channel shimmered in the morn-ing light as the twelve Spitfires with the Lions Rampant swept in at 3,000 feet over the endless stream of shipping which stretched, like an enormous bridge, right back to the Isle of Wight. Soldiers and sailors waved at their protectors; the Glasgow pilots, keyed up, eased out into battle formation as they approached the coast be-tween Cap de la Heve and the Cherbourg Peninsula. Not a sign of the Luftwaffe, but wherever they looked below, the battle raged. The cruiser *Augusta*, duelling with a heavy shore battery. Four des-troyers, cutting across the bay, wrapped in sheets of red flame as they loosed off salvo after salvo. Astern, the battlewagons, throwing fifteen inch shells twelve miles inland, as clipped-wing Seafires, hovering in pairs, called the falls of shot. And, as they came over the beaches, the hundreds of little ships running in to the shingle, pouring an endless stream of khaki and olive green ashore. Nobody waved here; they ran straight for the cover of dunes, burnt-out tanks or abandoned landing-craft. Still no sight of the Luftwaffe. Max took them inland, towards Caen, and back to Bayeux. Plenty of shellfire, but nothing to fire at.

Back to the beaches. Utah, where the Americans were already moving inland – and Omaha, the code name for a stretch of exposed shingle near Isigny where hundreds of Americans had already died. The bodies drifted slackly in the ebb tide; the beachhead was ceaselessly erupting as the German 88 mm shells rained down. 602, 500 feet above the slaughter, felt the frustration that would stay with them for much of the next two weeks. A flicker of movement caught Max's keen eye – a German truck a couple of miles inland risking a dash along a stretch of road. He raced towards it. He never fired; he didn't need to. The truck driver, seeing the Spitfire jumping the hedgerows, swerved into a wood and died as his vehicle burst into flames.

'Another one scared to death, Boss.'

'Shut up, Robbie.'

'I'm sorry, Boss. I just wish we could do something.'

'I know. Come on, it's time to go home.'

They came out over a destroyer, sinking amid a cluster of little boats taking off the survivors, and returned to Ford, where eager Intelligence Officers took down the details of the American landings. Swopping notes with other pilots, they heard with some relief that the British landings were going well. Above, the transports kept up their endless shuttle service – and then a Stirling appeared, coming down through the cloud base, with an engine out. It was clearly not going any further with its Horsa glider, so the tow rope was cast off, and the glider descended to land, safely, plumb in the middle of the airfield. Within seconds, the soldiers burst forth, machine guns cocked and ready, racing for the buildings and looking decidedly menacing. Only frantic shouts by their pilot – and some pointed gestures from the Spitfire boys – persuaded them they hadn't landed in France!

That day, 602 made three more flights, each one as uneventful as the first, as the invasion forces got the foothold they needed. The Boss flew each one, with his two Flight Commanders, Ken Charney and Frank Woolley. But the pilots worked in shifts. Max proudly wrote in his diary:

> I was able to put a team of twelve pilots into the air with a total number of operational sorties of 2,000, which averaged 166 per man. No other squadron has such experience contained within one unit, and it is unlikely that such an experienced team will ever fly together again in the future.

In the afternoon, they flew over the gliders which littered the landscape in the Cherbourg Peninsula, and kept the Germans' heads down as the Americans moved inland. Four hours later, as they circled over Omaha, some accurate flak brought rather sour R/T exchanges. And as twilight fell, they were back again over villages that burned, and dour French farmers who walked their terrified cattle home under the shells that tore the misty air.

As the Spitfires rolled to a standstill in darkness at Ford, Max gratefully accepted a lighted cigarette from his fitter, 'Harpy', and answered the eager questions of Dave, his rigger. Then, completely creased, he headed straight for his bed. The others dragged themselves in, and Hank Boyle, thoughtful as ever, appeared as if by magic in the doorway. Taking in the litter of discarded Mae Wests, flying boots, gloves and helmets, he said quietly, 'Don't worry about that. Just leave everything on the floor, I'll put it away later.' He stepped aside, and the orderly walked in, with steaming mugs of cocoa and biscuits. Quietly and quickly, 'Spy' got the intelligence information he needed, and slipped away. Hank started to arrange their gear.

'Bring my shaving water at dawn, Jeeves, there's a good chap.'

'Turn the toes of my socks in, would you, Claude?'

The banter was light, but the gratitude was in the eyes. They'd all seen him out on the apron, anxiously counting them back in after every operation. As the exhausted pilots fell asleep, he went round each one, placing the boots by the bed, and the Mae West under the pillow. He wiped the goggles carefully, and hung them over the boots.

'Goodnight Max – and good hunting tomorrow.'

But The Boss was deeply, dreamlessly asleep.

The next day, they flew four more – on the second flight, as they came back over the beachhead at Omaha, Jenkins shouted his warning of 'Look out, tracer!' Max felt the vibration as the Spitfire took hits around the tail; as they all climbed, they saw 'The Kid' going down trailing oil. He crash-landed right on the beach in a cloud of sand, radioed he was all right, and then poked his head cautiously out of the cockpit, to find himself in the middle of some sharp crossfire. Leaping out, he ducked and ran for some dunes, caught sight of US Marines in the grass, and crawled over to them. Meanwhile the squadron had posted Pilot Officer L.D. Kidd as 'Missing – believed safe'. He was, but only just.

Three days later, Fox, with uncanny instinct, found the same trigger-happy American gunner, and put his Spitfire down in exactly the same place. He was astonished to see The Kid's plane lying in a corner of the field, now a landing ground. What's more, he beat

The Kid back to Ford. While Kidd found himself stuck among red tape, Fox hitched a lift right back to Portsmouth.

They should have been among the first Spitfires to operate from France, but the Advance Landing Ground programme was bogged down around Caen and Bayeux, as the Allied forces met fierce resistance. Every day, 602 came over, shooting up anything that moved, and pleading for the Germans to put some aircraft up. Les Enfants Terribles got thoroughly fed up waiting, and decided to search out the Luftwaffe. Peeling off from a squadron sweep, 'Rem' and 'Closet', in loose formation, eyed the scene from 15,000 feet over Lisieux, taking in the great German airfields – Saint-André, Dreux, Beaumont-le-Roger. Nothing moved. Coming down in a wide orbit, Clostermann suddenly saw the outline of a pair of bombers under nets. 'Hullo, Jacques, look, two Heinkels down below.'

'Okay, Pierre, they're lovely.'

Together, the Spitfires went down, accelerating to fighting speed, guns and sights on, the pilots feeling their pulses quicken. They levelled out at zero feet, three miles from Dreux, and raced in over the hedges, blasting across the perimeter as a Messerschmitt 109G lifted off. Clostermann, striking panic into the hearts of the Germans on the ground, threw the Spitfire into a sharp bank, and rocketed round the edge of the field, taking in the details; twenty 190s warming up . . . another rank of fighters under the trees . . . a pilot leaping off a wing and diving for cover. The Spitfire, lean, grey, and deadly, flicked a wing up, drew thin white trails from her tips, and flattened out at only twenty feet, closing on the unfortunate 109. The cannons thumped, the black smoke whipped back over the wing, and the Messerschmitt stall turned, spinning straight in.

Over on the other side, Jacques leapfrogged a 109 as it landed, and blew a couple of minelaying Heinkels apart. At over 420 mph, the Spitfires jumped the boundary hedge, and raced for the clouds, emerging unscathed at 10,000 feet as the flak came up in all directions.

Back at Ford, The Boss, completely deadpan, tore them off a strip for their buccaneering. The next day, they knew all was forgiven. After the third patrol, over Caen, 602 were due to land in France for the first time, for a single night. As they approached the strip cut out of a wheat field near Bazenville, Max called them; 'Joystick Leader to Yellow 3 and 4, and Blue 3. You pancake first.'

Mon Capitaine, followed by 'Rem' and 'Closet', were first to land on French soil. They'd all put on their best blues.

Two minutes later, they wished they hadn't. The fine golden dust that was to clog nostrils, air filters and radiators for the next few months, billowed up in clouds as the Spitfires rolled in. In seconds, the pilots were more like flour factory workers.

As The Boss climbed out, he noticed his mechanic wearing the African Star. 'Home from home, eh?'

An even white grin appeared in the dust covered face, and the erk pushed up his goggles to leave two white circles. 'Bloody sight worse than anything Monty got me into – sir.'

'I suppose you know he's over here now, somewhere about Caen?'

'Is that right? Well, I wish he'd left the bloody desert back in Africa.'

On the 25th, they packed the Spitfires with every little item of personal kit they could squeeze in, and moved permanently to Normandy; as soon as they landed at Longues, the pilots leapt out and ran to the marquee, where the ground crews had the ceremony prepared. The Boss tugged at the string, and Mac McConachie hauled on the rope, as the Crossed Lion ran up the flagpole.

They'd already made their mark. A couple of days earlier, four of them – Ken Charney, Tim Burke the South African, Robbie Robinson and Mac – had taken on forty Focke-Wulfs right over the heads of the army. An appreciative audience cheered as Ken shot the tail right off one, Robbie and Tim nailed one apiece, while Mac, guarding their tails against the other thirty-seven, whipped round and snapped at another, which spun down out of sight. Robbie's and Tim's crashed close together, right on the banks of the Caen Canal – and Tim skidded across to hit a Messerschmitt which appeared over the scene. It fell away, billowing black smoke. The German fighter leader, with the odds in his favour now reduced from 10 to 1 to a mere 9 to 1, decided that discretion was the better part of valour. He gathered his charges, and made off to the south-east; the troops below were treated to the sight of thirty-five German fighters running for cover, hotly pursued by 602's four Spitfires, cannons and machine guns barking, to return a couple of minutes later and execute five victory rolls. Back at the airfield, Max wrote out a citation for the immediate award of a Bar to the tattered DFC ribbon Charney had earned in the angry skies over Malta.

*

Their first 'real' night in France was not so much an eye-opener as an eye-waterer. Mon Capitaine, anxious to be as hospitable as possible, vanished in the direction of Bayeux, to return a couple of hours later with several bottles of Calvados. Beaming in the light of the storm lantern in the tent, he withdrew the corks, and passed them round. He didn't bother to advise anyone to sip the fiery liquid carefully. Seconds later, the tent was nearly whipped from its pegs by a fusillade of coughs, which nearly drowned the noise of the gunfire around Caen. They slept soundly.

Clostermann celebrated his return by shooting down two German fighters right over their heads the next day, and added two more during the week. But mainly they concentrated on ground attack work, constantly patrolling the country lanes, shooting at anything military that didn't carry the large white star. Charney, Oliver, McConachie and Chalice became the experts – Bruce Oliver was particularly ruthless. One day, he fired at a Staff car until it burned and blew up. Twenty minutes later, spotting another near Essay, he hit it so hard it somersaulted twice. Three Germans crawled out of the wreckage – and Bruce went back and killed them where they lay. They were, by now, fighting a different war – a war where you saw the carnage, felt the pain of a nation recovering from the march of the jackboot, and found you'd become a murderer. In the tents at night, while the guns rumbled in the distance, the cigarette smoke formed a dense haze round the paraffin lamp, and the taste of the last gritty cup of tea was bitter in the mouth. Moose Manson planned his revenge for the fires that had almost consumed him once before; but the fires got him in the end, as his Spitfire entered a murderous cone of tracer and blew up in a sheet of flame. Jimmy Kelly poured out his hopes, his fears, and his plans for peace into the small hours, lying beside The Boss; four days later, he was gone. The Frenchmen would lie awake and wonder at the sullen, unco-operative attitude of their countrymen, the peasant farmers who just saw their livelihood threatened whoever was using their fields.

By day, the sights grew ever more terrible. Cows, lying dead and obscenely bloated in their hundreds . . . burnt out tanks with the flies and the carrion crows circling them in swarms . . . and grey-clad Germans scattered among the fields and hedgerows, sightless eyes staring at the skies where the Spitfires flew.

They finally grounded The Boss. After he'd slept continuously for nearly forty hours, John Lapsley broke the news gently.

'Max, you know, and I know, and all the boys know that you completed your tour months ago. You're only allowed 200 hours. How many do you have now?'

'Truthfully?'

'Yeah. This time.'

'Three hundred and sixty.'

'How many actual operations?'

'Two hundred and five.'

'Right. I order you to cease operations as of now. Consider it a well-deserved rest. That way, maybe the boys won't have to break the news you know Anna could never bear to hear. Come to my caravan tonight and we'll split a bottle.' Tactfully, he left, as Max found the tension snapping, his limbs trembling, and the tears flowing hot on his dusty cheeks.

During his last week in command, the boys went wild. The Frenchmen shot down three fighters, Ken Charney, who took over command in the air, got two more before they gave him command of 132 Squadron. Bob Stewart opened his 602 score sheet, and Jonssen got another pair, the DFC, and command of 'A' Flight.

When Max went back to Britain, so too did Frank Woolley, and Pierre Clostermann, who'd been presented with his first DFC in the field.

The new CO was everything they could have wished for – Squadron Leader J.J. 'Chris' Le Roux, from Patchetstroom in the Transvaal. A veteran of the early fighting in France, a Hurricane pilot in the Battle of Britain, a Flight Commander on 91 Squadron during the days of the Circuses, he'd then commanded 111 Squadron in Algeria and Tunisia, earning three DFCs by the time he took over 602. Within a week of his arrival, he'd added two Focke-Wulfs and three 109s to his tally, and pulled off one of the biggest coups of the Normandy campaign – though nobody realised it at the time. The date was 17th July, 1944. It was a red-letter day even by 602's standards. In furious fighting on a day when the Germans did decide to mix it for once, Le Roux claimed a Messerschmitt 109 definitely destroyed and another damaged, while Jonssen downed another two, before breakfast. They were still in their pyjamas. On the second flight of the day, Tim Burke, Danny Morgan and Bruce Oliver all scored kills, and Le Roux repeated his double. But it was in the late afternoon that they struck the killer blow.

15.40 hours: Feldmarschall Erwin Rommel, the 'Desert Fox', and now commander of the German forces in Normandy, concluded his visit to the HQ of the 1st SS Panzer Corps, where he had been discussing the situation with the SS Commander, Sepp Dietrich. About to drive back to his headquarters at La Roche-Guyon, Dietrich advised him to change his big staff car for a more manoeuvrable VW jeep. The fighter-bombers had been hitting everything in sight. Rommel, smiling, refused the offer. He directed his driver, Daniel, to stick to the side roads.

Approaching Vimoutiers, they had to turn back onto the main road. A couple of seconds later, Sergeant Holke called out, 'Look out, fighter bombers. Behind!'

'Try to make the village', Rommel rapped out. Daniel trod on the accelerator, and the car sped round the curve. But they were too late. Racing along the road from Livarot, less than 100 feet up, Le Roux saw the staff car, called in his section, and lined up his sights.

They felt the 20 mm shells ripping into the car, slicing through the upholstery and exploding through the left side of the vehicle as Daniel swerved in vain. He was hit in the shoulder, and slumped over the wheel. The car lurched to the right, and thumped into a tree, spinning back and coming to rest right across the road. Rommel, who'd struck his head hard on the windscreen, and was bleeding heavily, was thrown out. He hit the road, and fractured his skull.

Above, Le Roux saw it all as the flickering images of a slow motion film – the strikes, the car swerving, spinning, and the figure in grey flung like a rag doll across the road. He'd never know it, but he'd just written another page of The Legend. The hero of Africa, the general of Normandy, was never to return. Dragged off the road by other officers braving the Spitfires' guns, he was taken to hospital, and then put under close arrest when, days later, the Bomb Plot nearly killed Hitler.

*

Throughout the weeks of bitter fighting in Normandy, The Boss kept a paternal – and frequently operational – eye on 602. Max managed to get himself posted as a Forward Air Controller, which meant that he would run right up to the front lines in a Sherman tank, and call in the rocket-firing Typhoons and cannon-firing Spitfires by radio, directing their strikes as German shells burst all around the Sherman. On many occasions, 602 found him within 100 yards of the target as they came over low and fast, cannons thumping.

Max went into Vire with the 11th Armoured Division – shortly afterwards, 602, leapfrogging the other advanced landing grounds, moved in to a forward airstrip there, and carried on the slaughter. On the last day of July, they'd blown apart a dozen transports, together with escort, right on the front line, and HQ 2nd Army Group had signalled 'Congratulations. We had a grandstand view of your sharpshooting'. But it wasn't a war they enjoyed any more.

August was a bitter month.

It started with the loss of Jonssen, the Norwegian, shot down and killed while strafing a troop convoy. Bruce Oliver took over 'A' Flight. They settled into Vire, making it as comfortable as possible. They built their own pub, the 'Getsum Inn' constructed by the air-craftsmen and decorated rather luridly by Flight Lieutenant 'Fear-less' Pullman and Flight Sergeant Francis – who was noted for his 'wizard blondes', most of whom seemed to wear nothing but a smile. Stocking it was no problem. Spitfires would occasionally appear over the Channel with beer kegs on the bomb shackles; this was, of course, officially frowned on, but 602 found the answer. Long-range fuel tanks, suitably washed out, and refilled. One day, Thomas, the South African, appeared overhead in a Spit which was lurching all over the sky, as he lined up on his approach. Amid cheers, he finally got it down more or less in one piece.

'Wotcher, Dave. I don't suppose you switched to the wrong tank just then? She wasn't flying too straight.'

Thomas wore a beatific smile. 'Nope. Shpitfire handlesh great.'

'Have you been drinking?'

'Nope. Jusht checking the tanksh.'

A series of night recces around the airfield produced the rest of the stock – wine, and Calvados, to which they'd now taken a distinct liking. The pub was frequented by most of the squadron – and they needed something to take their minds off the sights, and smells, of the days.

It had been Ken Charney's voice which had first been heard on the radio with news of the Germans' breakout from the Falaise pocket towards the Seine. The Boss and his colleagues had called in the Tif-fies and blocked the bottleneck with burning tanks and transports.

Now the terrible slaughter began, as thousands of German soldiers were massacred day by day. Infantry brigades were strafed mercilessly as they attempted escape; even at 10,000 feet as they circled the killing ground like hawks, before pouncing on the first flicker of movement, the 602 men found themselves retching with the stench that drifted up from the rotting flesh of men, horses, and cattle torn by the cannon shells.

Thomas got himself shot down by an American Mustang – he radioed he was all right, but he came down behind the German front line. With the fighter bombers taking such a terrible toll, they worried about his chances of survival when the Germans picked him up.

On the 29th, Chris Le Roux disappeared. In foul weather, he set off on his second attempt to cross the English Channel. Nothing more was seen or heard of his Spitfire. With Bob Stewart temporarily in command, they carried on their low-level war against German machinery. Sickened with the slaughter in Falaise, they were now specialising in the destruction of transports, armoured cars, tanks, and self-propelled guns. They found the few chinks in the armour of even the formidable Tiger tanks, and by the end of the month held the record for the total number of 'flamers' in the 2nd Tactical Air Force. It wasn't a record they were particularly proud of.

On 17th September, as the disastrous Arnhem operation was launched, they moved into Belgium, the first squadron into Antwerp Municipal Airport. It was one of the strangest periods of the entire war for Bert Simpson and the rest of the ground staff. As they frantically worked to re-arm and service the Spitfires, flying up to seven missions daily, the German Storchs would hover over the airfield, spotting for the artillery which rained shells down on them. But when they went off duty, they would step out of the airfield and out of the war, boarding trams to take them into the city, where one of the sights was at the local zoo. Here a number of cages were occupied by citizens who had collaborated with the Germans. Now, they were treated – literally – like animals.

In the air, the pilots once again found themselves the witnesses of terrible slaughter, this time of the Allied airborne troops who'd landed in Arnhem. As The Boss worked his Sherman up the road to the Nijmegen Bridge, 602 shot the Germans out of the sky overhead, and the woods on either side, but the advancing armour couldn't break through. Sutherland, having pleaded in vain to be allowed to take some radios and relief equipment across the river to the beleaguered troops under cover of darkness, finally signalled 'Job finished. Tired of my rest from operations. Requesting posting to operational fighter squadron for a proper rest.'

They gave him back 602 Squadron. When he landed at Antwerp, there were only a few of the old faces left. Bruce Oliver, now sporting a DFC and a nervous twitch whenever he spoke; Robbie Robinson, debonair as ever, but now with a slight stammer; Mac, saying less than he used to; and Bob Stewart, who'd led them during the last few weeks, during which time he'd been hit by flak no less than nine times, the last time baling out in the nick of time at low level. That night, there was a party to beat them all. It wasn't until quite late the following day that Sutherland, starting his fifth operational tour, led them into the air, and back to Norfolk. There was one final battle to win – against the V2s.

*

Hitler's last – and potentially most threatening – secret weapon, the giant V2 rocket, was the first true intercontinental ballistic missile. Launched from sites around The Hague ('Big Ben' targets to the Spitfires), it rose to over 50,000 feet, before angling down on London and the airfields of Norfolk. Travelling faster than sound, it arrived ahead of any warning. 602, now based at Coltishall where they shared the airfield with 603, among others, at first found themselves flying escort missions to Liberators packed with black boxes designed to jam the V2s' guidance systems. They didn't.

Predictably, it was The Boss who came up with the answer. They'd dive-bombed the V1 sites – why not the V2 ones as well? 'There's just one problem, Sutherland. The sites are rather close to civilian installations. And they're pretty heavily fortified with concrete.'

Max discovered that the Spitfire XVI – basically a Mark IX with a Packard-built Merlin – had permanent bomb shackles under the wings, and had been stressed to take heavier loads. Having found his aircraft, he made sure 602 got the first batch available. They could sling 1,000 pounders under the fuselage, and a pair of 250 pounders under the wings. He already had the men he needed. Bob Stewart and Bruce Oliver went on well-earned rests, and the Flights were taken over by Dickie Pertwee and Scottie Waterhouse, who'd both won their spurs in the Middle East. Both could have commanded their own squadrons, but they jumped at the chance to fly with 602.

Raymond Baxter had joined them in Normandy. Looking like a swashbuckling buccaneer from the eighteenth century, he didn't say much about his experiences in the Mediterranean, but he'd flown Spitfires almost continuously since the middle of 1941; 'Bax' was as charming – and as professional – as they came. Then there was 'Steve' Stephenson, who'd actually broken his neck in a crash while training in the USA. After nearly recovering, he'd persuaded the medics to give him a flying category. Learning that they wouldn't let him fly on operations, he launched an intensive campaign, giving everyone around him such a hard time that they got rid of him – first to Britain, then to an OTU, and finally to 602. Now he was happy.

Tommy Love was a diminutive pilot from Rutherglen. In his youth, he'd read about the City of Glasgow Squadron – now, he'd realised his dearest ambition. 'Cupid' was popular on the squadron – particularly when he terrified the living daylights out of Controllers on foreign airfields as 602 came in to land. He'd drop right down out of sight, with the hood back and the hatch open, sighting along the side of the Spitfire's nose; the controllers would see only a Spitfire with an empty cockpit lurching around the circuit, looking for all the world as though the pilot had baled out.

And there was the Pole, Wroblewsky ('Double Whisky'). He'd been a music and singing teacher in Warsaw. When the city fell, he swore he'd never sing again until it was free. If ever 602 had faced a challenge, this was it. They had to get him completely plastered, of course, but by the time they left The Globe on the Yarmouth Road one night, the Fens had echoed to the most unbelievable rendering of 'I Belong To Glasgow', in a thick Polish accent.

Before the XVIs appeared, they flew interdiction missions throughout the Low Countries, hitting anything that could transport V2 materials, running the gauntlet of the flak every day, returning to the security of their red-brick mess in the evening, after which the faithful Rhona, their tiny WAAF driver, would take them round to their 'targets for tonight'. She looked after them like a hen with a bunch of troublesome chicks, never once failing to collect the whole brood and deliver them back to the nest.

In November, the new Spitties came, and Max worked them hard on the ranges until they could throw their bombs within ten yards of the target every time. Now, along with the Aussies of 453, they were ready.

'Wish you were here!'
602 in Normandy, July 1944

Armourers giving one of 'B' Flight's battle-scarred Spitfire XVIs a double punch. Note the long-range slipper tank under the belly. The Lion Rampant crest can just be distinguished through the oil streaking the cowling, above the cannon fairing. This pair of bombs were unloaded onto a V2 site in The Hague. Ludham, Norfolk, February 1945.

The last of the real fighters
Al Bowman in Spitfire F22 PK 395, October 1950.

Fast Lady
Vampire FB 5 at Renfrew, 1954. Note 602 crest on nose – and Grey Douglas flashes
beside roundel.

December 1st 1944. 11.45 hours: 602 took off on the first of the 'Big Ben' dive bombing attacks. Sutherland led them across the North Sea at 10,000 feet, with the Australians a mile behind. Approaching The Hague, the bomb switches went to 'on'; as they crossed the coast, the flak started, finding the range almost instantly. Max called, 'Attacking – *go! Go!*', stood the Spitfire on her wingtip, and went vertically down. White bursts of flak streaked past. Suddenly, there was an almighty explosion, and the rest of the squadron were horrified to see The Boss's plane disappear in a sheet of flame. The next thing they saw was his bomb – exploding square on the V2 site in the corner of the Hague-Bosche park, right beside the former Royal Palace.

Miraculously, Max saw the flame shooting up, felt the jolt as the shell struck his overload fuel tank under the belly of the Spitfire – and blew it clean off. Hurtling earthwards at 480 mph, hanging on the straps, he just had time to correct his aim and pull the bomb off before he hauled back, blacked out, and recovered to find himself shaking like a leaf.

The Palace was untouched.

In the weeks leading up to Christmas, they perfected their technique, knocking out site after site, and occasionally going further afield. On the 11th, six of them made the newspapers again, with what Sutherland himself described as 'The finest piece of dive bombing I've ever seen'.

December 11th 1944: CO and five others dive-bombed Statspoor Station in the Dutch capital with 250 pound bombs. This was a filling point for the lorries carrying liquid oxygen to the rocket sites. 10/10 cloud over the target. CO dived the squadron from 10,000 feet to 4,000 feet through a hole, North to South, then aileron turned in the dive, and dropped bombs North-West to South-East. Four bombs on East end of station, four in the centre, and two on the railway further east.

Extract, 602 Sqn Operations Record

The measure of their success was simple. After they started dive-bombing in the XVIs, the number of V2s arriving in Britain diminished. When bad weather intervened, the strikes increased again.

In the New Year, they kept it up. Big Ben attacks, escorting Beaufighters on shipping strikes off Den Helder, interdiction sorties against the transport systems which still survived, medium cover to the massed formations of Lancasters and Halifaxes which roamed free over Germany. As often as not, 602 would work a 'shuttle service', staging the Spitfires in and out of Dutch or Belgian airfields.

They entered the last phase in the middle of February. On the 14th, two trips – on the first, they dived from 10,000 feet to 2,000 feet over the Hague-Bosche and smacked a V2 site; landing at Ursel, they 'bombed-up', returned to The Hague and bombed and strafed the Hotel Promenade. Max went into the Line Book afterwards: 'Well, I couldn't decide what I was most frightened of – the flak bursts or my own cannon shells chasing me as they ricocheted off the hotel roof!'

On one of the V2 strikes, Cupid Love followed Baxter down, lobbed his bomb at the target, and screamed round to deliver a low-level cannon attack, as a diversion while the rest of the Spitfires dived. As he came back towards the target, there was a great gout of flame and smoke, and the monster rocket slowly rose up, belching fire. They'd attacked right in the middle of the countdown sequence. Instinctively, Cupid kicked the rudder bar, sighted, and let fly with his cannons; surely the first attempt to shoot down a ballistic missile in flight. Fortunately, he missed the warhead, otherwise he might have taken out half a dozen Spitfires too.

Then they were briefed for the trip to end them all.

March 18th 1945: 'This, gentlemen, is the Bataasher-Mex office building in The Hague. It houses V2 research scientists, laboratories, and German workers. While 453 create a diversion by dive-bombing the Big Ben on the racecourse, six aircraft of 602, in tight line abreast formation, will skip-bomb the Mex building. There must be no slip-ups. There is a church to the south-east – here – just thirty yards away, and on the other side Dutch civilian houses. It will be necessary to drop down over the wall into the garden, and release the bombs from window height. The bombs will be fitted with 11½ second delay fuses. I won't attempt to minimise the risks. There are estimated to be 200 plus light flak guns on the target approach. Good luck.'

Sutherland's 'Chosen Few' were Dickie Pertwee, 'Fearless' Pullman, Raymond Baxter, Flight Sergeant Zuber, and Steve Stephenson, who forced a wry smile when someone whispered, 'Looks like you're really sticking your neck out again, Steve.'

Not a word was spoken as they crossed the North Sea at low level. Five miles from the coast, they dropped right down on the water, and glanced up to where Ernest Esau's Australians were riding the flak bursts, at 8,000 feet.

They flashed across the beach at 350 mph, pulling up over the promenade house-tops as people flung themselves flat on the road-ways. As the streams of tracer criss-crossed their flight path, Max glanced out to check his position, swerved to miss a chimney, and Esau's voice came over – 'Dive bombing now, Max. Good luck.'

The Spitfire shook as tracer rattled on the wing, glancing off horizontally. Max prayed he'd get to the target before something vital was hit. The six Spitfires were now racing across The Hague, less than twenty feet apart, rocking in the flak bursts, vanishing behind taller buildings to reappear split seconds later; 'Target dead ahead 400 yards. Open fire.'

The cannons flashed, and the white face of the west wall of the office building was starred by the twinkling flashes. Windows dis-solved in showers of glass. Down below, people ducked as the hot shell cases cascaded from the Spitfires' wings. To the left of The Boss, Zuber's plane took two direct hits, and staggered drunkenly, dropping a wing to within inches of a roof. A crashing impact on the tail sent Sutherland himself skidding to the right, straight for Dickie Pertwee's Spitfire. Dickie lifted a wing obligingly, Max caught the Spitfire, and straightened.

Over the wall, they dropped fractionally, had a fleeting impres-sion of figures diving for cover behind the shattered windows – and of one man hurling himself out of a second storey window. Max held his sight under the roof line until the last possible moment.

'Bomb! *Bomb!* Go!'

As one, the Spitties leaped, freed of their loads, and rocketed over the roof. Max, fighting his shattered elevator controls, scraped over with inches to spare, his feet braced for the impact.

As the others raced past, he felt the Spitfire rising to 3,000 feet, sluggish on the controls. Cr-u-u-mp! Another hit on the tail. He glanced back, as the target disappeared in a cloud of smoke, flame, and red brick dust. They'd got it – the perfect strike. The church, and the tenements, were completely unscathed.

In seconds, they were beyond the flak, and as Max carefully climbed out between Rotterdam and The Hook, the other five cir-cled back.

'You all right, Boss?' Dickie Pertwee called.

'You'd better come and tell me – I haven't a clue.'

Bax came over, and slid his Spitfire beneath the tail of Max's.

'Your rudder is just a hole, Boss. The starboard elevator's like a colander. It's ripped to pieces,' he said quietly.

'Okay. Give me plenty of room in case I have to get out in a hurry.'

Twenty minutes later, as the others circled watchfully, The Boss, with infinite care, set the wounded Spitfire down gently at Ursel. As the Merlin died, the mechanic who'd come running over stopped in his tracks, staring at the tail.

'Blimey,' he breathed.

*

On 8th May, peace came to Europe, and celebrations to Coltishall. But in the middle of the release of tension, they gathered for a service. Under grey skies, pilots and ground crews bowed their heads and not a few felt the tears hot on their cheeks as they remembered the men who'd taken off in their Spitfires never to return.

'. . . at the going down of the sun, and in the morning, we will remember them. . . .'

The chaplain read from Pilgrim's Progress –

So when the battle was over, Christian said, I will here give thanks to Him that hath delivered me out of the mouth of the lion, to Him that did help me against Apollyon. Then there came to him a hand, with some of the leaves of the tree of life, which Christian took and applied to the wounds that he had received in battle and was healed immediately.

A week later, Max took command of a fighter Wing, and the City of Glasgow Squadron was disbanded.

*

The skies over Berlin filled with the sound of Merlins once again, as the Mustangs came over the city, escorting Winston Churchill's aircraft into Gatow Airport, prior to the Potsdam Conference.

As Berliners and Allied servicemen alike gazed up at the perfect formation, shimmering in the summer sky, there was a tiny flash struck from perspex as the Mustang leader peeled off from the formation, accelerating in a dive towards the heart of the city. As the fighter came down the sky, hearts on the ground started to race; but the Mustang didn't fire. Levelling off at only fifty feet, it swung round easily, and, arrow straight, went straight down the centre of the Wilhelmstrasse. The watchers, fascinated, saw the freshly painted Lion Rampant superimposed on the Cross gleaming on the polished cowling, as the fighter made them duck, and the Merlin's song echoed triumphantly round the grey stone walls.

The Boss was keeping his promise.

Epilogue

Saturday 22nd October 1983.

She sat there, silently brooding, her nose haughtily lifted towards the Eastern skies, her beautiful symmetry framed by the amber October sunlight, as the inevitable crowd gathered. Youngsters with their text-book enthusiasm eagerly checked the details . . . the bulges shrouding the late-model Merlin, the angle of the armoured glass, the clipped wings; 'I'm telling you, it's an LFXVIe, Billy'. Fathers and grandfathers smiled at the kids, and fell silent as their eyes were drawn back once again to the symbol of Britain's fight for freedom. And a few – a very few – strolled right up to her, as they had done forty years before, sharing a secret, intimate thrill as they touched the grey aluminium.

She too was a survivor. She was TB382, and though she bore different letters now, she had once proudly carried LO-Z on her slim fuselage, and the Lion Rampant on her cowling. 'Bax' had taken her screaming down the tracer-streaked skies over the Hague-Bosche and survived; Cupid Love had dived her right down to deck level over a railway bridge and flown through the brick dust as Jock Campbell's bomb went off; once, she'd even found herself under a tumbling 250 pounder as it soared over her starboard wing during a skip-bombing attack near Delft. She was a survivor all right.

She'd been honourably retired, and for many years guarded the gate at RAF Middleton St George – where the station CO, Sandy Johnstone, often gazed at her with affection. Now, she travelled the country, manhandled onto trucks, her wings whipped off and stuck on by unfeeling hands, wherever the Air Force was mounting a recruiting drive or commemorating a bit of history. On this October day, though, she'd finally come home to Glasgow. She stood outside the Rolls-Royce complex at Hillington, where once the Merlins had streamed off the production lines. The hour approached, and her admirers, a little reluctantly, left her, filed through the gate, and took their places beside a newly-erected hut.

Promptly at 14.15 hours, the three Phantoms of 43 Squadron boomed overhead, tearing the skies with the thunder of their passing, afterburners cutting fiery diamonds in their wake. The Fighting Cocks' salute to their comrades of 1940 at Tangmere.

Down below, the thirty three cadets of No 2175 (Rolls-Royce) Squadron, ATC, stood ramrod-straight, as their Commanding Officer, Bill McConnell, exchanged salutes with the Top Brass. Over the last eighteen months, the boys had been working like beavers on this project. It all started when they'd been presented with two panels from the Heinkel 111 which had been Archie McKellar's first victim; 'What about building a museum for the City of Glasgow Squadron?'

'Great idea. Who can we contact?'

They'd launched their search, through newspapers, magazines, radio, and the old boys' network. The foundations had been laid on the 19th July 1982. Now, at last, the work was done, and the squadron had come back to Glasgow. They were all there: Sandy Johnstone, full of praise for the boys' endeavours; George Pinkerton, recalling in clipped tones the story of that first kill; Hector Maclean, still limping on his tin leg and still smiling as he talked about it to an eager young reporter; Donald Jack and Dunlop Urie, who'd both dropped rank a year after the war ended to help 602 re-form, as Flight Commanders; Marcus Robinson who returned to command it, and who made sure they were the first to fly again in the post-war era, and Nuts Niven, who'd been invalided out with tuberculosis, but who had jumped at the chance to be part of 602 Squadron when Robinson offered him the role of civilian clerk.

In the years of peace, he'd seen the old faces gradually disappear, as newer and younger pilots became part of The Legend: Harbourne Stephen, who took over from Robinson, and who'd picked up a DSO, two DFCs, and nearly as many kills as Boyd; Jack Forrest, who'd flown rocket-firing Typhoons under 602's covering Spitfires; Alec Bowman, as hard and professional a fighter as any, with operations on 154 Squadron Spitfires and 234 Squadron Mustangs in his logbook; Jim Johnston, who'd picked up a DFC flying Mosquitos; Archie Robinson who won his on Pathfinders; he re-organised the pipe band.

For five years, Spitfires had once again flown from Abbotsinch and Renfrew – clipped-wing Mark XIVs, high-tailed, handsome F21s, and finally the F22s, with their un-Spitfire wings, huge tails absorbing the twisting airstream flung back from the five bladers, and jet-like bubble canopies.

In 1951, the jets came. A pair of Meteor trainers, and a clutch of neat little Vampires, adorned with the Grey Douglas flashes beside the roundels. The new generation added a few more laurels; Stuart Robinson, not only gliding his engineless Vampire fully 70 miles down the North Sea from 40,000 feet to a perfect landing at Leuchars, but guiding his Number Two – Jack Daly – all the way down with hand signals, following Daly's radio failure. They picked up the Cooper Trophy, and received the award of a Squadron Standard.

They nearly went to war again, too. With the Korean situation rapidly developing, and Sabre jets being shipped out from Glasgow, 602, along with 603 and 612, were called up, and went off to Leuchars for three months, in Vampires which rapidly acquired camouflage, and flying hours, as the Scottish Wing, under Group Captain Duncan Smith, worked up to operational efficiency. It was during this time that 602 made another little piece of history, when Flight Lieutenant Bill McGregor flew the last Spitfire operational sortie. The aircraft was LO-N, serial number PK651. The flight was from Leuchars to North Luffenham, and the date was 8th May 1951, exactly twelve years to the day from the arrival of the first four Spitfires at Abbotsinch. The City of Glasgow Squadron had the longest association of any in the Royal Air Force with the Spitfire; the only unit to notch up a dozen years with the fighter that will always be part of The Legend.

In March 1957, the Auxiliary Fighter Squadrons' story ended. In Glasgow, the Vampires were grounded, the Battle Honours laid up in the Cathedral, and the weekenders returned to their offices, factories and shipyards. Her Majesty The Queen wrote:

The history of the Auxiliary Air Force has been a glorious one. The first Auxiliary squadrons were included in the Air Defence of Great Britain in 1925. It was aircraft of these squadrons which shot down the first enemy bomber over this country; and Auxiliary squadrons were heavily engaged in the air over Dunkirk and throughout the Battle of Britain . . . and in Normandy, France and Germany.

I wish as Air Commodore-in-Chief to thank officers, airmen and airwomen of the Royal Auxiliary Force for all that they have given to the service of the country by their enthusiasm, their spirit and their devotion to duty in peace and war. I wish them to

know that they can look back with pride and satisfaction to service well done.

At Hillington, the formalities over, we entered the hut, and looked
back down the years, surrounded by photographs. Formal groups
at summer camp, and self-conscious pilots posing, caps at exactly
the right rakish angle, beside their Spitfires. Under glass, the
trophies won by those who could shoot straightest, punch hardest
and bomb most accurately; the yellowed logbooks, with their faded
ink, open at little feats of heroism; the artwork, patiently created by
deft brushes. Here, a couple of bits of Heinkel . . . over there, the
flying suit setting off that orange scarf . . . and the boys, faces alight
with the pleasure of the pilots.

The Legend at last had a home.

One by one, we drifted outside again, towards the Lady. The
autumn sun was lower now, striking golden highlights on her dark
grey wings, picking out the tips of the long propeller blades, the
muzzles of the cannons, the rim of the gyro sight. Her canopy was
back on its runners.

Three cadets were clustered round the port wing root, as Glen
Niven, in pin-stripe suit and spectacles, eased himself unhurriedly
into the bucket seat, swivelled his backside on a non-existent
parachute pack, and let his hands drop onto the throttle lever and
the spade-handle with the inch-round button under the thumb. He
began answering the torrent of eager questions:

'What was it like to fly, sir?'

'How fast could it really go?'

'How many Messerschmitts did you shoot down, sir?'

'Did you actually fly in the Battle of Britain, really?'

One by one, they got their answers, and wandered off, taking
their photographs and arguing over the technical details of this living piece of aviation history. We were left together in companionable silence.

Glen, who for years had kept trace of the pilots and ground
crews, turned round. 'These boys have done a hell of a good job,
you know.'

'Maybe they thought it was time somebody really said thanks for
what you did.'

'Uh huh. Listen, is there any chance of your book ever being
published? I'd like to read it.'

'I hope so. Like I said, maybe it's time we said thanks.'

He didn't hear me. The rudder flicked against the restraining locks, the ailerons twitched, and the Lady felt once again the touch of her master.

For a few, fleeting seconds, the feel, and the smell, of the Spitfire took her pilot winging into distant skies. The eyes behind the glasses misted a little; the grip on the stick tightened.

The vision flashed across the years; the baptism of fire over London at the height of the Battle of Britain . . . Donald Jack shouting a warning in the nick of time as the tracers converged on the Spitfire . . . the 109 he never saw which did hit, and the concern of the ground crew when the wounded Spitty landed. He'd come from the other side of Canada to fly with 602. He'd memorised the MO's eye chart before his medical – they never discovered he was blind as a bat in one eye. He'd binded like hell when they transferred him to 601, and later to 603. Back with 602, he'd watched in horror as Ritchie went down, shot through the head on his first sweep over France; throughout the nightmare days when Deere took them back again and again as close escort to the bombers, he'd stuck to his task, and developed a lasting respect for his aeroplane, especially when she'd delivered him safely home with the port wingtip shot off and the aileron shredded. He'd sweated, cursed, and whooped with joy in her tiny cockpit; towards the end, as the tuberculosis took a firm hold, he'd even coughed blood in her, and persuaded the crew to clean it up and say nothing, until the medics finally caught up with him.

I saw his left hand reach forward and lightly pat the cold grey fuselage as he climbed out. He'd always strenuously deny that he was a hero, an ace or a romantic. But he *was* a 602 Squadron fighter pilot. He caught my eye as he jumped down from the wing root.

'Bloody good aeroplane, that. Where's the bar?'

A young cadet approached, a little shyly. 'I just wondered, sir . . . were you . . . uh, are you, one of the aces?'

'Aw, nuts!'

The Few

602 Squadron pilots who flew operationally with 11 and 12 Groups during the Battle of Britain, July–October 1940. Rank is appropriate to the period of the list.

Aries, P/O Ellis W. — First operational during the Battle.

Babbage, Sgt. Cyril F., DFM — Slightly injured during the Battle.

Barthropp, F/O P.P.C. — First operational on fighters during the Battle.

Boyd, F/Lt. Robert Findlay, DFC — Flight Commander. At least 12 victories.

Bracton, Sgt.

Coverley, F/O W.H. 'Roger' — Killed during the Battle, over London.

Dunlop Urie, F/Lt., John — Flight Commander. Injured during the Battle.

Eade, Sgt. Alfie W. — Flew with 266 and 602 during the Battle.

Edy, P/O A.L. 'Jake', DFC — Killed later in the war.

Elcombe, Sgt. Douglas W. — Killed in the final stages of the Battle.

Farquhar, W/C A. Douglas, DFC — OC Martlesham Heath. Flew with 257 Squadron.

Ferguson, F/O P.J. 'Ian' — Injured in the last great 'Stuka Battle'

Fisher, P/O G.

Gage, P/O D.H. — Injured during the Battle. Later killed.

Gillies, F/Sgt. J. — Killed later in the war.

Hanbury, P/O O.V. 'Pedro' — Killed later in the war.

Hart, F/O J.S. (Canadian) — Transferred to 54 Squadron late in the Battle.

Hopkin, P/O W.P. 'John Willie' — Transferred from 54 Squadron during the Battle.

Jack, F/O Donald M. — Acted as Flight Commander.

Johnstone, S/L A.V.R. 'Sandy', DFC — CO during the Battle. At least 6 victories.

Lyall, P/O A. 'Pat' — Killed during the Battle.

McKellar, S/L Archie A., DSO DFC	CO of 605 Squadron. Killed 1st Nov. 19 victories.
MacLean, F/O Charles Hector	Severely injured during the Battle.
McDowall, Sgt. Andrew, DFM	Injured during the Battle. At least 9 victories.
Moody, P/O Harry W.	Killed during the Battle, over London.
Mount, F/Lt. C.J. 'Mickey', DFC	Flight Commander.
Niven, P/O H.G. 'Nuts' (Canadian)	Flew with 601 and 602 during the Battle.
Payne, P/O R.A. 'Agony'	Killed later in the war.
Phillips, Sgt. Randall F.P.	
Proctor, Sgt. J.	Killed later in the war.
Ritchie, F/O T.G.F.	Killed later in the war, with 602 over France.
Robinson, S/L Marcus	CO of 616 Squadron during the Battle.
Rose, P/O S.N.	
Smith, Sgt. L.E.	Transferred from 234 Squadron during the Battle.
Smith, Sgt. W.B.	
Sprague, Sgt. M.H.	Killed during the Battle.
Webb, F/Lt. Paul C.	Injured during the Battle, over London.
Whall, Sgt. B.E.P. 'Ginger', DFM	Killed during the Battle, over Arundel.
Whipps, Sgt. G.A. 'Wimpy'	Killed later in the war.

The Witnesses

In recreating exactly 'how it was', eye-witness accounts are, of course, invaluable. During the research for the book, and for two radio documentaries in 1980 and 1983, more than 120 people were interviewed, or corresponded with me. They were invariably helpful, and many took considerable time and trouble, in order to assist the telling of the story. Without them, the book would be dry, and I should like to record my indebtedness to them all.

It was of course inevitable that much of their evidence would overlap; valuable in corroborating particular parts of the story. The principal witnesses were:

Members of 602 Squadron

Wg. Cdr. P.P.C. Barthropp, DFC, AFC

F/Lt. Raymond Baxter

F/Lt. E.V.N. Bell

A.H. Bowman

Wg. Cdr. R. Findlay Boyd, DSO, DFC & Bar, AE

LAC R.B. "Nobby" Clark

LAC John F. Davies

Air Cmdr. A.C. Deere, DSO, OBE, DFC & Bar

LAC Sid Eveleigh

F/Lt. John S. Feather

S/L Rev. D. Noel Fisher

S/L J.A. Forrest, O StJ

S/L A.M. Grant, AE

Sgt. E.G. Hill

F/Lt. James Hosier Hodge

Ian D. Horne

S/L Edward A. Howell, OBE, DFC

F/Lt. John N. Hubbard

Wg. Cdr. Donald M. Jack, AE

Air Vice-Marshal A.V.R. Johnstone, CB, DFC

F/Sgt T.L. 'Cupid' Love

Wg. Cdr. C.H. MacLean, AE, BL

AC2 Duncan MacLeod

S/L A. Denis McNab

P/O H.G. Niven

S/L J.B. Niven, DFC & Bar

Sgt. R.F.P. Phillips

Gp. Capt. G.C. Pinkerton, OBE, DFC, AE

Wg. Cdr. A. Rintoul, CBE, AE

Gp. Capt. Marcus Robinson, CB, AFC, AE

Air Marshal Sir Anthony Selway, KCB, DFC

F/Sgt. G.R. Simpson

LAC W.R. Smith

S/L H.M. Stephen, DSO, DFC

F/Lt. John Strain, DFC, AFC

Wg. Cdr. R.A. 'Max' Sutherland, DFC

Wg. Cdr. J.D. Urie, O StJ, AE

Air Cmdr. P.C. Webb, CBE, DFC, AE

The Others

Chaz Bowyer

Dugald Cameron

Norman L.R. Franks

Peter G.M. Fyfe

The Duke of Hamilton & Brandon, K StJ

Mrs Johan Irvine

F/Lt. W. McConnell

Thomas McRoberts Snr.

Ronald D. Penhall

Mrs Florence M. Russell

Paul Sampson

Malcolm Spaven

SELECT BIBLIOGRAPHY

Select Bibliography

Published Sources
Cajus Bekker: The Luftwaffe War Diaries
    Macdonald & Co., 1967
Paul Carell: Invasion! They're Coming!
    Harrap, 1962
Wing Commander Pierre Clostermann: The Big Show
    Chatto & Windus, 1951
Basil Collier: The Battle of Britain
    Batsford, 1962
Richard Collier: Eagle Day
    Hodder & Stoughton, 1966
Group Captain Alan Deere: Nine Lives
    Hodder & Stoughton, 1959
General Adolf Galland: The First and The Last
    Methuen, 1953
Wing Commander E.H. Howell: Escape to Live
    Longmans, 1947
Air Vice Marshal A.V.R. Johnstone: Where No Angels Dwell
    Jarrolds, 1969
Air Vice Marshal A.V.R. Johnstone: Enemy In The Sky
    William Kimber, 1976
Air Vice Marshal A.V.R. Johnstone: Adventure In The Sky
    William Kimber, 1978
Group Captain J.A. Kent: One Of The Few
    William Kimber, 1971
F.G. Nancarrow: Glasgow's Fighter Squadron
    Collins, 1942
Alfred Price: The Hardest Day
    Macdonald & Jane's, 1979
John Rawlings: Fighter Squadrons of the RAF
    Macdonald & Jane's
Denis Richards: Royal Air Force 1939-45
    HMSO, 1953

Bruce Robertson: Spitfire: The Story of a Famous Fighter
  Harleyford, 1960
D. Wood & D. Dempster: The Narrow Margin
  Hutchinson, 1961
The Pilots' Book of Everest
  Hodge, 1936

Unpublished Sources
Air Ministry Records (Public Record Office).
  602 Squadron Operations Record Books: Ref. AIR 27/2073 –
    2078
  Station Record Books: Ref. AIR 28
  602 Squadron Combat Reports: Ref. AIR 50/166
  Miscellaneous correspondence, including short squadron his-
    tory by F/Lt John Pudney.: Ref. AIR 20/6188.
  Correspondence with C-in-C, Fighter Command: Ref. AIR 14/
    449
Wing Commander E.V.N. Bell: Outline of a history of 602 Squad-
  ron, 1947/8.
Wing Commander R.A. Sutherland: Collection of diary notes
  and letters.

Short manuscripts and correspondence from a number of pilots
and aircraftsmen.

A large number of notes, logbooks and letters kindly lent by squadron members and their relatives, together with written archive
transcripts from the BBC, for which I am indebted.

INDEX

Index

Ranks, where stated, are appropriate to the period and events covered by the text.